THE LDS GAME BOOK

REVISED EDITION

Family Reunions · Family Night Games
Party Games and Ideas · Neighborhood Parties
Girls' Camp · Youth Groups and Conferences
Fathers and Sons Outings · Scouts

ALMA HEATON

THE **LDS** GAME BOOK

REVISED EDITION

Family Reunions · Family Night Games
Party Games and Ideas · Neighborhood Parties
Girls' Camp · Youth Groups and Conferences
Fathers and Sons Outings · Scouts

CFI
AN IMPRINT OF CEDAR FORT, INC.
SPRINGVILLE, UTAH

ISBN 13: 978-1-4621-1198-5

Published by CFI, an imprint of Cedar Fort, Inc.
2373 W. 700 S., Springville, UT, 84663
Distributed by Cedar Fort, Inc., www.cedarfort.com

Cover design by Shawnda T. Craig
Cover design © 2014 by Lyle Mortimer
Edited and typeset by Deborah Spencer

Printed in the United States of America

10 9 8 7 6 5 4 3 2 1

Printed on acid-free paper

Other Books Written by Alma and Marie Heaton

After Retirement

Attention Getters and Forfeits

Behind the Taj Mahal

Double Fun

Enjoy Yourself—It's Later Than You Think

Experience of a Lifetime

Family Recreation

Finding Gold in Your Golden Years

G-Rated Jokes Vol. I

G-Rated Jokes Vol. II

Games with Gospel Themes

Games Our Pioneers Played

Gospel Criss-Cross Mazes

Gospel Crossword Puzzles

Gospel Learning Motivators

The Joy of Living Your Religion

The LDS Game Book

Live & Learn

One Liners

Party Starters and Quiet Games

Planning Enjoyable Reunions

Playway of Teaching Games

Teaching with Objects

Tools for Teaching

Traveling Games

Visual Lessons

Contents

Contents

Contents

Contents

Contents

Foreword

The author has drawn heavily upon years of classroom and other related experiences to bring into focus a practical and philosophical view of the place of recreational activities in individual and family living. His effort has been to show that the home is a laboratory wherein family members can perfect themselves by living the gospel in its fulness. Recreational activities in the home, intelligently and purposefully planned and developed, may make gospel principles blossom in the lives of all family members.

This book, *The LDS Game Book*, is divided into four parts. Part one includes a philosophic orientation—"Family Togetherness." The remaining parts include sequential development of fun activities as they may be applied to family night, family reunions, the family and neighbors, and the family in the Church. The basic purpose of each of these discussions is to translate gospel lessons into the lives of family and Church members through recreational activities. Family reunions are viewed as being extensions of "family nights."

Happiness and joy need to be developed through living great principles of gospel truth in all phases of family life. The author believes that man is born to be active. The gospel is not only an idea, a concept; it is also an activity to be experienced. These great truths of life and eternity may be learned through the physical body and through the mind. It is through the activities which invoke both body and mind—the active level—that people are converted and fellowshipped into spiritual activity and full Church membership. The play way of teaching places the person in a correct attitude for learning. When gospel principles are applied to games and recreational activities those concepts become increasingly meaningful.

This publication is designed as a text for classes in recreational activities and as a source book for parents and leaders in recreation.

—Dr. Milton F. Hartvigsen, dean of Brigham Young University's College of Physical Education, 1956–1974

Acknowledgments

Acknowledgments go to all the family recreation classes of the past three years for submitting information for this publication and also to seminary and institute teachers who contributed information in the recreation leadership class.

To our family—Randel, Hal, Rochelle, and Debra—who have tested and experimented with the family nights and gospel games and given their suggestions.

It has been a great pleasure to work with the editor, Mrs. Boyd Robertson. She has shown much patience in testing and rewriting the games.

I would like to acknowledge Ernest Olsen, a recreation major from Brigham Young University, for his very impressive cartoons and art work.

Introduction

Today in our world of modern inventions and miracles, people have more leisure time than ever before. Yet in their attempt to use this time, they have, in many cases, only sped up their pace of living rather than more effectively using their moments of leisure. As a result, the most basic and fundamental unit of man, the family, has suffered greatly. Never before has the family found such a wide spread in the interests and pleasures of its members.

This book has been compiled in an effort to help the modern family in its search for the art of creativity and recreation through participating in activities together.

The LDS Game Book has been prepared for all those teachers, parents, and future parents who may have difficulty making religious lessons a part of the lives of children. The manual is divided into four units with a complete index. How individuals apply the recreation and fun technique of teaching depends on the enthusiasm, training, and study of each individual. Each person should analyze his or her specific situation and apply the games and lessons needed. This text has been prepared for the guidance of all people interested in their family, friends, and neighbors in seminaries, institutes, priesthood, and Sunday School classes. It is the desire of the author that many families may find the help needed to further their family unity within these pages.

FAMILY RECREATION

A. Games for Family Home Evening

B. Traveling Games

C. Paper and Pencil Games

D. Active Games

E. Quiet Games

Introduction

Games in this first section are not merely designed to provide gospel games for your family home evenings but also are intended to give suggestions for games that will add fun and excitement to your family's other activities and to those quiet evenings at home when you want to entertain each other.

Games For Family Home Evening

These games are not to take the place of the home evening lesson. After reading over the home evening lesson, look through this section on games for family home evenings and find a game that can be applied to the lesson. Often parents can make better applications than are suggested here. The lesson will be learned faster, retained longer, and recalled more quickly if a game is associated with it. Taking the lesson from the printed page and applying it to the lives of individuals has always been a teacher's greatest challenge. Jesus made the application through parables. We are doing it through games, allowing the lesson to come alive.

It is sometimes better to play the game before the lesson. In this way a parent can talk about the experience and it will be meaningful for the child.

Pre-Opener Games for Family Home Evening

Raise the Devil

Place the tips of your fingers lightly against the corresponding fingertips of your opposite hand. Then bend the long center fingers of each hand down so that the knuckles of the center fingers touch. These represent trouble. Now try to move each of the matching sets of fingers individually. The thumbs represent the sons—note how you can get action out of them. The little fingers represent the daughters good action there, too. The index fingers represent the mother. You can get action out of her. The ring fingers represent the father. Try to move him. You can't move Dad without raising the devil (center finger knuckles)!

Note: "Raising the devil" is an old phrase for getting into trouble.

Guess Who You Are

Write the names of famous scriptural or Church history characters on small cards, one on each card. Pin one of the cards on the back of each player. By answering yes or no questions, each family member guesses the name on their back.

Mystery Games for Family Home Evenings

The Storyteller

The leader tells a story to the group. While telling the story they do several things such as mopping their brow, buttoning their shirt, untying their shoelaces, and so on. When the story is finished, the group is asked to list the things the leader did in the order that the leader did them, rather than what the leader said. The person with the most accurate list is the winner.

Gospel Application: Our actions speak louder than our words.

Cannibals and Missionaries

Players are in lines. (There may be multiple lines playing at once.) Two players in each line are cannibals, and two are missionaries. The missionaries must devise a way to get the two cannibals to the other side of the river. Only two people may be in the boat at one time. If the cannibals outnumber the missionaries, the cannibals growl and that line loses. The line that wins shows the group the correct way to get the cannibals across the river. Solution: A missionary takes one cannibal across the river, comes back and gets the other missionary, then goes back and gets the other cannibal.

Gospel Application: We must follow certain laws of the Lord in order to obtain certain goals in life.

How Many Times Did the Train Stop?

This is a math problem. Tell the group of an imaginary trip you took, and as you name each place, tell them how many people got on and off the train. Make the numbers easy to add and subtract. When you are through, ask, "How many times did the train stop?" Usually the players have been keeping track of the number of people on the train, not the train stops.

Gospel Application: This illustrates the subtleness Satan uses to lead us down the wrong path. We so often look for the wrong things in life.

Staying on the Straight and Narrow

Blindfold a person and stand them on an ironing board or plank. Have two assistants lift the ends up about two to four inches and hold it there. Ask the blindfolded victim to put their hands on the two assistants' shoulders. Tell the person they are going higher, as the assistants slowly squat down. The victim thinks they are rising. Then tell them to jump down.

Gospel Application: Be sure your steps are taking you upward, and that you are not standing still but that you are progressing.

Knock

A person who has the "key" to the game goes out of the room. The "key" is the knowledge of how to win the game. Another person, their partner, remains in the room, and everyone chooses someone to be "it." When the person who left the room returns, they try to guess who has been chosen. The partner knocks on a player's chair and asks, "Is it Mary?" The person guessing says, "No." And so on. When the partner knocks on the side of the chair, the next person they name is "it," and the one guessing will be able to yes.

Gospel Application: Find ways to apply this game to the gospel for your family's family home evening.

Entrance

The group must be in a circle and have a leader who knows how to play the game. With a stick, the leader "draws" a circle on the floor and says, "Here is the man in the moon. Here is an eye; here is an eye; here is his nose; and here is his mouth." They clear their throat and then hand the stick to the next person, who is required to do draw the man in the moon. The secret of the game is that the next person must copy the artist exactly, including clearing their throat, or they have not drawn the picture correctly. When a player catches on to the secret, they can hand the stick to the next person.

Gospel Application: Apply this to the gospel by drawing parallels to baptism, for example. We must follow ordinances exactly in order to progress.

Telling Time

The group picks an hour on the clock face while the leader is not watching. They take this number—four, for instance—and start counting to themselves, beginning with five, as the leader taps on the clock face, until they reach twenty. They tell the leader to stop—and lo, it is the number they chose. (The leader counts taps to themselves, beginning with one, and taps anywhere on the clock face until the eighth tap, which the leader lands on twelve. The leader then taps counterclockwise until the group tells the leader to stop. If the group has counted correctly, the leader always stops at the number the group chose.

Gospel Application: There are no mysteries or miracles to God. As with this game, which we think of as a mystery or a miracle, it is based upon laws we do not yet understand.

Tommy, Tommy, Tum

Hold up the left hand, fingers spread. Touching each finger with the right index finger, starting with the little finger, say, "Tommy, Tommy, Tommy, Tum" and (making a loop from the index finger down to the base and up to the tip of thumb) "whoops Tommy." Then touching each finger again in turn, down to the little finger, "Whoops, Tommy, Tommy, Tommy, Tum." Then bring the hands down casually to the lap, clasping them with the fingers interlocked. (Game is best played while seated.) The trick is in clasping the hands.

The players try to do likewise, the leader saying "yes" if correct or "no" if they do not clasp hands.

Gospel Application: We should judge a person by what we see them do rather than on what we hear.

Learning Games for Family Home Evening

Articles of Faith

Have the players stand back about eight feet and throw a bean bag into a muffin tin. The muffin tin has numbers in the bottom. The person has to say the Article of Faith corresponding to the number of the muffin cup the bag lands in.

Name a Temple

Divide the family into two equal groups. Have the leader question each person on each team for temple names—any temple—but the leader must keep a list of the temples named. Each team member whispers the name of a temple to the leader. The winning team will be the one naming the most temples without repeating a temple the other team has named. Team members may listen to the opposite team's answers and avoid repeating those temples.

Know Your Standard Works

The leader calls out the name of a book from the standard works and the family names the particular work from which it comes. **Example:** Peter. **Answer:** New Testament.

Gospel Scramble

Scramble some gospel words that apply to the evening's lesson and have family members unscramble them. Pick out one word and give a two-minute talk on it.

Message Relay

Divide the group into several smaller groups of equal size. Have a scripture written or typed out (one for each group), divide it into single words, and put them in a container for each group on a chair in front of them. Once signaled, one person from each group picks up a word and brings it back to the group; then the next person does the same, and so on. The group then assembles the scripture. When a group has its scripture figured out, they deliver it to the leader written out on a piece of paper. The winner is the first group to correctly identify the scripture.

Gospel Relay

Have players in two lines. In front of each line, have a basket filled with slips of paper. On each paper is written one of the Ten Commandments, without the verse number and missing several key words. The first player will run to the basket, find the first commandment, and place it on the floor, filling in the blank spaces with the correct words. The second player does the same with the second commandment, and so on. The winner is the first group that has the commandments in order and correctly filled in.

Question Bee

Have the family write ten questions each on the lesson being reviewed. Then have them divide into two groups in a spelling bee–like manner, only instead of sitting down when missing a question, the player goes to the end of the line on the other side. When one side misses a question, the other side gets a point.

Scriptures

Provide the players with paper and pencils. Quote familiar scriptures and have the contestants write (or say, if they are small children) the part not quoted.

Truth or Consequences

Each person has two cards, one marked true, the other false. The following statements are read (or you may make up statements applying to the evening's lesson). Award one point for each correct card held up. The family member gaining the most points win. The "consequence" each loser must pay is performing or displaying a talent.

1. The Bible says Jonah was swallowed by a whale.
2. A leader is always unselfish.
3. Joseph Smith was the second president of the Church.
4. The Bible is made up of many small books.
5. The bishop is sometimes called "the father of the ward."
6. Faith in the Lord Jesus Christ is the first principle of the gospel.
7. Daniel was put in a lion's den.
8. Shadrach, Meshach, and Abednego were the three young men who were put in the furnace.
9. We never have to repent.

Prophet Race

Divide players into two teams. Have each team race to a pad of paper, one player at a time. Each member must write down a different prophet's name. The team members must leave their piece of paper near the pad so the next team member may see what has been listed previously. There is to be no talking while waiting to race for the pad, except for cheers or other noise, and no team member may prompt other members whether at the pad or waiting to get to it. The winner is the first team to write down correctly, in a given amount of time, the most names of prophets without repeating any.

Hymnal Artists

Each player is given a piece of paper with a hymn title on it and requested to draw, to the best of their ability, something to represent the title. When the picture is drawn, the title is folded under and the sheet passed to the leader. The pictures are next held up for all players to study for a prescribed time. The players try to identify the hymns depicted and write down what they think each picture depicts. The player with the most correct answers wins the game.

Spelling Baseball

Divide the group into two teams. The pitcher (leader) "pitches" a Bible word to the batter. If the batter spells it correctly, he goes to first base. If he fails, he is out. Base runners may only advance by the next runners spelling words correctly. When three are out, change sides. Play for nine innings and keep score. In order to make it fair, have two lists of words, one for smaller children and another for the older ones.

Family Baseball

Prepare two copies of a list of questions reviewing what the family has been studying. Divide the family into two groups and let them sit on opposite sides of the room. Let each team select a pitcher and have him come to the front of the room and stand in front of the opposing team. Draw a baseball diamond and scoreboard on a whiteboard (or chalkboard). The pitcher then "throws" a question to a member of the opposite team. The father or mother acts as umpire and determines whether the answer merits an out, base hit, two-base hit, and so on, and draws or indicates the runner's position on the board. They also keep track of the outs and runs. Generally follow the rules of baseball (three outs and the other team gets a chance to "bat"). The team with the most runs wins.

Flash Cards

Divide the family into two or more teams. Number the members of each team. Use large cards that each bear a letter of the alphabet for the questions. The leader proceeds by asking questions like the following to each team in turn, usually to be answered by one or a few words:

"Number three, name an Old Testament character whose name begins with this letter."

"Number four, tell something about a prophet whose name begins with this letter."

"Number two, name a city in the history of the Church that begins with this letter."

Some sample categories for the Bible or Church history are cities and villages; rivers and mountains; countries or lands; prophets; kings or queens; important people from the Bible or Church history; and so on. After each question is asked, the leader flashes the card bearing the letter. The team member whose number was called answers the question. If the member answers correctly, they score a point for their team.

Pass It On

Prepare a list of questions beforehand that can be answered briefly and objectively. Pass an object about the room while counting or playing music, and stop without warning. (You can use any method of making the object being passed stop indiscriminately. If it stops with the same person twice in a row, have the last one who touched it and who has not had a turn answer the question.) The person who is caught left holding the object chooses a number (from within the total number of prepared questions) and answers the appropriate question. There should be at least one blank number, so that there is an opportunity for someone to choose a number for which there is no question. You may keep score if desired, but this is not necessary.

"Era of Youth"

This is an adaptation of a spelling bee. Divide the family into teams and have them stand or sit in rows facing each other. Number one of Team A asks number one of Team B a question about something in the current month's *New Era*. If the latter answers the question correctly, they in turn ask their opponent a question. If the one questioned cannot answer, or their answer is incorrect, they must go to the end of the line on the opposing team. The side with the most players after everyone has had a turn wins the game.

Gospel Charades

The family is divided into two groups. Group A leaves the room to return and pantomime the meaning of a biblical word or phrase that Group B is to guess. Sometimes help is given, such as "This is a three-syllable word," or "This is familiar prophet," or "This is a proverb," and so on. If Group B guesses correctly, they have a turn to present their charade. If, however, they fail to guess the answer after a reasonable time, Group A gets a point and presents another charade.

Guessing Hymns

A person claps only the rhythm of a known hymn. The other players try to guess the hymn.

Articles of Faith

Divide into two lines. The purpose of the game is for each person in turn to say one word of a specified article of faith. When the person does not know the next word the rest of the team act it out.

Who Are You?

Divide the family into several teams. The mother chooses someone to be "it," and to represent a character from the scriptures (Old Testament, New Testament, Book of Mormon, Church History, and so on). By asking the person who is "it" indirect questions in turn, each team tries to find out whom the player represents. When a team feels that they knows who the "it" player represents, they call for a conference, and go into a huddle to discuss the possibilities. Each team may make only one guess and the team that correctly names the character scores a point. An incorrect guess puts the team out of the game until another person is chosen to be "it."

Questions should be yes or no questions. They must be of an indirect type such as: Are you one of the prophets? Did you die a natural death? Is there a book of the Old Testament by your character? Are you one of the judges of Israel? Did you predict Israel's downfall? The "it" player should refuse to answer direct questions (at least at the start) like the following: Are you the son of Jacob? Are you called "Father of the Faithful"? Did you love Delilah? Were you the first King of Israel? Was Abigail your wife?

Musical Spelling Bee

Divide the family into two groups and have them face each other.

The leader plays or hums portions of tunes (Church songs or hymns). If the first player at the head of the line cannot name the song, they sit down. Then the player at the head of the opposite line guesses, and so on down the two lines. The last one remaining is the winner.

Scripture Finding

Divide the family into two teams. Call out a Bible (Book of Mormon, and so on) reference. The first team to have all its members find the passage in their copies of the scriptures wins a point.

Animal, Vegetable, and Mineral

Pick two family members to be the panel and seat them at the front of the room with their backs to a whiteboard (or chalkboard). Choose your subject and indicate to the panel what category it fits in (Peter's sword, which is mineral; or Jesus's robe, animal). Write the subject on the board so the family can read it, and then allow the panel twenty questions in which to identify it. Don't use the same panel too long at one time.

Picture Recognition Contest

Hang around the room pictures depicting scriptural events (or gospel activities such as family prayer, blessing a baby, blessing the food, and so on). Be sure to cover the titles Give each picture a number. Let family members go around and identify the scene or tell something about the event pictured.

Scripture Quoting

The family divides into two teams. Each side has a captain, who calls which members can participate. Take turns until all on that team have had a turn. A referee counts time allowing a point to the opposite team when one side stalls five seconds. One team quotes a passage of scripture that the opposite team must explain. If that team cannot explain it, a point goes to the team that quoted it unless that team also cannot explain it, in which case a point is lost by their team. Teams take turns.

Famous Pioneers

Someone gets up and tells the history of a famous pioneer. The person who guesses it then tells the history of another pioneer, and so on.

Solo Singing

Each family member selects a hymn and begins to sing it as the leader points to him. Each person in order must have a hymn ready to sing with no delay. Anyone missing a beat and breaking rhythm must sing a solo.

Frustration

Have a leader go around the circle of players and give the name of a hymn. Then the leader points to a person and counts to ten. The player pointed to must begin singing the first verse before the leader finishes counting.

Who Am I?

Divide the players into two groups. To begin select a player from one of the groups to be "it." This person decides on a character from either the scriptures or Latter-day leaders and announces their source to the players (scriptures, *Ensign*, and so on). This person then gives a clue; for instance, if the person chose Moses, they could say, "I went up a mountain." Each group has one guess and if a group gives the correct answer that side receives ten points. If no correct answer is given, another clue is offered for nine points, and so on. When the answer is given or the count gets to zero the other side chooses someone to be "it."

Apostle Rhythm

Play "rhythm" by clapping hands on knees twice and clapping hands together once. Seat in a circle and give each player the name of an apostle. Maintain a hierarchy in the circle, with a leader at the "start" of the circle and around to a lowest position. When a person's apostle name is called, the player with that name calls another name to the rhythm. When someone misses, they go to the "end" of the circle and the others move up.

Gospel Quizzing

Fill in the missing blanks by correctly matching the columns below (Did you see the theme of each book in the existing letters?):

FIRST & SECOND SAMUEL	BOOK OF EXODUS
1. S	1. .. .. .. A ..
2. .. .. H	2. .. .. L ..
3. E	3. .. .. O .. ..
4. P	4. .. .. N .. ..
5. H	5. .. G .. .. ..
6. .. E	
7. .. .. R ..	6. J .. ..
8. D	7. .. .. .. O ..
	8. .. .. U ..
9. .. .. K	9. .. .. R .. .. ..
10. .. .. I	10. .. .. N .. .. ..
11. .. .. N	11. .. E ..
12. G	12. .. .. Y

First & Second Samuel

1.	First King of Israel	(Saul)
2.	David's best friend	(Jonathan)
3.	High priest who trained Samuel	(Eli)
4.	A man who speaks for God	(Prophet)
5.	Mother of Samuel	(Hannah)
6.	Father of David	(Jesse)
7.	David's musical instrument	(Harp)
8.	Author of many of the psalms	(David)
9.	Sacred chest stolen by Philistines	(Ark)
10.	David's weapon	(Sling)
11.	David's son and successor	(Solomon)
12.	Giant whom David killed	(Goliath)

Book of Exodus

1.	Mountain where Moses received the Ten Commandments	(Sinai)
2.	Tent used as a place of worship	(Tabernacle)

3. Graven images (Idols)
4. Food supplied by God to Israelites (Manna)
5. Land from which the Israelites escaped (Egypt)
6. Old Testament word for God (Jehovah)
7. Moses's brother and spokesman (Aaron)
8. "Long Journey" book of Old Testament (Exodus)
9. Moses's sister (Miriam)
10. The promised land (Canaan)
11. Number of plagues placed on
    Egyptians by God (Ten)
12. Years Israelites were in the wilderness (Forty)

Question Draw

Place enough questions in a box to accommodate the group. Divide the family into teams. Choose a member from Team A by number and draw a question out of the question box. If the player answers it, they get five points and draw a second time. If they answer the second question, they get ten points, and the third time, fifteen points. Then give Team B a chance. Keep track of the points and score by teams.

Gospel Seeds

Each person in turn follows a line drawn on the floor by placing the heel of one foot against the toe of the other. About every three feet they must stop and place a seed (from which the gospel may grow) in a small receptacle set about one and a half feet from the line. When they reach the end, they run back and tag the next person who plants their gospel seeds in the same manner. Great to play with multiple teams racing against each other.

Scripture Shout

Divide players into several groups. One group yells a scripture simultaneously, each individual shouting one assigned word. The remaining groups try to figure out the scripture; the first group to do so correctly wins.

Books of the Bible Game

All the titles to the books of the Bible can be found among these letters. Those books which are prefixed with Roman numerals appear only once and so there are fifty-seven titles to be found. Draw a circle around each title as you find it. The titles are written forward, backward, up, down, or diagonally in any direction.

```
P P S E L M S E G D U J O S H U A Z H A C I M
R R O C E D R E H T S E T S A I S E L C C E O
O E T E K U L E T R S O F C S U D O X E S S Z
V I I H W X O E K O H N O N S E H E B R E W S
E H M L E R Q Z V J S L A P E A O W N Y L P U
R C O E H S S R T I O E U I I H J M M L C H S
B A T I T U S A H S T N I N T V E O K U I I N
S L H N T X T A S A R I A H W A N M H S N L O
M A Y A A Y E I L P G H C H P O L L I N O I I
L M Z D M B A R K O P G S U R P A A K A R P T
A E M K I N G S B E N T A E S E B K G I H P A
S Z C M S B E F Z P C I T I H R T J I S C I L
P E S N A M O R G A I U A M O S S E N E J A E
N K A A I R P H I L E M O N M B L H P H H N V
O I M H A T K U S D Q P O N S O O I G P K S E
M E U U H E S R H A I M E R E J L F X E L Z R
O L E M M E H O S E A V W H A I R A H C E Z K
L M L A M E N T A T I O N S H X U A L E O J E
O O J A K U K K A B A H K P Y Z T E C T V E E
S W B O S E M A J A C O R I N T H I A N S D L
A E B C H D E B O B A D I A H C D F G H I U E
J R E L H U B G E N E S I S R E B M U N O J Y
```

Merge the Phrases

Prior to family home evening, write the following statements on separate slips of paper:

"Thou shalt have no other gods before me." (Exodus 20:3)

"Thou shalt worship the Lord thy God, and him only shalt thou serve." (Matthew 4:10)

"Thou shalt love the Lord thy God with all thy heart, and with all thy soul, and with all thy mind." (Matthew 22:37)

After you have written these sentences, including references, cut the sentences apart into phrases. Put the phrases to all the sentences into a dish. Tell your family to put the phrases together in the right order so they will make three complete sentences. The completed sentences will have an important message for each member of the family.

If you prefer, make two sets of the scripture verses. Cut them up as before and put each complete set in an envelope. Divide your family into two groups and give each group an envelope. The side that puts the verses together first wins.

Have the verses repeated aloud after they are in place.

Active Games for Family Home Evening

Satan Says

The leader does things usually involving quick physical movements. The group are to do whatever he does when he precedes his instruction with the words, "Simon says." However, if the leader tells the group, "Satan says," the group should not obey. The object is to see how long each person can follow directions without doing what "Satan says." To make the game more illustrative, prepare mashed potatoes to look like ice cream, and for the last order say, "Satan says have some ice cream." All those who fall for this will discover that the food is not ice cream, even it looks enticing.

Gospel Application: Withstand Satan's temptations.

Advance

This game should be played on a short stairway, bleachers, and so on, but it also may be played on a tile floor or in a living room by marking off boundary lines about twelve inches apart with string, magazines, or ribbon. One person is chosen as the leader and stands in front of the others who sit on the bottom step. The leader holds a penny in one hand. They hold their hands behind them and clench the penny in one hand. Then the leader holds both clenched fists in front of themselves and lets the players choose the hand they think the penny might be in. After all the players have guessed, the leader opens their hands for them to see. Those who guessed right may move up one step and the others remain where they are. The leader then hides the penny and the players guess again. When a player has reached the top of the stairs, they begin to come down. The one who first gets back to the starting point is the winner and may be the leader next time.

Gospel Application: Use this game in object lessons.

Back to Back

The family is arranged in pairs. They stand back to back with their elbows hooked. One player (not in a pair) is chosen to be "it." At the signal "everybody change," players must find other partners. Players are not safe unless elbows are hooked. The odd player tries to get a partner and the one who is left out is "it."

Gospel Application: We have to be prepared or else we may be left out and not be able to receive blessing.

Character

The leader tells a story describing how Satan is trying to get all of us to use our valuable time in wasteful activities. He does this one thing at a time until we gradually become so wrapped up in what attracts us that we have no time or ability to do other things that are more worthwhile. Some of the things Satan has us do may be the following, which the group now does as the leader demonstrates:

1. Rocking chair (rock back and forth)
2. Bouncy ball (dribble with right hand)

3. Fan to keep cool (fan with left hand)
4. Bicycle (pump with left leg)
5. Sewing machine (treadle with right leg)

Now we are too busy to do anything else. And we got here one step at a time.

Gospel Application: Satan leads us into darkness one step at a time.

Captain, May I?

Have all players stand on a line, and choose one to be the captain. The captain gives orders to each player who takes their turn stepping toward a goal line. Before they carry out their assigned orders, they must say, "Captain, may I?" The leader will say, for example, "You may take two steps forward." If movement is made without permission, the player must return to the start. The first person to the goal line wins. (Taking longer steps should help players get to the goal line.)

Gospel Application: To gain our goal of the celestial kingdom, we must be obedient to the commandments of the Lord.

Let's Go with the Pioneers
(Especially for small children)

The group repeats what the leader says and imitates the leader's actions. With each action the leader says, "Let's," and the group says, "All right."

"Let's go with the pioneers." "All right," the group says.

"Let's go with the pioneers."

"Let's pack the food and bedding in the wagon." (Lift boxes into the wagon.)

"Let's get started." (Shout to horses, slap thighs to make sound of hoof beats. Do this each time you go.)

"Let's cross this river." (Make swish-swish, swimming actions.)

"Oh! The wagon got stuck. Let's push." (Make grunting sounds)

"Oh! The wagon broke. Let's fix it." (Pound with fist on palm of other hand.)

"Let's climb this big hill." (Go slowly)

"Oh! It's going back down." (Go fast) "Crash!" (Make a loud slapping noise)

Gospel Application: Learn about courage and how to withstand hardships as the pioneers did.

Golf Ring Toss

Throw rings at pegs placed at various distances from a starting line. The nearest peg could represent baptism; the next, confirmation; the next, temple marriage; the next, the first resurrection; and the furthest peg, the celestial kingdom. Players must progress in order from closest to most distant peg. Pegs are placed far enough apart that a person generally has to throw several times to get the ring over the peg. Players cannot progress to the next stage until they have thrown the ring over the peg (or have shown they've developed the skill required to progress to it, for small children). The pegs could have the stages written on them.

Gospel Application: Eternal progression is gained slowly and only as one progressively meets requirements of higher laws. One must live the "lesser" law before they can live the "greater."

Pin the Tail on the Donkey

Blindfold each player. Each attempts to pin a tail on the donkey.

Gospel Application: We fail to reach right goals without the light of the gospel.

Sardines

One player hides in a closet or behind a door, a big rock, a clump of bushes, trees, and so on. The rest of the players hunt separately to find where the one player is hiding. When a player finds the hidden player, they wait until no one is looking, and then hide with the player. The hunt continues until everyone finds the hiding place. This is a good game for indoors or outdoors.

Gospel Application: Our families should be united in truth. When one member of a family joins the Church, they should consistently invite other members of the family to the gospel, and seek to be sealed together.

Washer Toss

Give each player five washers (or buttons or coins) and have them toss one for each turn from behind a line five feet from the goal. The person who gets his washer across the line, but the closest to it, wins all the washers tossed during that turn. The person who finally gets all the washers wins.

Gospel Application: The closer we remain to the Lord, the greater the rewards we'll receive.

Happiness

Have everyone lie on the floor in a rough circle, each with the back of his head on someone else's stomach. The first person to begin says, "Ho, ho, ho," and then the second says, "Hee, hee, hee," the third, "Ho, ho, ho," and so on around the circle. Soon everyone will begin to laugh and can't stop.

Gospel Application: Happiness and joy are contagious. Be cheerful and everyone among your associates will be affected by your cheerfulness.

Slide Right

All players, except one, are seated in a closed circle that contains one empty chair. One player is "it" and stands in the center. This player tries to seat themselves in the vacant chair that is continually being taken by the person next to it. The "it" player calls "slide right" or "slide left" and thus controls the direction the group moves. When they call "slide right," the person who finds the chair on their right empty must slide into it. When "slide left" is called, each player is responsible for occupying the vacant chair on their left. When "it" gets a chair, the person who should have taken the chair becomes "it."

Gospel Application: Beware of Satan's spirits, who are constantly trying to get into our lives.

The Thin Line

Place a dime in the bottom of a cup. Fill the cup with flour. Turn the cup upside-down. The dime is on top of the flour. Each person takes a turn cutting away some of the flour until the dime falls. The person causing the dime to fall has to pick it up with his teeth.

Gospel Application: If a person gets too close to the line between good and evil, he has to pay the penalty.

Prone to Safety

One player, selected to be "it," chases everyone, trying to tag anyone who is not in a "safe" position (for example, in a kneeling position with arms folded). A player who is caught then becomes "it" and the previous "it" player becomes a runner. Players should not remain in one place, but should move about freely within the play area.

Gospel Application: If you stand in holy places (the safe positions), you'll be safe.

Cotton Bowl Relay

Set two large bowls on two small tables. Sprinkle around the empty bowls small cotton balls. Divide the players into two teams. Blindfold the first player on each team. Hand each a large spoon (wooden, plastic, or metal). At a signal, ask each one to spoon into the bowl as many cotton balls as the player can in one minute. Since the balls have virtually no weight, the blindfolded player cannot tell whether they are scooping balls or missing them. When the first two players are through, count the number of balls in each bowl and remove them for the next player's turn. Let each member of the team compete. Add the totals at the end of the game. The team with the most cotton balls in the bowl is the winner.

Gospel Application: We cannot always rely on our senses; we must have faith to assist our senses or do what they cannot achieve.

The Coyote and the Sheep

The sheep and the shepherd form a line, one behind the other each with his hands on the shoulders of the player in front of him or holding hands. The shepherd is at the head of the line. The coyote approaches the shepherd, and the shepherd asks, "What does the coyote want?" The coyote says, "I want good meat." The shepherd replies, "Then go to the end of the line where the best lambs are." The coyote tries to tag the end lamb. The shepherd and sheep try to keep the coyote from getting the last lamb. The sheep and shepherd must not separate. If they do, the lamb or player who lets go becomes the shepherd. If the last lamb is caught, the shepherd becomes the coyote—the latter joins the middle of the sheep line for the next game, and the second in line now heads the line as shepherd.

Gospel Application: We must help each other do the will of the Lord.

Newspaper Race

Each contestant is furnished with two pieces of newspaper. Each step in the race must be made on the newspaper. Thus, the player puts down a sheet, steps on it, puts down another sheet, steps on it, reaches back to get the first sheet, and so on until they reach the goal line. The first player to reach the goal line wins.

Gospel Application: The newspapers represent steps in practicing the gospel and reaching the goal line is like obtaining a blessing (or like arriving at church on time, having completed the necessary steps to get there).

Who Are Your Neighbors?

Give each member of the family a biblical name. Seat them in a circle, and have each person learns the names of those sitting next to them. Choose one player to be "it" and have them walk inside the circles, suddenly stop, and, pointing at someone, say, "Who are your neighbors?" and count to ten. That player must give the names of both their neighbor on the right and left before the "it" player counts to ten or else they must exchange places with the "it" player. The person chosen to be "it" may vary their question by asking the name of the neighbor to the right or the left.

Gospel Application: Getting to know our neighbors usually helps us to love them more.

Traps

Two people face each other and join hands, holding their hands high so that the marching group can go under them. Players march around in a circle in two by two formation, similar to the popular game "London Bridge Is Falling Down." When the music stops, the pair holding hands lowers their hands and attempts to catch as many other pairs as possible in the trap. Each pair caught forms a new trap across the circle. The aim is to be the last couple caught.

Gospel Application: Do not get caught in Satan's trap.

Hot and Cold

A player leaves the room while the others select something the player should do, such as standing on a chair or opening the window. The player is brought back into the room but is not allowed to ask questions. When the player is close to, or nearly attempting, the stunt, the whole group loudly sings "Do What Is Right." When the player is not on track, they sing the song softly. They modulate the volume according to the player's closeness to the required action. When the player actually does the desired act, they choose someone else to be the next one to leave the room.

Variation: Hide an object while the player is out of the room and have them search for it, using the song's volume to help guide the player to the hidden object.

Gospel Application: We must be in tune with the Spirit in order to be guided to the best course of action.

Forgiveness

One of the group leaves the room. While he is out, the other members of the group choose an object in the room that is in plain sight. The person returns to the room and guesses what the object is. For instance, they might say, "I guess that it is the piano." The group does not tell them whether their guess is right or wrong at this point. The player must go on and ask a question to try to verify their guess. They may ask any question about size, position in the room, color, texture, and so on. For example, if they wish to check whether or not it is the piano, the player would ask, "Is it more than four feet long?" If the answer is "No," the player knows it is not the piano and says, "I've made a mistake." When the player says this, the group tries to help them by giving them a clue to guide them. The player then makes another guess but is not told whether they are right or wrong until they ask a question to check their guess. If the player is wrong again, they say, "I've made a mistake," and they get another clue. Again they must ask a question. If they are wrong at the end of three guesses, the group will tell them what the object is.

Gospel Application: The purpose of the game is to emphasize the idea that saying "I've made a mistake" brings benefits; in this case the benefits are the clues given by the group to help them. If the player fails to say, "I've made a mistake" when they guessed wrong, their turn is over. If their guess is right, they should be told so at the end of their question. Allow each member of the group to have a turn going out of the room and coming back to guess an object.

Gospel Steps

All players stand in a line except for a leader who is in front, about thirty or forty feet away. The leader calls out the name of a person in the line and tells them they may take one, two, or three "gospel" steps (as big a step as possible); or one, two, or three "heavenly" steps (length of one's shoe); or one, two or three "faith" steps (a jump forward as far as possible). The person must say "May I?" and the leader may say, "Yes, you may," or "No, you may not. You may take . . . steps," saying another type of step. The first one to get to the leader's line takes the leader's place.

Gospel Application: You must do the right things to progress in gospel living.

Pick-Up

Parents will have gathered five personal items of each member of the family without their knowledge and put them into a sack. One parent calls out "Pick-up," and throws the things around the room. (Make sure things collected are unbreakable.) Score one point for everything picked up by each person, and two points if they can return it to its rightful owner.

Gospel Application: Respect for others and their things.

Obstacles in Man's Life

Explain that the purpose of this activity will be to see if each one can listen to and follow the instructions of the leader and not be prevented from reaching their goal by all the persuasion and heckling of others. Point out that this is exactly what each of us must do to be a faithful steward.

For this game you will need dry beans (or like objects) and a butter knife. Place the beans on a plate. Very young children should probably use a spoon instead of the knife. The leader of the game instructs the player to scoop up three beans with the knife (fewer if preferable) without using their other hand. Then the player is to carry the beans without spilling them to a table or chair about ten feet away. Warn the player that others will try to get them to drop the beans or to stop or to disobey the instructions, and part of the test is to see if he can disregard them and reach his goal. It may add interest to the game to place a low stool (or a box) and a chair in his path, and tell him to step over the stool and walk around the chair.

As the player walks toward the goal, family members may heckle them and persuade them to disobey instructions. However, they may not touch the player. In the case of the young children, this should be done with care and in a spirit of fun, so they will not become so frustrated that they will not try. If they succeed in reaching the goal in spite of the heckling and without spilling their beans, clap for them and give them a treat, such as a piece of candy.

Patriarchal Game

Make some kind of obstacle course by moving furniture around, and then have each member go through it—the youngest of the family going through only once, the next oldest going through twice, and so on.

After this is finished, ask the children who they would want to lead them through the course again, but this time they would be blindfolded. Ideally they would want the most experienced person to lead them through. At this point, draw an analogy between the person with the most experience and the parents of a family, who can offer good advice through experience.

Quiet Games for Family Home Evening

Drawing in the Dark

Blindfold several family members and have them attempt to draw an object. The results will usually be quite distorted. Let them try it again without the blindfolds. Compare this to show how our lives would be without the light of the gospel to help us on our way. Without it we are in the dark and can easily lose our way and become confused.

Gospel Application: We need the gospel's light to guide us.

Revelation

The leader begins by whispering to the person on his right. The phrase or sentence is passed silently around the room from person to person. A check of the original message against what the last person says they heard reveals that it has become distorted in the process.

Gospel Application: Truth originates in only one place, God, and He may convey that truth through revelation. Seek the proper source of true and heed the counsel given. Seek to confirm the truths you hear by the Spirit.

Count Your Blessings

All players are seated in a circle. One player starts off with "I am grateful for apples (or something beginning with the letter A). The next player is grateful for something beginning with B, like "I am thankful for my brother." The third, C, might say, "I am grateful for children to play with." The game continues around the circle and through the alphabet. If a player fails to think of a word beginning with the proper letter, he drops out of the circle. The winner is the one remaining in the circle longest.

Gospel Application: We should express gratitude for our blessings.

Overtake

Count off around a single circle by twos, and give an object (ball, bean bag, balloon, and so on) to a number one and to a number two across the circle. At the starting signal the number ones pass their objects to the right, to number ones only, at the same time trying to catch the object passed by the number twos. Number twos are also trying to catch the number ones' object. When the whistle blows, passing stops, and a point is given to the team whose object has gained the most distance around the circle on the other.

Gospel Application: We must strive every day to live the gospel or we will fall behind.

My Eyes Are Open

Choose an object to hide and show it to the group. Send one to four people out of the room and hide the object in plain sight. The people come back and try to see the object. When a person sees it, they return to their seat and say, "My eyes are open."

Gospel Application: Sometimes we can't see things that are right before our eyes. Some people look but never see.

Talking Pictures

One person holds an object hidden in their hand and as they describe it, the other players have to draw a picture of it.

Gospel Application: This is the way we know of God and His attributes. Only by experiences in the Church can we visualize the things of God.

Following Instructions

Instruct the group to close their eyes and each to hold both hands in front of their bodies, with the index fingertips touching, and about twelve inches from the nose. Announce that you are going to give them a coordination test. Tell them to raise the right hand six inches, lower the left hand six inches, move the right hand six inches away from the body and the left hand six inches toward the body. Continue this type of direction until everyone's index fingers should be touching again, and then instruct the group to open their eyes.

Gospel Application: We are not able to follow the gospel teachings until we learn to listen and follow instructions.

I Have a Kindness

Have each member of the family write on a piece of paper some act of kindness they may perform for someone else. Have them sign their names. Put the papers in a box and pass the box saying: "I have a kindness." The next person says, "Do you?" You reply, "Yes, I do," and hand the box to that person. That person repeats the action with the person next to them, and so on. Set a timer, and when it sounds, the person holding the box takes a paper from the box. They will then receive the kindness written on the paper.

Gospel Application: We should show kindness and love to other family members.

Organization

The first player draws a head and neck without permitting the others to see what he has drawn. He then folds the paper and passes it for the next player to draw the trunk (or torso) of the body with the arms and hands. The paper is again folded and passed for the next player to draw the legs and feet. After the "work of art" has been completed, the paper is unfolded and the creation is put on display.

Gospel Application: When churches or people are not properly organized, they "go all to pieces." The head bone should be connected to the neck bone, and so on (see Ezekiel 37 or Ephesians 4:11–12).

Poor Kitty

The players are seated in a circle with a person chosen to be "Kitty" in the center. Kitty moves to any individual, kneels, and begins to meow. The player must stroke Kitty's head three times and say, "Poor Kitty, poor Kitty, poor Kitty," each time without smiling. Any player who smiles while Kitty is kneeling or acting before him must take his place. Kitty may create humorous situations to make the players laugh.

Gospel Application: We need to have deep convictions, good control, and turn to Christ in order to resist temptation.

Fowl, Beast, or Fish

The person who is "it" stands before the seated players, and suddenly points his finger at someone and says, "Bird," (beast, or fish) and counts to ten. The person pointed at must give the name of a bird, beast, or fish not mentioned before in the game. If the player is able to give the name before the player who is "it" finishes counting, then the "it" person must endeavor to trap another person. A player failing to answer correctly or mentioning a name already given becomes "it."

Gospel Application: Learn the animals God created.

Creation

Modeling clay, play dough, or an edible play dough can be used. Each person is given a piece of dough and a small piece of cardboard to work on. Give toothpicks to help model the dough. Each family member models something that is connected with the Creation.

Gospel Application: Teaching children about the Creation.

Stocking Surprises

Provide each player with a pencil and paper. Pass around large stocking (filled with objects like a spoon, a toothbrush, a toy horn, a small ball, and so on), and allow each person two minutes to feel the contents. After passing the stocking along, have the players write what they think they felt in the stocking. When all have had a turn, show the contents to the players as they check their papers.

Gospel Application: Things are not always what they appear to be and Satan will try to deceive us.

In the Beginning

Choose a player to be "it," who says, "In the beginning, God created something that begins with . . . (any letter)." The other players try to guess what it is. The first person to raise their hand gets the first guess. The correct guesser becomes "it" for the next time.

Gospel Application: Learn about the Creation.

Horizons

Close one eye and hold a penny out in front of the other eye and tell what you see. As you bring it closer, tell what you can see each time. When it gets up to your eye, you won't be able to see anything but the penny.

Gospel Application: Avoid narrow horizons. Life is composed of many elements.

Matthew, Mark, Luke, and John

The family will arrange their chairs in a semicircle. On each chair is placed the name of one of the books of the New Testament (named in consecutive order). The one sitting in the seat of Matthew starts. This player gets all players going in a count-of-three rhythm, usually by hitting the knees twice and snapping fingers for three. On the count of three, Matthew calls the name of one of the other books. On the next count of three, the person with that name must call out the name of another book and so on until a person misses, in which case they go to the end of the semicircle and everyone else moves up a seat, each person checking the name on their new chair. The object is to be in Matthew's seat.

Gospel Application: Memorize the books of the New Testament.

Do What I Say

Everyone puts their hands straight in the air and on the count of three, they see who can put them down the fastest. The leader counts "one, two," and then brings his hands down really fast without saying three. You will find that others will do the same.

Gospel Application: Example speaks louder than words. People are converted by what they see people do, not by what they hear alone.

Time

With the group seated, the leader looks at his watch and says, "Go." All players try to judge when a minute is over. When someone thinks a minute is up he stands up quietly. The person who stands up closest to the minute wins.

Gospel Application: Be accountable for every minute of your life here on the earth. Be aware of time and do not waste it on meaningless activities.

Family History

One player provides information for clues to some ancestor or some family member. The others try to guess who it is they are describing.

Gospel Application: Learn to know our family members. We are endowed with a great heritage.

Habits

Wrap a string around someone's wrist and have them break it. This is fairly easy. Then wrap it around again; they can still break it quite easily. Wrap it several times (six or seven) and it cannot be broken without considerable damage to the wrist.

Gospel Application: Habits are hard to break; the longer we have a bad one, the more difficult it is to overcome.

Steps to Heaven

I'm going on a trip to Heaven and the steps are as follows. (These are just examples):

A. Attending Church	J. Joy
B. Baptism	K. Kindness
C. Celestial Living	L. Love
D. Dependability	M. Mission
E. Eternity	N. Nice
F. Faith	O. Obedience
G. Goodness	P. Prayer
H. Honesty	Q. Quiet
I. Inspiration	R. Repentance

S. Sunday School	W. Worship
T. Tithing	X. Excellence (X-cellence)
U. Unselfishness	Y. Youth
V. Voice	Z. Zion

Other words may be used. Each player must say what the person just before them said and add their own step to heaven.

Gospel Application: Learn the principles of the gospel.

Integrity

Have each member of the family break down the word "integrity"—I-N-T-E-G-R-I-T-Y—and, by using each letter, write a word or two which would be an attribute of integrity. (Example: I— interest in others.) Place a time limit. The winner is determined by the number of attributes written.

I Am My Brother's Keeper

The players sit in a circle. Each person selects a personal item that is easily identified as their own (shoe, tie, wallet, glasses, and so on). The first person, who is the leader, exchanges their item either one, two, or three players to the left. The person on their right exchanges their own item in the same manner only to the right. Each neighbor must try to prevent their brother or sister (neighbor) from getting back their personal item. If a person gets back their own item then their neighbors, right and left, have to pay a penalty (chosen by the person who got their item back). Moves or exchanges are made in order, one after another, and can only be made in the direction from which the turn for exchange came, either right or left. Each player should have one or two penalties in mind for their neighbors to do.

Gospel Application: When the game is complete, ask the players the following question: "What gospel lessons can be shared from this game?"

Quick Recall

A player chosen to be "it" goes to someone seated and calls out a name (or date, and so on) pertaining to the lesson and then counts to ten. The other person must respond with something about whatever was called.

Example: The player chosen to be "it" says, "Abraham, 1, 2, 3," and so on. The person pointed to calls, "Sarah," or "father of nations," and so on. If the player fails to respond correctly, they must be "it" at that point.

Stop Me if I'm Wrong

Tell a story or discuss a gospel subject. Make the story up so that you can give misinformation. Have a member stop you whenever you make a mistake. A point is earned for each correction.

Guess Who Loves Me

A player chosen to be "it" thinks of something that someone in the family has done for them that showed love for them. The rest of the family tries to guess who did it. The one who guesses right is "it" next time.

Sliced Words

Write the letters of certain words pertaining to the lesson on separate slips of paper (a set for however many pairs) and mix the letters thoroughly. Divide the players into couples and give each couple a similar set of letters. The pair who first arranges their letters into the word gets one point. Then distribute another set of letters to be made into a word, and so on. Five points wins the game.

Appreciation

Select a player to be "it" to start the game. He will choose an officer in the Church, such as a bishop, and say, "I am the bishop. I am happy when . . . (think of something that would make the bishop happy)." Then, beginning at the player's right, each member of the family in turn says, "I am the bishop" and names some way that people can make the bishop happy. For example: "I am the bishop. I am happy when the priests are reverent at the sacrament table." When a family member names what player chosen to be "it" is thinking about, that person becomes the new "it."

Peace

Players each take a paper and pencil and, at a given signal, jots down five items found in the home that remind them of peace. The first one finished receives a treat after explaining why each item listed reminds them of peace.

Charades

Divide the family into two groups. The groups separate and each chooses a law of the gospel its players will act out for the other side to guess. The acting is in pantomime only. Choose laws, such as those from the following list, which can be demonstrated without irreverence.

Each side figures out exactly what its players are to do. There are many ways of acting out each law. The more original a group is the better. A side choosing number one from the list below might have one player tear up bits of paper and let them fall to the floor. Another player accuses them of it by pointing to the paper and then to them. They deny by tapping themselves on the chest and shaking their head. They accuse another player by pointing to them and then to the paper.

1. Do not bear false witness
2. Honor father and mother
3. Keep the Sabbath holy
4. Do not steal
5. Do not covet what others have
6. Pay your tithes and offerings
7. Obey the Word of Wisdom
8. Help and serve one another
9. Teach the gospel to others
10. Be tolerant with those who are different from you
11. Return good for evil
12. Be a peacemaker
13. Do unto others as you would have others do unto you
14. Honor the priesthood
15. Obey the laws of the land

Purity

Each person receives a pencil and paper with the word "purity" printed down the left side of the paper. The object of the game is to see how many words you can make starting with each of the letters P-U-R-I-T-Y. These words must in some way pertain to purity or describe something about it.

Example:

P. Patience, prophet, principles, practice, partner, and so on.
U. Understanding, unblemished, untouched, and so on.
R. Righteous, rule, reality, ruler, and so on.
I. Important, interested, insistent, and so on.
T. Time, trial, taught, teach, and so on.
Y. Years, young, and so on.

Variation: This can be played with small children by having a group of pictures depicting words that might have something to do with purity.

Hear No Evil, See No Evil, Speak No Evil

Seat the family in a circle formation. The leader stands in the middle and explains that when they point to a person in the circle that person is to cover their eyes. The person on the right is to cover their ears and the person on the left is to cover their mouth. If they do not do this by the time the leader counts to ten, they are to get up and help the leader test the rest. The last three to remain seated are acclaimed "those best prepared against sin."

Messages

Pass pencils and paper with six groups of letters arranged on it in the following way. Tell the family that there are six messages to them in code. They are not to change the order of the letters but they are to group them in such a way that they can decode the messages. You may use the following messages or make up ones that apply to the evening's lesson.

1. Rec ogn ize t hat i co vet so met imes.
2. The rea reso met hing sic ann otdo.

3. Wor kon myo wnt ale nts.
4. Ic an wo rkh ard er.
5. Se tmy hear ton wor thw hil ethi ngs.
6. I wi llr ejo iceint hes ucc ess ofo the rs.

When the letters are correctly grouped they will read as follows:

1. Recognize that I covet sometimes.
2. There are some things I cannot do.
3. Work on my own talents.
4. I can work harder.
5. Set my heart on worthwhile things.
6. I will rejoice in the success of others.

Traveling Games

Family trips and outings are fine when we finally arrive at Aunt Mary's or Yellowstone National Park, but long hours of riding can make everyone restless. The entire trip is sometimes spent in complaining and fidgeting. Why put up with that when there are many interesting and enjoyable games that can be played in the car, on a train, or on a bus? Mom can be the scorekeeper and Dad the referee, or Mom and Dad can compete against the children just to see who's quicker.

License Plate Math

See who can add all the numbers on the license plates of surrounding cars the most quickly. As a car approaches (or passes), the one who first correctly adds the numbers on the license plate is the winner.

Out of State

The person who spots an out-of-state license plate first yells, "Out of state!" The first one to recognize the state yells its name. The first person receives one point, and the second receives two points.

Which Animal?

One person sees an animal and imitates one of its characteristics. The others guess the animal and write their answers on the paper. After all have had a turn imitating an animal, the one with the most right answers is the winner.

Spinning Yarns

One person begins telling a story about anything they want. When they reach an exciting point in the story, they stop and the next person continues until all have had a turn.

Foresight

Everyone guesses what time the car will arrive at a particular town on the route. The one who guesses most accurately is the winner and may select the restaurant, motel, gas station, or whatever applies.

Nursery Songs

In turn each passenger begins singing a nursery rhyme to the tune of "Solomon Levi" (an Internet search will give the tune if no one in the group is familiar with it). All join in and continue until no one can think of another rhyme. The last person to begin a rhyme is the winner.

Teakettle

One person is instructed to place their hands over their ears so that they cannot hear. The remaining players decide on a homophone—a word that has a double meaning or spelling (pane versus pain, for example). Then the one who could not hear the word is asked a question by each player using the word "teakettle" instead of the word which has been selected. (For example: "Did you ever throw a rock through a 'teakettle'?" or "Did you ever have a 'teakettle' in your head?") The player whose sentence gives away the "teakettle" word then places their hands over their ears, and the game continues.

Variation: This game can be played with verbs in place of homophones.

"I'm Going on a Trip . . ."

The person begins by saying, "I'm going on a trip and I'm going to take . . . (two things)." (The secret is that the two items begin with the player's first and last initials, respectively.) The next player must detect the clue and learn to do the same with their initials until all catch on to it. Have players choose other patterns that the rest of the group must decipher to continue playing other rounds.

Quiet Game

The object of this game is to see who can sit still and be quiet the longest. It is designed for quieting the children when they get too active.

It Takes a Bit of Looking

Locate items such as the following while traveling. The first person to complete the list wins the game. (Adapt the list as needed to include local items.)

SIGNS

.... Barber pole
.... Sale sign
.... Fire prevention sign
.... Oil sign
.... Ice cream sign
.... Church sign
.... Keep to Right sign
.... No Parking sign

.... Fast food sign
.... Sign with word "Zone"
.... "No Vacancy" motel sign
.... Sign indicating distance
.... Picture of bell on sign
.... Sign to reduce speed
.... Sign on tree

FOR YOUNGER CHILDREN

.... Horse on left side of road
.... Animal tied by rope or chain
.... Red or gray chicken
.... Horse on right side of road
.... Calf on left side of road
........White chicken
.... Sheep on left side of road
.... Calf on right side of road
.... Animal drinking water
.... Pig on right side of road

.... Long-haired dog
.... Short-haired dog
.... Cow lying down
.... Goat
.... Black and white animal
.... Cow eating grass
.... Red and white animal
.... Duck, goose, or turkey
.... Pony
.... Animal scratching itself

GOING THROUGH A CITY

.... Weather vane on building
.... Outdoor telephone booth
.... School
.... Church
.... Red roof
.... Ladder
.... House under construction
.... Two-color roof
.... Green roof
.... Broken window in building
.... Building being built
.... Brick fireplace
.... Stone fireplace
.... Wall without a window
.... Brick house
.... Canvas awning
.... U.S. flag on building
.... Church with colored window
.... Round or oval window
.... Venetian blinds in house
.... Glass block in building
.... Metal building
.... Building damaged by fire
.... Government building

FOR A FAST TRIP

.... Car with hood open
.... Station wagon
.... Car making left turn
.... Car with top luggage carrier
.... Six-wheel truck
.... Convertible
.... Jeep
.... Foreign car
.... Semi/Eighteen-wheeler
.... Bicycle
.... Road-building equipment
.... Train
.... Gasoline transport truck
.... Blue sedan
.... Car with visible spare tire
.... Dump truck
.... Two-tone car
.... Car same color as your own
.... Car with trailer hitch
.... Car with door open
.... Truck with canvas cover
.... Truck with refrigeration
.... Car with printing on door
.... Cattle or sheep truck

Billboard Alphabet

Go through the alphabet using the letters found on billboards along the highway. Only one letter may be taken from each sign-board, and letters must follow in alphabetical order.

Variation: Start with zero and count as high as possible using the last digit on license plates. The first one to reach the goal wins.

Guess and Count

Count animals, red cars, bridges, or any other object. Before beginning, guess how many will be seen in a certain distance.

Distance

Locate a church spire, a hill in the road, a silo, or another noticeable object in the distance. Everyone guesses the distance and watches the odometer to see who comes the closest.

"I Have Something in Mind . . ."

Each person takes a turn saying, "I have something in mind that is . . . (the color of the object)." Others try to guess what it is. The number of guesses taken to locate the object is the score given to the one who had the object in mind. The highest score wins. (Also called "I Spy" and begins "I spy with my little eye something . . . [the color of the object]")

Geography

One person begins by naming a river, country, state, city, body of water, island, mountain, or peninsula. The person on their right has to think of another geographical object that begins with the last letter of the preceding word. (For example: Kansas, Salem, Montana, Amazon.)

Gas Game

Each person selects the name of a popular gas company. For each gas station passed, one point is scored to the person assigned that company.

"Who Am I?"

One person thinks of another person while others try to "read their mind" by asking them questions. They can only answer by saying "yes" or "no." For variation, limit questions to twenty; use geographical names, books, plays, songs, and so on.

Cattle Drive

Divide the family into two teams, and assign to one team the right hand side of the road and to the other, the left. The teams count cows (round up the cattle), winning one point for every cow seen, and five points for every all-white cow seen. A total of so many points is agreed upon in order to win the game.

Paper and Pencil Games

Although paper and pencil games are appropriate for almost any occasion, they are especially good for those quiet evenings at home when homework and dishes are done and baths are taken. It isn't quite bedtime and the children are eager for something to do. These games can be adapted for almost any age.

Scrambled Names

Animals

act........(cat)

ogd........(dog)

areb........(bear)

owc........(cow)

art........(rat)

edyonk........(donkey)

ipg........(pig)

uesmo........(mouse)

kcud........(duck)

eosog........(goose)

erde........(deer)

abribt........(rabbit)

hrseo........(horse)

Trees

rucesp........(spruce)

eechb........(beech)

neip........(pine)

nutestch........(chestnut)

oplarp.........(poplar)

ckoryih........(hickory)

plema........(maple)

olcuts........(locust)

ayosmcre........(sycamore)

wilolw........(willow)

colkmeh........(hemlock)

radec........(cedar)

martakac........(tamarack)

prcyess........(cypress)

irf........(fir)

sha........(ash)

Countries

ainid........(India)

mernagy........(Germany)

tlyai.........(Italy)

lngande........(England)

lolahdn........(Holland)

anadac........(Canada)

racfai........(Africa)

njapa........(Japan)

achni........(China)

fanlndi........(Finland)

razilb........(Brazil)

Fruits

plepa........(apple)

heacp........(peach)

ngeroa........(orange)

ruitferapg........(grapefruit)

reap........(pear)

mulp........(plum)

ricotpa........(apricot)

wotemlaern.......(watermelon)

Religious Hymns

Identify the correct titles of these songs which have been written with opposite meanings from the true titles.

How Loose a Roof	(How Firm a Foundation)
Drop Off	(Carry On)
Go, Go, You Devils	(Come, Come, Ye Saints)
Later the Night Will Begin	(Now the Day Is Over)
Low Off the Valley Bottom	(High on a Mountain Top)
Go Away You	(Come Follow Me)
Later Permit Us to Cry	(Now Let Us Rejoice)
Oh, How Awful Was the Evening	(Oh, How Lovely Was the Morning)
Sour Is the Play	(Sweet Is the Work)
The Devil Is Your Dark	(The Lord Is My Light)
Gather Moonbeams	(Scatter Sunshine)

Famous Latter-day Saints

What prominent Latter-day Saint man was Secretary of Agriculture in the cabinet of a president of the United States?

(Ezra Taft Benson)

Which Mormon baseball player was named "Outstanding Pitcher of the Year" in the major leagues in 1960?

(Vernon Law)

Name the Latter-day Saint man who was the world's middle-weight boxing champion.
(Gene Fullmer)

What famous Mormon was once United States ambassador to Mexico?
(J. Reuben Clark, Jr.)

What Latter-day Saint once held more speed records for automobile racing than any other man?
(Ab Jenkins)

Who was the first Latter-day Saint to run for president of the United States?
(Joseph Smith)

Name the Latter-day Saint woman whose name has become synonymous with quality bathing suits.
(Rose Marie Reid)

Name a famous Latter-day Saint golfer.
(Billy Casper)

Name the Latter-day Saint man who grew up in Germany during WWII and was a commercial pilot.
Dieter F. Uchtdorf

Name the Berlin Candy Bomber.
Gail Halvorsen

Name a Latter-day Saint who is New York Times Best Seller.
(Stephenie Meyer, Orson Scott Card, and so on)

Developing the I. Q.

Complete the following. Each blank calls for either a number or letter or word to be filled in. Every line is a separate item. Take the items in order, but do not spend too much time on any one.

1 2 3 4 5 __	(6)
white black short long down__	(up)
AB BC CD D__	(E)
Z Y X W V U__	(T)
1 2 3 2 1 2 3 4 3 2 3 4 5 4 3 4 5 6 5 __	(4)

NE/SW E/W N/__   (S)
escape scape cape__   (ape)
oh ho rat tar mood __   (doom)
A Z B Y C X D __   (W)
tot tot bard drab 537__   (735)
mist is wasp as pint in tone __   on)
57326 73265 32657 26573 __   (65732)
knit in spud up both to stay __   (at)
Scotland landscape scapegoat __ee   (goatee)
surgeon 1234567 snore 17635 rogue __   (36425)
tam tan rib rid rat raw hip __   (hit)
3124 82 73 154 46 13 __   (6)
lag leg pen pin big bog rob __   (rub)
two w four r one o three __   (r)

Check Your Ize

Match the descriptive term which best fits the word ending in "ize." Use each word only once, but use all of them. (Letters in parentheses are the answers.)

(t) Limiting eyes	a. legalize
(b) Smallest eyes	b. minimize
(f) Frightened eyes	c. advertise
(y) Talking eyes	d. dramatize
(h) Candy eyes	e. specialize
(i) Complaining eyes	f. terrorize
(a) Lawful eyes	g. baptize
(l) Classifying eyes	h. caramelize
(ff) Gregarious eyes	i. criticize
(m) Substitute eyes	j. analyze
(n) Last eyes	k. chastise
(w) Musical eyes	l. categorize
(k) Corrective eyes	m. deputize
(p) Coordinating eyes	n. finalize
(r) True eyes	o. organize
(o) Musical eyes	p. synchronize
(v) Feeling eyes	q. defies
(x) Sufficient eyes	r. realize
(u) Substantial eyes	s. paralyze
(s) Immovable eyes	t. rationalize

(q) Rebellious eyes   u. materialize
(aa) Perfumed eyes   v. emotionalize
(e) Professional eyes   w. harmonize
(bb) Seeing eyes   x. satisfies
(d) Acting eyes   y. verbalize
(j) Examining eyes   z. modernize
(c) Announcing eyes   aa. deodorize
(z) Up-to-date eyes   bb. visualize
(dd) Teaching eyes   cc. jeopardize
(cc) Dangerous eyes   dd. moralize
(g) Watery eyes   ee. franchise
(ee) Exclusive eyes   ff. socialize

Armchair Tour of the U.S.A.

The names of all fifty states of the United States can be found among the letters below. The names read forward, backward, up, down, and diagonally. Draw a pencil line around the name of a state when you locate the sequence of letters that spell it.

```
S T T E S U H C A S S A M T R S M Z A O U R
R E T S K C I K P L B V R S Y A V E M A A W
A N O Z I R A I N I G R I V T S E W I D N Y
A I N R O F I L A C U A Z X Y S R G N I A K
N O T G N I H S A W U N A B S T M E N R I C
S O U T H D A K O T A N E E J J O O E O S U
M A R Y L A N D L M I H N N N C N R S L I T
O P U T A H R S T L N N U E J V T G O F U N
A K A X H O A W O I E Y Z A V E R I T S O E
K R L S B C D R E T F C I J K A R A A X L K
S O A A I N A V L Y S N N E P M D S N O P E
A Y S X H C S R N A G I H C I M N A E T U R
R W K E H O W Y O M I N G V S A X Y S Y A H
B E A T C E M F I L H J T I K L I K I E O O
E N U K L M N A H M I H E R C A R T N H D D
N O R T H D A K O T A N A G L B N I D U A E
S R I R U O S S I M I T A I S A A S I K R I
N E W H A M P S H I R E B N O M O R A E O S
X G I P P I S S I S S I M I V A V W N S L L
Y O C I X E M W E N D E L A W A R E A Z O A
X N I S N O C S I W R T S A N A T N O M C N
T T U C I T C E N N O C S I O N I L L I X D
```

"Did You Ever See?"

Each player in turn adds to the following list or pays a forfeit. See page _ for forfeits. "Did you ever see . . ."

a sea coast	a cat nip
a wheel barrow	a door step
a chicken run	mountain ears
a cattle cross	a heart burn
a cracker box	an alley way
a board walk	a cow hide

Scrambled Animals

1.	ALMAL	(Llama)
2.	ANOGARKO	(Kangaroo)
3.	BEDRAG	(Badger)
4.	BRAVEE	(Beaver)
5.	BRAZE	(Zebra)
6.	CEMHIZANEP	(Chimpanzee)
7.	COOTEL	(Ocelot)
8.	ERGIT	(Tiger)
9.	EWLRENOVI	(Wolverine)
10.	EHGROP	(Gopher)
11.	KEMYON	(Monkey)
12.	LOFUBAF	(Buffalo)
13.	NEEPTHAL	(Elephant)
14.	NETHARP	(Panther)
15.	OMASHIC	(Chamois)
16.	ONAPEELT	(Antelope)
17.	ONIBS	(Bison)
18.	OSUME	(Mouse)
19.	PASOTUMPOIPH	(Hippopotamus)
20.	PHESE	(Sheep)
21.	RATOGUNAN	(Orangutan)
22.	ROBA	(Boar)
23.	TARBIB	(Rabbit)
24.	TAWLCID	(Wildcat)
25.	YENOKD	(Donkey)

Know Your House

Have all the children gather in one room. Then one of the group takes a pencil and paper and goes about the house jotting down various questions about familiar objects. For example, they might write, "How many windows are there in the house? How many electric floor plugs?" When the list has been prepared, all the players are given pencils and papers. Then the person who has made up the list reads the questions one by one, and the others write down their answers.

When everyone is finished, the questioner repeats the questions, and each player reads his answers in turn. Ten points are given for a correct answer. The one who has the highest score becomes the next one to make out a list.

Body Parts

Each of the phrases below represents some part of a person's body.

Part of a wagon	(Tongue)
A school child	(Pupil)
Tropical tree	(Palm)
Edge of a saw	(Teeth)
Weapons of war	(Arms)
What a dog buries	(Bone)
A cad	(Heel)
A place of worship	(Temple)
Top of a hill	(Crown)
What you put to the wheel	(Shoulder)
What the tortoise raced with	(Hair)
Part of a river	(Mouth)
To keep tools in	(Chest)
Sometimes it locks	(Jaw)
A type of macaroni	(Elbow)
Used by a carpenter	(Nail)
What you should keep out of other people's business	(Nose)
"I have Two Little__"	(Hands)

Scrambled Wedding Terms

1. DRBIE   (Bride)
2. MROGO   (Groom)
3. VLOE   (Love)
4. ULEB   (Blue)
5. QUETOUB   (Bouquet)
6. AECK   (Cake)
7. CREI   (Rice)
8. TESBNMA   (Best Man)
9. DAIRBIDSEM   (Bridesmaid)
10. RECRPHEA   (Preacher)
11. RECFITITACE   (Certificate)
12. DEIWNGD GRIN (Wedding ring)
13. MIDAODN   (Diamond)
14. YOOMHEONN   (Honeymoon)
15. NUJE   (June)
16. PLOEMTENE   (Elopement)
17. MANEGNTEGE (Engagement)
18. LOPROASP   (Proposal)
19. LIEV   (Veil)
20. YASRREVNNIA (Anniversary)
21. ROTHEMNIWAL (Mother-In-Law)

Scrambled Pies

1. KIPUPMN   (Pumpkin)
2. COCTOUN DRAUTSC (Coconut Custard)
3. PAELP   (Apple)
4. HEACP   (Peach)
5. REWYRABTRS   (Strawberry)
6. KRECEHUYLBR (Huckleberry)
7. PRYBARERS   (Raspberry)
8. LMUP   (Plum)
9. ANANAB MERCA (Banana Cream)
10. TRUNCRA   (Currant)
11. CIENM   (Mince)
12. NEURP   (Prune)
13. TRUBETTOSCCH (Butterscotch)
14. NEMOL GRENEUMI (Lemon Meringue)
15. NAIRSI   (Raisin)

16. HARUBRB	(Rhubarb)
17. TRIOPAC	(Apricot)
18. RELEUBYBR	(Blueberry)
19. PERAG	(Grape)
20. YELKABCRBR	(Blackberry)
21. TAEM	(Meat)
22. CYRANBERR	(Cranberry)
23. REHCRY	(Cherry)
24. PAPNELPEI	(Pineapple)
25. LOCTAHOEC	(Chocolate)

Home

Place the letters from the word "home" in the spaces provided so as to complete the word.

1. .. .. t .. .. r	(Mother)
2. C .. r	(Chrome)
3. .. .. y	(Homey)
4. S .. .. t .. .. r	(Smother)
5. .. .. .. l .. c k	(Hemlock)
6. .. .. l y	(Homely)
7. S o .. .. w	(Somehow)
8. .. .. i r l .. o ..	(Heirloom)
9. .. .. r	(Homer)
10. S .. .. o t .. .. n	(Smoothen)
11. .. .. a g ..	(Homage)
12. .. a n d s	(Handsome)
13. S .. .. w .. .. n	(Showmen)
14. T .. .. .. r e ..	(Theorem)
15. .. .. a d .. .. s t	(Headmost)

Family Quiz Game

For adults:

1. Who was the Roman god of war?
2. Is tarragon a spice or an herb?
3. The French designer who created the look of white boots and short tunic dresses in 1964 was . . . .
4. What is the name of the federal government's preschool program designed to help the culturally deprived child?

5. Which constitutional amendment deals with income tax?
6. Name the Broadway play on which Richard Rodgers's musical "Do I Hear a Waltz?" is based.
7. Who was the first woman to be a presidential candidate?
8. Which of the following is not a civil rights organization? CORE, SNCC, SANE, and NAACP.
9. What was the "Manhattan Project?"
10. Anthracite coal is (a) hard (b) soft.
11. How long is a fortnight?
12. True or false? The pound is a unit of mass.
13. What is Robert Ford noted for?
14. In which year was Abraham Lincoln killed?
15. What are the two major religions in India?
16. Who wrote *Crime and Punishment*?
17. What does the Latin phrase *pro tempore* mean?
18. In what motion picture of Charles Chaplin's did he first speak?
19. In what year was the King James version of the Bible published?
20. Who played the brave sheriff in the movie *High Noon*?

For youth 10 to 15:

1. If A has 29 votes, B has 21 votes, and C has 25 votes, A wins by a .... of four votes over their closest opponent.
2. What Spanish explorer discovered the Mississippi River?
3. What state was Andrew Jackson's birthplace?
4. Who wrote *Robinson Crusoe*?
5. What is an ion?
6. An angle that is less than 90 degrees is often called an .... angle.
7. What is an amoeba?
8. Who shot Abraham Lincoln?
9. True or false: Thomas Jefferson was the third president of the United States.
10. What two individuals wrote the famous Broadway musical "South Pacific"?
11. What star is closest to our planet Earth?
12. The speed of a boat is measured in ....
13. What country was Cleopatra queen of?
14. How many sharps are in the key of D major?
15. The Amazon is a famous river in what continent?

16. What is the popular title given to the federal government's program to aid the poor?
17. How many people usually sit on an American court jury?
18. What baseball player hit the most home runs in a single season?

For youngsters 6½ to 9 years:

1. We get ivory from what animals?
2. Is the weather hotter or colder as one nears the equator?
3. Which of our states is the largest in area?
4. The longest river in the United States is . . . .
5. What was the name of the girl who flew away with Peter Pan?
6. Which president of the United States freed the slaves?
7. Is James Bond the author or the leading character in the popular spy movies and novels?
8. What is name of the ocean on the west coast of the United States?
9. Which state is farther north—Maine or Florida?
10. What part of speech are names like Robert, Empire State Building, and so on?

For youngsters 5 and 6 years:

1. True or false: The teepee was a home built by American Indians.
2. In the story, "The Ugly Duckling," what does the ugly duckling become?
3. Which is closer to the Earth—the moon or Mars?
4. How many fingers do you have?
5. What is the name of the famous Walt Disney mouse?
6. The name of the fairy tale character who has glass slippers is . . . .
7. How many hours are there on the face of a clock?
8. What does the yellow traffic light mean?

ANSWERS

For adults:

1. Mars
2. An herb
3. André Courrèges
4. Project Head Start
5. Article XVI
6. "Time of the Cuckoo"
7. Victoria Woodhull, 1872
8. SANE-Committee for a Sane Nuclear Policy
9. A committee established in 1942 by President Roosevelt to investigate the uses of nuclear energy for military purposes
10. (a) Hard
11. Two weeks
12. False (The pound is a unit of weight)
13. He shot Jesse James.
14. 1865
15. Hinduism and Mohammedanism
16. Fyodor Dostoyevsky
17. "For the time being"
18. 1940, "The Great Dictator"
19. 1611
20. Gary Cooper

For youth:

1. Plurality
2. Hernando de Soto
3. South Carolina
4. Daniel Defoe
5. An atom, or group of atoms with an electrical charge
6. Acute
7. A microscopic one-celled animal
8. John Wilkes Booth
9. True
10. Rodgers & Hammerstein
11. The sun
12. Knots
13. Egypt
14. Two, f# and c#
15. South America
16. The War on Poverty
17. Twelve
18. Roger Maris, 61 in 1961

For youngsters 6½ to 9:

1. Elephant, walrus
2. Hotter
3. Alaska
4. Mississippi, Missouri, Red Rock River
5. Wendy
6. Abraham Lincoln
7. Leading character
8. Pacific Ocean
9. Maine
10. Proper nouns

For youngsters 5 and 6:

1. True
2. A swan
3. The moon
4. Ten

5. Mickey Mouse
6. Cinderella
7. Twelve
8. Slow or caution

Hemisphere

In the diagram below draw six straight lines across the rectangle in such a way as to separate each small circle from every other small circle.

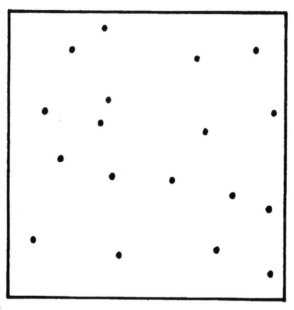

Answer:

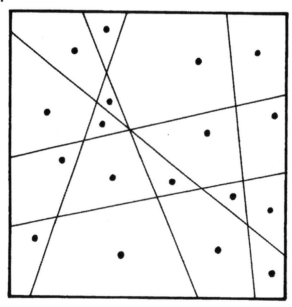

Cross Country Run

Sheets of paper or cardboard are marked out into a number of small squares, each one numbered, but not in rotation. Each player is given one of these sheets. The "run" consists in following with a pencil a course from square to square, in consecutive numerical order (1, 2, 3, 4, and so on). The first to connect all his squares in this consecutive fashion wins.

11	58	39	13	53	34	20	5
21	48	22	60	27	57	6	43
35	61	1	44	12	7	33	26
41	56	18	62	19	47	14	59
10	46	32	3	28	36	4	40
31	45	2	55	37	63	25	51
17	23	64	16	52	30	15	54
24	50	9	49	38	8	42	29

Song Titles

Draw a picture of the following titles, or come up with titles of your own:

1. "When the Moon Comes Over the Mountain"
2. "He'll Be Coming Around the Mountain When He Comes"
3. "Smoke Gets in Your Eyes"
4. "Down by the Old Mill Stream"
5. "There's a Long Long Trail Awinding"
6. "Did you Think to Pray?"
7. "High on a Mountain Top"
8. "Sowing, Sowing"
9. "I'm Dreaming of a White Christmas"

10. "Tea for Two"
11. "Joseph Smith's First Prayer"
12. "Catch the Sunshine"
13. "Ere You Left Your Room This Morning Did You Think to Pray?"
14. "Put Your Shoulder to the Wheel"
15. "What Shall the Harvest Be?"
16. "America"
17. "When It's Spring Time in the Rockies"

Western Scramble

Western Characters

Attyw Pear	(Wyatt Earp)
Cod Dalihay	(Doc Halliday)
Rknaf Semaj	(Frank James)
Sejes Masej	(Jesse James)
Dilw Ubi Ockickh	(Wild Bill Hickock)
Nanei Yekola	(Annie Oakley)
Fabulfo Lbil	(Buffalo Bill)
Libly Het Idk	(Billy the Kid)
Veyda Troctkec	(Davey Crockett)
Mji Wiobe	(Jim Bowie)
Msa Toushon	(Sam Houston)
Asm Tloc	(Sam Colt)
Lilw Sogrre	(Will Rogers)
Ellbe Rrats	(Belle Starr)
Rogemoni	(Geronimo)
Hocecis	(Cochise)
Seopc Blli	(Pecos Bill)
Yro Gesror	(Roy Rogers)

Western Towns

Agvniiri Ycti	(Virginia City)
Nocsut	(Tucson)
Nneechey	(Cheyenne)
Roft Ratng	(Fort Grant)
Tenosbmot	(Tombstone)
Lervis Ticy	(Silver City)
Taans Ef	(Santa Fe)

Torf Thorw   (Fort Worth)
Sonrac Yict   (Carson City)
K. O. Orarlic   (O. K. Corral)
Moala   (Alamo)
Tobo Ilhl   (Boot Hill)
Aderol   (Laredo)
Gdoed Iytc   (Dodge City)

Indian Tribes

Uipte   (Piute)
Vjonaa   (Navajo)
Piho   (Hopi)
Ecahap   (Apache)
Tue   (Ute)
Soshheno   (Shoshone)
Nokbanc   (Bannock)
Faeteblck   (Blackfeet)
Ehekorce   (Cherokee)
Mcecohna   (Comanche)
Monlesei   (Seminole)

Objects of the West

Surps   (Spurs)
Sdedla   (Saddle)
Ledrib   (Bridle)
Lacror   (Corral)
Ester   (Steer)
Lafc   (Calf)
Lubl   (Bull)
Erhos   (Horse)
Bocyow   (Cowboy)
Doore   (Rodeo)
Slosa   (Lasso)
Spachu   (Chaps)
Rembroso   (Sombrero)
Urrob   (Burro)
Dranb   (Brand)
Lsohetr   (Holster)

Brain Teasers in Science

1. What year is MCDXCII, and what happened that year?
2. What is the purpose of a barometer?
3. "212 degrees Fahrenheit" is most commonly used to designate the . . . of water?
4. What travels at the rate of 186,300 miles per second?
5. What scientific principle was discovered through the fall of an apple?
6. Milk that has been heated to partially sterilize it is called what?
7. If a repair man speaks of a carburetor, what is he repairing?
8. Try this scientific riddle: What goes up and down in winter?
9. Who discovered what by using a string, a key, and a jar?
10. What did Eli Whitney invent?
11. What did Fulton invent?
12. What invention does the name Westinghouse stand for?
13. What electrical terms do AC and DC stand for?
14. True or false: The temperature is 60° below zero eight miles from Miami.
15. If you burned a pan of fudge what would you call the remains?
16. What happens when carbon and oxygen unite in the body?
17. We breathe in oxygen and breathe out what?
18. What causes day and night?
19. How long does it take the earth to travel around the sun?
20. What is the imaginary line around the center of a globe called?
21. Why do the wires in an electric toaster glow and get hot?
22. What does "supersonic speed" mean?
23. Is it true that Galileo invented a telescope for studying the stars?
24. Which of the following is not a protein food: chicken, cheese, beans, or cabbage?
25. What vitamin prevents rickets and helps to make good teeth?
26. Are capillaries larger or smaller than veins?
27. In what way are people usually protected against smallpox?
28. How does a prism in a spectrograph affect a ray of light?
29. Name a fish famous for migrating.
30. What Polish woman discovered radium?
31. For what is Albert Einstein most widely known?
32. Why does an iron ship float?

33. If you had an omelet made from the biggest egg, which egg would it be?
34. Why is distilled water used in a car battery?
35. Why is a storage battery better than a dry cell?
36. Why do fuses in your house sometimes "blow" out?
37. Which of the following conducts electricity: glass, rubber, or copper?
38. Why are several cylinders in an automobile better than one?
39. What idea did James Watt get from a steaming teakettle?
40. What heavenly body affects the tides of our oceans?
41. Which is larger, Earth, Jupiter, or Mars?
42. How is mitosis associated with making two for one?
43. Explain why the word "pasteurization" comes from the name "Pasteur."

ANSWERS

1. 1492, Columbus discovered America
2. To record atmospheric pressure and forecast weather
3. Boiling point
4. Light
5. Gravity discovered by Newton
6. Pasteurized milk
7. Gasoline motor
8. Mercury in a thermometer
9. Ben Franklin, electricity
10. Cotton gin
11. Steamboat
12. Air brake
13. Alternating current, direct current
14. True, 8 miles straight up
15. Charcoal or carbon
16. Heat is produced
17. Carbon dioxide
18. Rotation of the earth on its axis every 24 hours
19. 365¼ days
20. Equator
21. They are made of a substance that resists electricity
22. Speed faster than that of sound
23. Yes
24. Cabbage
25. Vitamin D

26. Smaller
27. By vaccination
28. Bends each color a different amount thus separating the colors.
29. Salmon
30. Madame Marie Curie
31. Theory of relativity
32. Inside hollow, filled with air
33. Ostrich egg
34. No minerals, no ruin
35. Dry cell can't be recharged
36. Too much current, metal in fuse melts and breaks the circuit
37. Copper
38. More power and even flow
39. Using steam for power
40. The moon
41. Jupiter
42. Reproduction by direct cell division
43. Louis Pasteur discovered bacteria

Brain Teasers in Math

1. What is 3.14 called in mathematics?
2. You have ¾ glass of juice and pour out ⅜; how much is left?
3. How much money is two bucks and two dimes?
4. If someone gave you 20 cats and 20 dogs, what would you have?
5. Give three four-letter words that mean a measure of length.
6. What figure has five sides?
7. If ¼ inch equals 4 feet, how long will a hall be if the drawing is 2¾ inches?
8. You have 2½ pies to serve 10 boys; how much will each get?
9. If you use a pole to lift a log, which is the resistance, and which is the lever?
10. On a common seesaw, where is the fulcrum point?
11. Are fire tongs, a monkey wrench, and a nut cracker all levers?
12. What is the main advantage in using a pulley to lift a weight?
13. If 55% of American people live in cities, what percent do not?
14. If your allowance is $5.25 and you spend $1.50, how much is left?

15. How do you find the perimeter of a rectangle?
16. How do you find the area of a rectangle?
17. If you get 3 pencils for 10 cents, how much would 12 pencils cost?
18. How do you change minutes to part of an hour?
19. If 54 loaves are wrapped in a minute, how many are wrapped in an hour?
20. Add $9^3/_5$ and $6^2/_5$.
21. How many pint bottles will 8 quarts of milk fill?
22. Harry is 16 and Alice is 8. How many times as old as Alice is Harry?
23. How can an improper fraction be changed to a mixed number?
24. How is an equilateral triangle different from any other kind of triangle?
25. If you got a $90 typewriter at a 15% discount, what would you pay?
26. If you ate 6 chestnuts out of 60, what fraction did you eat?
27. How many quarts make one gallon?
28. How many marbles do you get for 9 cents if they are 3 for a penny?
29. In Roman numerals, what does "V" mean?

ANSWERS

1. Pi
2. $^3/_8$
3. $2.20
4. A fight
5. Inch, foot, yard, mile, pace, hand
6. Pentagon
7. 44 feet
8. $^1/_4$
9. Log—resistance; pole—lever
10. Where the board touches its prop
11. Yes
12. You can change the direction of pull
13. 45%
14. $3.75
15. Add length of sides, or 2(w+l)
16. Multiply the length by the width
17. 40 cents

18. Divide the minutes by sixty
19. 3,240
20. 16
21. 16
22. Twice
23. Divide the numerator by the denominator
24. All three sides are equal
25. $76.50
26. $^1/_{10}$
27. 4
28. 27
29. 5

Active Games

Slam Bang

Seat players around a table and provide each with an empty thread spool tied with a piece of string about three feet long. While the players hold the end of the strings, the leader assembles all the spools in the center of the table under a container, such as an inverted empty can, a pan cover, and so on. For each turn the leader holds the cover about eighteen inches above the assembled spools and throws two dice. Anytime the dice add up to seven in any combination the leader slams down the cover while the players jerk away their spools. Any player whose spool is trapped is eliminated, and the last player remaining is the winner.

Jack Horner

Blindfold two players. Give the players five marshmallows each and tell them to feed each other. This is great fun for all.

Hold Fast! Let Go!

Four players stand up. Each player grasps a corner of a square of paper. A fifth player commands "Hold fast!" or "Let go!" Players are required to do just the opposite. When "hold fast" is called out, players let go. When "let go" is called out, players must hold fast. Players who fail to do the opposite of the command drop out. The last player grasping the paper accurately is the winner.

Guess Who

A person selected to be "it" is blindfolded. Other players form a circle around the blindfolded player. This player walks to one of the players in the circle and by feeling only the player's head and shoulders tries to discover their identity. If their guess is right, the player whose identity has been guessed is "it" for the next game.

Hunt the Ring

A person selected to be "it" stands in the middle of a circle of players. A piece of string long enough to go around the circle is slipped through a ring and the ends of the string are tied. All players in the circle grasp the string. The "it" player counts to ten with their eyes closed so as not to see the ring passed initially. The ring is concealed under a player's hand and is passed from player to player. The "it" player must find the player under whose hand the ring is concealed. The player caught with the ring becomes "it."

Swat the Mosquito

Select a player to be the swatter. Blindfold them and provide them with a rolled newspaper as a swatter. Seat them in the center of the room on a stool or box. The players (mosquitoes) tiptoe up to the swatter and buzz in their ear, quickly withdrawing when the swatter strikes at them. Anyone hit becomes the swatter. The swatter may swat only when they hear a buzz. Instruct the players not to buzz constantly, but only when they are very near to the swatter.

The game is sometimes played by having the players say "Chickadee" instead of buzzing.

Deer Stalking

The "hunter" and "deer" are both blindfolded. They stand at opposite ends of a long table. The hunter attempts to catch the deer, and the deer tries to avoid being caught as they both move around the table. The family should remain quiet so that the hunter can stalk the deer through any movements they make. The game is exciting and full of suspense for the spectators as well as for the players. Sometimes, to add to the fun, the hunter is allowed to make an occasional noise by rapping on the table. This gives the deer more chance to get away. The variation is amusing, for often the hunter decides to rap just when, without knowing it, they have practically caught the deer.

Spoon Click

All but one of the players stand in a circle. The one player is blindfolded and placed in the center. They are given two spoons. The players in the circle clasp hands and move around until the blindfolded player clicks the spoons together, at which signal the circle must stand still. The blindfolded player then goes up to anyone in the circle and, by feeling over their face and head with the bowls of the spoons, must identify the player. The player may not feel on the shoulder or around the neck; only on the face and head. A player may stoop to disguise their height for this, but otherwise may not evade the touch of the spoons. If the blindfolded player correctly identifies the person before them, they change places. If their guess is incorrect, the play is repeated.

Obey the Law

Players arrange their chairs in a circle. One player, called the lawgiver, stands in the center. As they give the laws, the other players obey. If the players are not alert, they will disobey the law, and the lawgiver can take the chair of the disobedient player, who then becomes the next lawgiver.

Use "laws" similar to the following list, or use some of your own. The laws should be given in rapid succession so that the players must stay alert.

> Stand up.
> Sit down.
> Stand on the left foot.
> Move two chairs to the right.
> Move one chair to the left.
> Move to the second chair on your right.
> Move to the third chair on your left.
> Lift both feet off the floor.
> Turn around.
> Raise both arms.

What's Gone?

One player is the leader and must collect a miscellaneous group of objects, about ten in number, such as a spoon, string, pencil, tack, and so on. These are placed on a table and, at a command from the leader, all players turn their backs. The leader takes away one of the articles and says, "ready." The players turn back to the table and the leader calls upon one of them to name the missing article before they can count to ten. A player who misses is becomes the leader.

Blind Bell

All the players but one are blindfolded and scatter. The one who is not blindfolded carries a bell loosely in one hand so that it will ring with every step. This bell may also be hung around the neck on a string. The blindfolded players try to catch the one with the bell who will have to use considerable alertness to keep out of the way. Whoever catches the bell player changes places with them.

Lost Lover

Players are seated in a circle with one player who is "it" blindfolded in the center. The "it" player tries to find a seated player and then drops to their knees and says to the one seated, "Are you my lost lover?" The victim answers with a disguised voice. They may bark like a dog, meow like a cat, growl, or answer in any manner they wish, as the person who is "it" tries to recognize who they are. If the player who is "it" guesses correctly, the victim becomes "it." If not, the "it" player tries again.

Quiet Games

Nature Hunting

A player chosen to be "it" chooses a subject and must give clues for the others to guess the what the subject is. The player may say "I am thinking of a tree," or "an animal," or "an insect." Clues may be given to help the group locate the particular subject. For instance, the "it" player may say, "The bird I have in mind has a red stripe on a black wing and is often seen on swaying cattails in a swampy land."

Slammers, Creepers

Divide the players into two groups with a leader or captain for each. Teams sit on opposite sides of the table. A coin is passed from hand to hand under the table by one team in an effort to conceal its movements from the other side. When they wish, the leader of the opposite team says, "Arms up." All the coin-passing group must then raise closed fists and show them to the challengers. The same leader then says either "slammers" or "creepers." When "slammers" is called, palms are slapped onto the table with enough noise to cover the clink of the coin. When "creepers" is called players place their fists on the edge of the table and slowly extend the fingers, trying to conceal the location of the coin. The captain of the other team now points to hands that his team wishes raised. After the hands are raised, they should be put on the owner's lap. The object is to find the hand covering the coin as soon as possible. For each hand left on the table there is a point for the guessing team. Teams alternate with the coin.

Imitation

The leader tells a story about birds and animals. Whenever the leader mentions a bird, all the children wave their arms like a bird flying; but if, by mistake, someone waves their arms when animals are mentioned, then the culprit must take the place of the storyteller and go on with the story.

Purchase

A player says, "I'm going to Chicago. What shall I buy?" The player on that player's right must respond with three things beginning with the first letter of the town the first player mentioned, such as "Candy, corn, and chowder." The second player then says, "I'm going to St. Paul. What shall I buy?" The next player names three things beginning with the letter *S*. The purchases must be named before the next player can count to ten.

Forfeit

Everyone gets in a circle and passes a pillow around. When the leader says stop, the person with the pillow must forfeit something they have with them, like a sock or a pair of glasses. After several people have given up something, the leader takes their objects and asks one of the people to sit in front of the leader. The leader tells the person, "Here is a thing and a very pretty thing. What shall the owner do to redeem it?" The person asks, "Fine or superfine?" (Fine means it's a boy's object; superfine, a girl's.) The leader tells them which it is; then the person thinks of a penalty suitable for either a boy or girl as the case may be, such as doing a cartwheel or telling a joke. The person to whom this object belongs is now required to do the penalty if they'd like their object back. This continues until all the objects are returned.

My Grandmother

Begin a conversation by saying, "I have a strange grandmother. She won't sit on a chair; she'll only sit on a stool. She won't wear shoes; she prefers boots. She doesn't like peaches, but she loves strawberries." Someone else in the group may be cued to come back with similar remarks about his grandmother. The others must discover the trick.

The key is the double letters. Grandmother likes only things with double letters. A similar game is "My grandmother doesn't like possums." Then any word containing *p* doesn't suit grandmother.

Common Sayings

One person leaves the room and the rest select a familiar saying or proverb, the words of which are distributed one by one, in the order of their sequence, among the players. If there are more words than people, the older players may have more than one word. The person then returns and asks something of each of the players in turn, who must try to introduce in the reply the special words allotted to him in such a way as to escape the notice of the questioner. The person from whose answer the person guesses the proverb then becomes "it."

Examples:

1. Don't count your chickens before they hatch
2. Early to bed, early to rise
3. Don't throw the baby out with the bath water
4. We'll cross that bridge when we get to it
5. Keep your friends close but your enemies closer

Pick-Up-Sticks

You can use toothpicks or regular pick-up-sticks. Usually two to six people play. Gather the sticks, drop them, and have each person take a turn picking them up one by one with another stick or their fingers. If a player moves a stick they are not picking up, they lose their turn. Once all the sticks are all picked up, the one with the most sticks wins.

Harmony

One player begins the game by saying, for instance, "I am thinking of something in the room that rhymes with 'fair.'" The others ask, "Is it chair?" "Is it hair?" "Is it pear?" and so on until they guess it. The one who guesses correctly starts another. The game may be varied by enlarging the boundaries so that one is not confined to the room for his thought, or the limits may be determined by some classification, such as nature, geography, Church history, and so on.

What's the Trick?

Have one person leave the room. Inform them before they leave that they are to ask questions when they are called back into the room. While they are out, tell the remaining persons they are to answer not the question asked them, but the question of the person just previously asked. The first person need not answer. The person returns to the room and tries to figure out the game.

Barnyard Music

The leader gives each guest the name of a barnyard animal to imitate. Assign to the victim the task of braying like a donkey. At the signal each shouts his call. All goes well the first time, and then the leader quiets everything down to give the signal to start again and asks all to start their call quickly and loudly when the leader waves their hand. The signal is given and not a sound is heard except from the victim, who sounds forth loudly with a donkey solo. This is a great trick to play on Dad. Be sure to explain the game to all other players apart from the victim.

What Is My Thought Like?

The players are seated. The leader states that they are thinking about something but will not say what until later. The leader says to each player, "What is my thought like?" The first player might say, "A blue jay"; the second, "A patrolman," and so on. As each answer is given, the leader jots it down. When all have answered, the leader goes to the first and says, "My thought is about my tie. Why is my necktie like a blue jay?" The player must think quickly and might answer, "It's pretty loud." The leader then asks the next player why their tie is like a patrolman, and the player might answer, "Always getting on somebody's neck." The interest in this event centers around the humor of the answers and, in any family, many clever remarks will result.

The Queen's Headache

Blindfold one of the family and seat them at one end of the room. Place an empty chair to the side of them. Then announce that the "queen" has a headache and doesn't want to be disturbed. The players try to walk up to the empty chair without disturbing the queen. The queen groans as soon as they hear footsteps approaching and the one who is walking must sit down wherever they are. Keep up the game until a player succeeds in getting to the empty chair.

How, When, and Where?

A player leaves the room while the group selects a noun, for example, "trip." The player returns and asks each person three questions: "How do you like it?"; "When do you like it?"; and "Where do you like it?" The answers might be, "Long drawn out," to the first; "In the fall," to the second; "In the hills," to the third. The player whose answer reveals the chosen word is the next to leave the room.

Poison Object

A person (not playing) holds a whistle. The players form a single circle facing center. Give one person an object. At the starting signal, they pass it around the circle to the right. When the whistle blows, the person holding the object is out. The last person in the circle is the winner.

Up, Down, Up

The leader places an object in their hand, puts their hands behind their back, and goes to someone with both fists closed as if there were something in both hands. The leader then says, "Up, down, up," while changing the position of their fists from top to bottom. The person the leader is facing tries to guess which hand the object is in. If the person guesses correctly, they become the leader.

Funny Face

The players sit in a circle with a solemn expression. One player is "it." They suddenly burst out laughing and, as suddenly, stop, wipe the smile from their face and toss it to another who in turn bursts out laughing. This continues. Any player who laughs and is not supposed to, drops out of the game. The last player in the game is the winner.

What's Wrong?

One player leaves the room. In his absence the others change the position of the chairs or other small furniture. Only these changes are permitted. The "it" player is called and upon their return must point out the changes. If they are successful another person is chosen to be "it."

Listen

One player is blindfolded and seated near one end of the room. The other players line up and one at a time attempt to pass the blindfolded player without being discovered. Players whom the blindfolded player hears passing them drop out. The last player left in the game wins. First player caught is blindfolded for the new game.

Make a Body

Make a cube and paint the following letters on the sides: B-H-A-L-E-M (or have numbers stand for these letters on a regular die). A player rolls the cube. They must get the letters in order and can only draw the part of the body as they throw the correct letters.

B body (beautiful)—make one
H head (healthy)—make one
A arms (agile)—make two
L legs (lovable)—make two
E eyes (educated)—make two
M mouth (merry)—make one

If they successfully toss the needed letter the player takes another turn. If they toss something they already have or something out of order they lose their turn. A player cannot start drawing their body until they gets a *B* for body. The first player to complete their body is the winner.

Imaginative Hunting

One player decides on a place of hiding. Bounds have been set by common agreement, such as "in the house," "in the room," "in the yard." The player who guesses correctly has the privilege of deciding on a place of hiding next time. If the bounds are confined to the room, the player may hide in a vase, in a desk drawer, behind a flower pot, and so on, since this is an imaginative game.

Out the Window

Players take turns looking out the window. When all have had a turn the playing starts. In order, each player tells one thing that they saw but they must not repeat an object given by a previous player. As players can no longer give new items, they drop out. The last player to mention a new item is the winner.

Alphabet Draw

Draw each letter of the alphabet on an index card. Place these cards in the center of the table. Each player, in turn, draws a card until some player draws letter A, which he keeps. The other cards are returned to the center of the table and shuffled into the stack, and drawing continues until a player draws letter *B* whereupon remaining cards are again put in the center. This continues until the entire alphabet has been drawn in order. The player with the greatest number of cards in his possession is the winner.

Touch

All players except one are blindfolded The player who is not blindfolded selects a group of objects such as a match box, pencil, small toy, and so on. Each player is handed an object and told to identify it. As a player misses, they drop out. The game continues until only one player remains.

I'm Thinking

The players are seated. The person chosen to be "it" says, "I'm thinking of something that begins with A." This can be anything, an animal, fish, person, flower, word, and so on. The other players ask leading questions and try to guess in turn. The "it" player can answer only "yes" or "no" to the questions. As each player guesses and fails, they drop out. The one who guesses correctly wins and is the next person to be "it." Should all players fail to guess, the original "it" player has another turn.

Taste

All players except one are blindfolded. The player who is not blindfolded hands each player something to taste, such as sugar, salt, vinegar, and so on. Each player, after tasting, must identify the item. As players miss they drop out. The game continues until only one player remains.

Earth, Air, or Water

The players sit around the room. The first player has a handkerchief which he tosses to one of the others; as he tosses he says one of these words: earth, air, or water. The catcher must instantly name a creature which lives in the realm named. If they fail to name a creature or are wrong in their answer they drop out of the game. No creature can be named twice in the same game. The player who repeats drops out as well. The last player left is the winner.

Smell

All players except one are blindfolded. The player who is not blindfolded hands each player something to smell, such as vanilla, orange, onion, and so on. Each player, after smelling, must identify the odor. As players miss they drop out. The game continues until only one player remains.

I Am Thinking of Someone

The person who is "it" will describe some family member by describing a distinctive trait that person has or a specific act they have performed. (Negative traits or actions are ruled out.) The rest of the family will try to guess which family member is being described. No one should guess until they are fairly sure they are right. If the guess is wrong, the person is not permitted to guess again in that round. The person who is "it" is allowed to give several clues. The one who guessed correctly will have the next turn to describe someone. The game continues until everyone has been described at least once. The person being described may not guess that he is the one.

The person who is "it" should avoid telling whether the one being described is male or female. Speak of the person as "this person." It will add to the fun of the game if the clues are vague and general at first and become more specific as the game proceeds. It might be well, especially if the children are small, for a parent to start the game in order to make the playing procedure clear. For instance, the parent might say, "I'm thinking of someone in this family who is almost always happy. This is someone who is kind and helpful. This person picked up little brother's toys the other day without being asked. This is someone who doesn't get angry when teased but plays with the one who teases."

What Do You Know about Me?

Each person in the family in turn will ask a question about their preferences and call on different family members to answer. If after three or four tries the group is not able to do so, he will tell them the answers. The same question may be used by different players. The person who explains the game might read aloud the following list of questions to start the thinking. Family members could ask one of these questions or any other they choose. The game continues as long as desired, each player in turn asking a question about themselves. Score one point for each correct answer given.

1. What is my favorite color?
2. What is my favorite food?
3. What is my favorite TV show?
4. What is my favorite game?
5. What is my favorite flower?
6. What is my favorite subject in school?
7. What is my favorite time of year?
8. What is my favorite song?
9. What is my favorite Bible story?
10. Who is my favorite friend?

National Anthem

Players all stand up and face the leader. Everyone sings the national anthem. The leader has the words and watches the group to see who doesn't know the words. When they see someone miss, they have that person turn around and face the opposite direction. The last one turned around wins.

Music

The person in the center of the circle names a musical instrument and explains or demonstrates the act that accompanies it. The act must involve three people. For example: A guitar might be one of the instruments. The person who is in the center, "it," walks up to a person and says, "guitar," and starts to count to ten. The person they point to could put their arms up as if holding a guitar, and the one on the guitarist's left would finger it with his left hand, and the one on the right would strum it with his right hand. If the action is not completed before the person who is "it" counts to ten, the person to whom they pointed must exchange places with them. Similar actions could be done for other instruments such as drums, trumpet, trombone, and so on.

Modern Art

The leader blindfolds all of the players and gives them a piece of paper and a pencil. The leader then says, "Draw a house." In the following order they instruct the players to complete the picture with suggested details: "Put a chimney on the house with smoke coming out of the chimney." "Draw a horse on a trail by the house." "Draw a man on a horse." "Draw a hat on the man." "Put a fence around the house." After they have completed their "masterpieces," the leader has them take off their blindfolds and look at their work. A judge may be selected to determine the winner of the contest.

Do This and More

One player begins the game by doing something, such as putting their thumbs to their ears and wiggling their fingers; then they point to another player who must repeat that action and add one of their own, such as putting their hand under their chin and wiggling their fingers. The next player may add sticking out their tongue, and so on. Each successive player must repeat, in order, all of the actions of the other players and add another. No player may be called on more than once unless they request it.

Gospel Word Puzzle

Fill in each of the twenty-five squares below with as many five-letter gospel words as you can fit in horizontally and vertically. If you can't get five-letter words, get four-letter words. Get as many as you can. Each five-letter word is worth three points and each four-letter word is worth one point. The player with the most points wins.

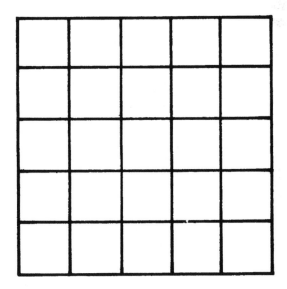

A Group of Fingerplays

Rain

Patter, patter, pat.
(Clap, clap, clap)
Down the raindrops fall.
(Hands up, fingers moving as hands lower)
To give the thirsty flowers a drink.
(Cup hand, finger tips together)
And help them stand up tall.
(Stand straight)
The petals open wide to say
(Cup hands, gradually open wide)
Thank you, sky, for rain today.

The Church

Here is the church
(Lock fingers upside down)
And here is the steeple.
(Raise little fingers)
Open the doors and see all the people.
(turn hands over)
Close the door and hear them pray.
(Close hands)
Open the doors and they go away.
(Palms up)

Ten Little Fingers

I have ten little fingers and they belong to me;
I can make them do things,
Would you like to see?
I can shut them up tight,
I can open them wide,
I can put them together
Or make them all hide.
I can make them jump high,
I can make them jump low
I can fold them quietly

And hold them just so.
(Do motions as words are said)

My Mother

I have a mother kind and sweet.
(Point to self)
She dusts and sweeps our house so neat.
(Make dusting motions)
She washes dishes, irons our clothes.
(Actions)
When I need help, she always knows
Exactly what is good and right
For her—a special prayer tonight.

Wash Day

Here is a little wash bench.
(Little fingers touching, palms bent to right angles)
Here is a little tub.
(Hands cupped)
Here is a little scrubbing board,
(Hands outstretched along side each other)
And here is the way to scrub.
(Scrubbing motion)

Five Little Ducks

Five little ducks that I once knew
Big ones, little ones, there were too.
But the one little duck with a feather in his back
He rules the others with his quack, quack, quack.
(Dramatize, leaving out the quack, quack, quack.)
Down to the river they would go—
Wibble, wobble, wibble, wobble, to and fro.
But the one little duck with the feather in his back
He rules the others with his quack, quack, quack.

A Teensy, Weensy Spider

A teensy, weensy spider
Climbed up the water spout.
(Fingers climb upward on top of each other)
Down came the rain
(Wiggle fingers to make rain)
And washed the spider out.
(Hands flung downward and outward)
Out came the sun
(Hands form circle)
And dried up all the rain.
And teensy, weensy spider
Climbed up the spout again.
(Fingers climb upward as before)

I'm a Little Teapot

I'm a little teapot short and stout.
Here is my handle, here is my spout.
When I get all steamed up, here me shout,
"Tip me over, pour me out."

1. Each child places a hand on a hip for the handle and holds the other arm outstretched for a spout;
2. At this last line, they bend slowly to the side of the outstretched arm.

Five Little Kittens

This little kitty said, "I smell a mouse."
(Raise first finger)
This little kitty said, "Let's go creepity creep."
(Raise fourth finger)
This little kitty said, "Meow, meow, meow."
(Raise thumb)
"I saw him run in his hole right now."
(Place all fingers around thumb)

Ten Little Indians

One Little, two little, three little Indians,
Four little, five little, six little Indians,
Seven little, eight little, nine little Indians,

Ten little Indian boys.

(Hold up the appropriate number of fingers as poem is said or sung—Then reverse, "Ten little, nine little, eight little Indians, and so on" and bring fingers down one at a time.)

The Wind and the Leaves

Leaves are floating softly down;
(Raise arms and let them flutter down)
They make a carpet on the ground.
(Spread arms, palms down, to indicate carpet)
When, swish! The wind comes whirling by
And sends them dancing to the sky.
(Sway and whirl)

Two Little Dickie Birds

Two little dickie birds sat upon a wall,
(Place hands together with thumbs up)
One named Peter, and one named Paul.
Flyaway, Peter; flyaway, Paul.
(Hands behind back one at a time)
Come back, Peter; come back, Paul.
(Hands return individually)

Kittens and Puppies

One little, two little, three little kittens
(Hold up three fingers on one hand, one at a time)
Were napping one day in the sun.
(Bend fingers over)
One little, two little, three little puppies
(Hold up three fingers of the other hand, one at a time)
Said, "Come, let's have some fun."
Up to the kittens the puppies went creeping,
(Puppy fingers creep slowly to kitten fingers)
As quiet as quiet can be.
One little, two little, three little kittens
Went scampering up a small tree.
(Right fingers go up left arm to shoulder)

Put on a Smile

I have something in my pocket
That belongs across my face.
You will never, never, guess it
Till I put it in its place.

1. Hold the left hand, cup-shaped, to represent a pocket.
2. Next, describe a smile on your face with the right hand, pointer finger.
3. Then shake your head as you point to one of the children.
4. And last, pretend to take a smile out of the pocket and use both hands to tuck it on your lips.)

Five Frogs

Five little speckled frogs
(Hold up five fingers)
Sat on a speckled log
Eating some most delicious bugs, yum, yum;
One jumped into the pool
(Take down one finger)
Where it was nice and cool.
Now there are four little speckled frogs—glub, glub.
(Repeat verse using four, three, two, and then "one little speckled frog.")

The Balloon

This is the way to make a balloon.
So, so, so.
(Hands together, palms meeting)
This is the way to blow the balloon.
Blow, blow, blow.
(Pretend blow into palms)
This is the way to fly the balloon.
Go, go, go.
(Flying motion)
This is the way to break the balloon.
Oh! Oh! Oh!
(Clap hands at word "break")

The Man and the Rabbit

There was a little house in the middle of the wood,
(Make shape of roof)
And by the window a little man stood.
He saw a rabbit hopping by,
Knocking at the door.
(Bob two fingers up and down, and knock at door)
"Help me! Help me! Help me!" he said
(Throw hands up three times)
Or the hunter will shoot me dead.
(Make gun with both hands)
Come little rabbit, come with me.
(Make motion of beckoning)
Happy we will be.
(Hold two fingers up and pet them with other hand)

PARTY GAMES

A. Pre-Opener Game

B. Blindfold Games

1. Teens and Adults
2. Children

C. Indoor Party Games

1. Teens and Adults
2. Children
3. Riddles, Puzzles, and Jokes

D. Outdoor Games

1. Relay and Running Games
2. Active Games
3. Swimming Games

Introduction

Four main divisions are in this second section, along with smaller subdivisions. The games in this section are especially designed for neighborhood parties, any type of outdoor recreation, and parties for adults, teens, and children. Like the games in the other sections, they can be easily adapted for use in the family. Some of the games shown in the outdoor section can readily be played indoors and vice versa.

Pre-Opener Game for Neighborhood Parties

As guests enter the room, direct them to a table containing the following objects with cards of directions by each object (Have the necessary items to gauge the correct answer):

1. A glass jar of beans (Guess how many)
2. A small ball of string/rope (How long?)
3. An orange (How many seeds?)
4. ¼ of a newspaper page (How many words?)
5. A stick (How long?)
6. A large dictionary (How heavy?)
7. Part of a deck of cards (Number of cards?)
8. A can of water (How many quarts?)
9. Photo of a child or animal (Age?)
10. A block of wood (How thick?)

Blindfold Games
Teen and Adult Blindfold Games

A Night at the Opera

No matter how poorly some of your guests may sing, everybody present can take part in this game.

One of the group is blindfolded and seated in a corner with his back to the other guests, who are lined up at the far end of the room. Then, one at a time, each person in the line attempts to sing a song, disguising their voice as much as possible.

The blindfolded person is given one guess to determine who the singer is. If they fail to guess correctly, the next person in line sings, and the blindfolded player guesses again. This keeps up until the identity of one of the singers is correctly guessed, whereupon the blindfolded person takes their place in the line, and the singer who was discovered has to put on the blindfold.

Egg Blindfold

Newspapers are spread on the floor along with about two dozen raw eggs placed on top. A person is selected and asked to study the positions of the eggs, after which they are taken into another room. Meanwhile the eggs are removed and in their place are put some egg shells and crisp crackers. The person is then brought in blindfolded. They are asked to make their way through the crackers and shells; they still think there are raw eggs there. For the best results ask the person to take off their shoes.

Getting Dressed

Put three or more people (preferably boys) in the center of the group. Explain that they must attempt to put on a nylon stocking while wearing cotton gloves. Blindfold and give gloves to each but substitute a nylon scarf for the stocking, or sew the stocking tops closed.

Blind Man's Lunch

Two players participate in this event, but it is greatly enjoyed by the spectators too. Blindfold the two and seat them on the floor just within arm's reach of each other. Give each two crackers. They attempt to feed each other. The winner is the one who is more successful in actually feeding the other player the crackers.

Fun with a Piñata

Fill a piñata with candy. Blindfold a person who then tries to break the piñata with a heavy stick or broom handle. Everyone scrambles to get the candy.

Who Hit Me?

Two players lie side by side in the center of the floor with their face covered with a blanket or towel while the group stands in a close circle around them. It is explained that one of the group will hit one of the "sleepers" with a rolled magazine, and the latter must uncover their head and identify the hitter before they get back to their place. In reality one of the "sleepers" is part of the trick, and they do the hitting. They hit themselves occasionally for effect. It is a great source of entertainment for all watching the game.

Pudding Eating Contest

Four participants are each covered with large bibs. Blindfolds are put on them and they are each given a bowl of pudding and a spoon. The object is to feed the pudding to the person on the opposite side of the table. The first one whose bowl is empty wins.

Obstacle Relay

Make two teams and set up an obstacle course. Each member of the individual teams has to try to get through the obstacle course blindfolded. The first team to have everyone through, or the team with the fastest time, wins.

Find Your Hometown

Place a map on the wall (or a cork board) and the participants are blindfolded and given pins. The one who can stick his pin closest to his own hometown wins the game.

Monday

Half of the players are blindfolded. The other half are given several articles of clothing and clothespins. Pair up one blindfolded person and one person with clothing. The clothing person hands one article and two clothespins to the blindfolded partner, who races down to a clothesline. There may be a clothesline for each pair or one large one that is strung from one end of the room to the other (between two chairs). The blindfolded player hangs up the article with the two clothespins. They return for another and another until they are all hung up. Their partner can coach from the sideline. The one who returns to base first after hanging all pieces wins a prize.

Tightrope Walking

One person is blindfolded and walks on a rope that is stretched out on the floor. If they step off the rope, they are out. This game can also be fun if made into a competition between two teams, with the purpose to see which team can get the most members across.

What Was That?

Certain guests are selected and shown a number of objects, such as a rubber ball, a pencil, an apple, and so on. They are then blindfolded and told to listen while the objects are dropped to the floor. As each object is dropped, the blindfolded guests must identify the object correctly.

Blowing Out the Candle

A lit candle rests on a table. A player is blindfolded, moved back three steps, turned around in a circle, and permitted to take three steps before blowing. The object is to blow out the candle. This game can also be a relay race.

Walk the Straight and Narrow

Divide into two groups; each group stands in front of a line which has been drawn on the floor. Four or five obstacles are placed on these lines. Each member of a team is blindfolded one at a time and must walk their line. Teammates help by telling when they are off the line and when they are about to come to an obstacle. The first team with all its members at the other end of the line is the winner.

Straight and Narrow

The idea of this game is to walk across the room blindfolded while holding hands with another blindfolded person. Blindfold three couples who must keep holding hands as couples. At the word "go," let them try to find their way to the goal at the other end of the room. They must not let go of one another or they will be disqualified. The couple reaching the goal first wins.

Children's Blindfold Games

Grunt, Piggy, Grunt

Players stand in a circle facing the center. A person chosen to be "it" is in the ring. This person is blindfolded and given a long stick (blackboard pointer, yardstick, broom, or rolled-up magazine or newspaper). This person is turned around several times after being blindfolded; then they go toward the edge of the circle, holding their pointer before them. When the pointer touches a player in the circle, the "it" player says, "Grunt, piggy, grunt!" The person who is thus spoken to must grunt or make some similar sound while the "it" player tries guess their identity. If they guess correctly, the grunter becomes the next "it." If the "it" player fails to identify a person, they move to a new player and continue to try. Players must avoid giving away their own identity with talking or laughter or the blindfolded person may quickly shift and point to someone they believe they know by position in the circle and guess their identity. If the circle group is large, two persons can be "it" simultaneously.

One Step

A person is blindfolded and put in the middle of the group. The group is given a certain amount of time to move away while the blindfold person tries to touch someone in the group. The children in the group are allowed only one step to get away.

Red Light! Green Light!

Blindfold one person and stand them in the middle of a circle. When the blindfolded player yells, "Green light," everyone moves to a different place until the blindfolded player says, "Red light." Everyone then stops wherever they are. The blindfolded player searches around until they find someone; then they have one guess to identify the person. If there is a large group, three guesses would be better.

Slipper Slap

Select one player to be "it" and blindfold them. The remaining players stand in a compact circle around the blindfolded person, shoulders touching and hands behind backs. Give one of the players a swatter or a rolled-up a newspaper.

The swatter is passed around the circle behind the players' backs. At every opportunity the players swat "it" and quickly get rid of the swatter by passing it around the circle behind their backs. The "it" player tries to catch whoever is swatting them. If they succeed they exchange places; if not the blindfolded player continues until they are successful.

Pin the Face

Cut out various parts of a face from paper. Draw a huge oval, representing a head, and put it up on the wall. Guests are blindfolded one at a time and given one cutout and told to place it correctly on the blank face. This is a game that creates lots of laughs.

Pickup

Blindfold two people and get them to pick up handfuls of coins or other small objects dropped on the floor. The one picking up the most wins.

Good Morning

One player is blindfolded and stands in the center of the circle, which moves around him initially to start the game. The circle stops and one of the players says, "Good morning, (player's name)." The blindfolded player answers at once by pointing to the speaker and saying, "Good morning, Mary," or whoever they think the speaker is. They have three guesses. The third time the blindfolded player fails the circle moves around again, and the blindfolded player begins to guess again with another player saying good morning.

Bag Blind Man's Bluff

The children stand in a circle. One player, carrying a large, stout paper bag, walks around the outside of the circle. They clap the bag down over the head of some player. As soon as the player does this, all the rest of the players take three long steps in any direction they choose. The "blind man" immediately shouts, "One, two, three, halt!" At the word "halt," everyone must stand still. The "blind man" walks about and touches someone. They ask this person three questions to find out who it is and the other must answer promptly, though they may disguise their voice. If the "blind man" guesses correctly, the bag is drawn down over the other one's head, and they become the "blind man." If not, the original "blind man" cries out, "One, two, three, halt," all the players taking three more steps, and the "blind man" must guess again.

Note: Do not use a plastic bag because it is dangerous. You could also use a blindfold but it takes the extra time to tie it before the play starts.

The Whistle

The player who is "it" is blindfolded and a whistle is attached to his back with a string and safety pin. The players, one at a time, try to sneak up and blow the whistle. "It" must catch the whistler and identify them if they can.

Pirate

One person is blindfolded. They sit on a chair and listen for their opponent, who is trying to steal their treasure (any object placed under the chair). If the blindfolded person hears them and thinks they know where their opponent is, they point with their finger and shoot (bang!). They may use a gun that shoots ping-pong balls. They have three shots to succeed, and if they don't, they try again with another opponent. If they do succeed, the opponent takes their place.

Can-Can

Players make a large oval around an open space about twenty-five feet long. They may stand or sit on chairs or on the floor. Place a chair or box for goals at each end of the oval. Place six cans, cartons, or other objects at random in the oval. Select two players. One player must find and place three of the objects on his chair, one at a time. The other must find and place three of the objects under his chair. However, they are both blindfolded! If one player gets to their rival's chair by accident, they may remove their rival's objects one at a time and take them to their pile. The first to get three cans in the correct place wins. The other players cheer for their favorite and keep the players from stepping out of the playing area.

Peep Peep

One person is blindfolded and sits on someone's lap. They try to figure out whose lap they are sitting on by the voice of the person they are sitting on when that person says, "Peep, peep."

Teamwork

Divide the group into two or four smaller groups. Each team chooses two players to represent them. After one person from each group is blindfolded, take a ball or other article and place it somewhere in the room. The other person chosen from the group will direct their teammate to the ball, calling only directions. The first team to find the ball is the winner.

Indoor Party Games
Teen and Adult Indoor Party Games

Uncle Josh Died

Call five or six persons to the front of the room and have them perform for the enjoyment of the rest of the group. All stand shoulder to shoulder, fold arms, and then sit on heels and balance on toes. The leader turns to their left-hand neighbor and says, "Uncle Josh died last night." The neighbor says, "How did he die?" The leader replies, "A-winkin' his eye," and immediately starts winking their own eye. The neighbor repeats the bit of gossip and also the action down the line to the next person and so on, until it comes back to the original leader, who this time repeats, "I heard Uncle Josh died last night." Their neighbor says, "How did he die?" "A-winkin' his eye," and adds, "with his face awry," and pulls up one corner of their mouth. The next time the leader adds, "One foot in the sky," and finally "A-wavin' good-bye." Whenever a new motion is added, it is continued for the remainder of the game. The leader then concludes by saying, "Let's go bury him" and gives their neighbor a push so that each player falls over on their neighbor.

What Happened?

After a brief rehearsal, two or three members of a group come out and perform an unusual scene. Perhaps one of the group starts to sing, another hits them over the head with a mallet, and the third member starts to scream and pull the rug from under the assailant. All three fall down, pat each other on the back, and leave the room hopping on one foot.

Following their exit, each guest at the party is asked to write down on paper an account of exactly what happened. The papers are collected, and the eyewitness accounts are read. The variety of facts presented is always amazing.

What Did She Wear?

The hostess selects a girl to dress up in all the extra clothing, jewelry, and so on that she can wear. She then enters the room, walking slowly back and forth twice, while the guests are asked to observe everything she is wearing. This should be made as difficult as possible, by including hat, coat, scarf, earrings, bracelet, handbag, and any other item that might be handy.

After the girl leaves the room each guest is asked to write down on paper a list of the girl's complete wardrobe. The person who is most accurate wins.

Laws

There are two teams; team one is Do and team two is Don't. Give each team one minute to write down as many laws as they possibly can, team one writing "do" laws and team two writing "don't" laws. After each team has completed their list, a box of candy can be given as a prize to the team with the longest list. Each team may tell why they listed such laws and give a one-minute speech on each.

Examples:

1. Do things for people. Be a giver, not a taker.
2. Don't compete with your coworkers. Compete against yourself. You can't lose.
3. Do always have an alternative. Remember Murphy's Law, "If anything can go wrong, it will."
4. Don't be a perfectionist. Folks who wait to get "all set" seldom get started.
5. Do give yourself little subgoals. They'll lead you into the big ones—and it's fun to write them off!
6. Don't enjoy self-pity. It's a time-waster.
7. Do try the new. Don't put it off.

Patience

This skit is a fun trick for a large group. It is presented in five acts. The characters are an old prospector and his donkey looking for water.

Act I: Prospector leads donkey across room; the donkey says, "Water, master, water!" The prospector replies, "Patience, donkey, patience!"

Act II: Same as Act I.

Act III: Same as Acts I and II.

Act V: Usually as you begin this act someone asks what happened to Act IV and the prospector turns to that person and says, "Patience, donkey, patience!"

Movie Stars

Seat the group in a circle around the room. Each player must choose the name of a movie star as his own. These names are told aloud to the group, perhaps twice so the players may more easily remember the names. A person chosen to be "it" stands in the middle of the circle with a folded newspaper in his hand. Another player inside the circle begins the game by standing and saying the name of one of the movie stars. The person whose name is called must then stand, say another name, and sit down before the "it" player hits them with the newspaper. If the speaker fails to do so, they become "it."

This Is a Fork, This Is a Spoon

The group is seated in a circle. One player has a fork and a player seated beside him has a spoon. Each turns to the person on their other side and says, "This is a fork (spoon)." "A what?" says the person addressed. "A fork (spoon)," is the reply. That person then turns to the next player saying, "This is a fork (spoon)." "A what?" The player then turns back to the original fork (spoon) holder and asks, "A what?" The original holder replies, "A fork (spoon)," and the second player says, "A fork (spoon)," to the third player. This continues around the circle until the fork and spoon reach the original players. The greatest fun occurs as the fork and spoon cross each other in the middle of the circle.

Situation

Ask someone how much nerve they have or tell them their balance is going to be checked. Then put a pie plate of water up against the ceiling and have them hold it there with a broom handle. After a while they won't know what to do or how to get it down.

Wink

Half of the players are seated in chairs facing a circle. There is one empty chair. Behind every chair stands the other players. All the standing players start with their hands stiffly at their sides. The standing player behind the empty chair becomes "it" and must get a sitting player to fill their chair. When they see a sitting player they would like to have sit in their chair, they winks at the player.

The sitting player must slip away from their chair before the standing player at their back can restrain them by putting their hands on the sitting player's shoulders. If the sitting player escapes, their standing player becomes "it" with their empty chair and must try to get another sitting player for their chair.

Car

Any number of players may play this game. There are seats for all of the players but one, who stands in the center of the group. Each person sitting down takes the name of some part of a car. The person in the center starts to tell a story about a car and whenever he mentions the name of a part of the automobile, the person who represents that part must get up, turn around, and sit down again. When the word car is spoken, everybody must get up, turn around and sit down again. At the end of the story, the person in the middle says, "The car overturned in the ditch." Then everyone has to change seats, the leader, of course, trying to get a seat in the general confusion. The person who can't find a place to sit has to be the next storyteller.

Cup Game

Parlez-vous français
La ree, la raa, la ree,

Parlez-vous français
La ree, la raa, la ree,

The above verse is sung in rhythm as the players sit in a circle and pass cups to their right. On the accented beat, each player grasps the cup just placed in front of them by the player on their left, and on the next beat puts it in front of the player on their right. On the last line each holds the cup in front of them, moving it in a back-and-forth motion—first to the right, then to the left, then right again, and then passing it on. As the game proceeds, verse and motion speed up. Those losing the rhythm or getting more than one cup in front of them are eliminated.

Cane Ringing

Hang a bracelet or teething ring by a string or rope so that it hangs at shoulder height. Players hold a broom handle or a stick about three feet long in the right or left hand and hold it out to the side at shoulder height. They walk toward the ring with the right or left (matching the hand) eye closed, attempting to put the end of the cane through the ring. Score one hundred points for each successful try. Take five tries each.

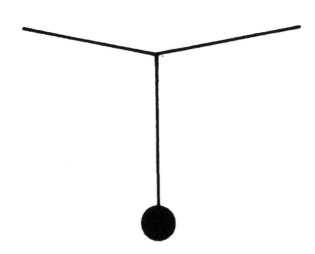

Heel Toss

This game is made by drawing nine squares on a two-foot square piece of wood. Number the squares as shown in the diagram and paint the different squares various colors. Cut five rubber heels into discs about the size of a dollar. Players stand eight feet from the board and toss the five heels so they will land flat on the board. Score is according to the numbers in the squares.

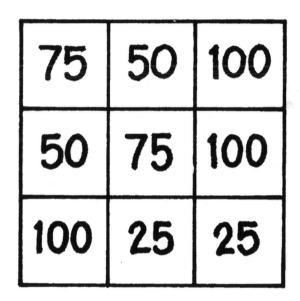

Ball Bounce

For this game, you'll need a waste basket or similar container and five bouncy balls. Bounce the balls on the floor from a line eight feet away from the container with the object being to bounce the balls into it. Score one hundred points for each ball remaining in the container.

Pool Golf

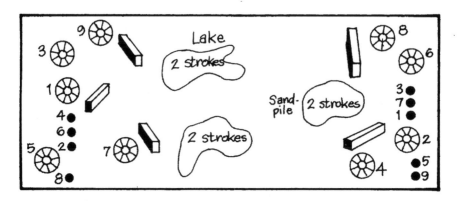

This game can easily be constructed. Use two flat pieces of wood five feet by three feet by a fourth inch. Use the top piece to drill holes for the greens, which are the large, detailed double circles in the illustration. Drill only the inner circle a half inch in diameter. Glue both boards together making the result a half inch thick. The board with the drilled holes will be the top board. The little circles with numbers in them represent the tees for the holes; they should be only painted spots. Paint in the lakes and sand pile also. Construct little obstacle blocks (painted red) before greens.

Rules: This game should be played like golf except that you use pool sticks and discs. The object of the game is for a player to tee off from tee number one to hole number one. See how many strikes (by use of the pool stick) it will take to reach the hole. Shoot for other holes until you reach hole nine. The player who reaches hole nine with the least strokes wins. If a player lands in the lakes or sand pile they lose two strokes. Any number can play.

Muffin Pan Bounce Ball

Use an ordinary muffin pan that contains a dozen cups. With small pieces of tape, mark different values by each group of cups. Place the pan near a wall if possible. Players stand eight feet away and attempt to bounce ping-pong balls so they will land in the cups. Score as indicated in the diagram. See also "Ping-Pong Bounce" (p. 108).

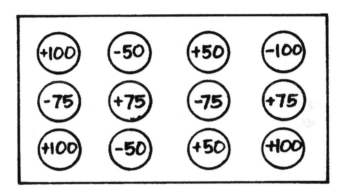

Pendulum Swing

Tie a rope to the top of a doorway so that it may swing freely. Tie a ball to the lower end of the rope so that the ball hangs about four inches from the floor. Stand a tenpin, or similar object, by the ball. The player must swing the ball past the tenpin and hit it as the ball swings back. Each successful try nets one hundred points. Each player gets five tries.

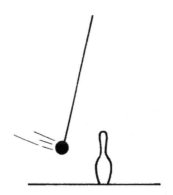

Scoop Golf

This game is great for kids and adults. It is made by fastening a can to the top of an eighteen-inch broom handle. A two-foot string is threaded through a sponge rubber ball and the free end tied to the broom handle under the can. To play the game, toss the ball in the air by swinging the stick upward. Try to catch the ball in the can. Score one hundred points for each successful try. The ball must remain in the can. Each player gets five tries.

Gulping Jim

With fun for the whole family, this tossing game is made by cutting eyes, nose, and mouth in an eighteen-inch by twenty-four-inch board. Give it some color. Hang or lean the board against a wall. Toss bean bags at the face with an underhanded swing from a distance of eight feet. Score: Eyes are worth a hundred; nose, seventy-five; mouth, fifty.

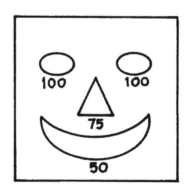

Shuffle Board

Draw the following diagram on a piece of quarter-inch plywood, eight inches by twenty inches and assign each square a point value. Place a checker on the base line and with the thumb and finger flip it for the squares on the target. Score according to the square in which most of the checker rests. Each person gets five tries.

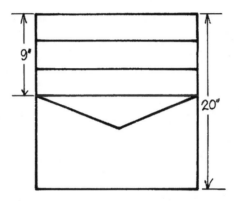

Quoit Shield

Cut out a piece of quarter-inch plywood in the shape of a shield and place two-inch right angle screws or hooks as in the diagram. Stand eight feet away and toss five four-inch rope quoits (rope rings) at the target. Score as numbered.

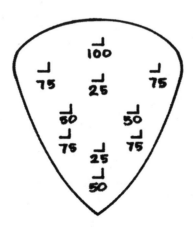

A-B-C

Players name objects shown in a picture, each trying to complete the alphabet without an omission. That is, number one finds an object such as "arm," number two finds "ankle," and number three may fail to find something beginning with the letter A within the time limit of fifteen seconds. Each player records the number he or she discovers. Number two has first turn in finding B, number three first at C, and so on. An object may be named only once during the game.

Ping-Pong Bounce

Place a muffin tin in the center of a table. This game may be played one team against another or for individual scores. Bounce five or six ping-pong balls into the muffin tin (one ball at a time). The ball must bounce on the table first and then into the muffin tin. Also, the ball must leave the player's hand at the edge of the table. Award ten points for each ball that stays in the muffin tin or a different number of points depending on each little cup. Similar to "Muffin Pan Bounce Ball" (p. 105).

Reading Temples

The leader must have an accomplice who is sent out of the room. The group is told that thoughts can be transmitted through the hand. The group decides on a number between one and ten and the accomplice is recalled, who places their hands on the leader's temples and after considerable "stage business," names the number.

(The number is transmitted by the leader, who clinches and relaxes his jaw the required number of times. This gives a movement of the temples that can be felt but not seen.)

Which Match?

Scatter a half-dozen matches on the floor in the center of the circle of seated players. The leader must have an accomplice, who is sent out of the room, and the players decide upon one match. The player is recalled, and the leader says, "Is it this match?" pointing to one match after another, until the selected match is pointed to and the player says, "Yes."

The method is that the leader stands still in pointing to the matches except when he points to the selected match. In this case, they make a very slight movement of their right foot.

Variations: Three matches are placed in a row on the floor. The players select one match and the accomplice is recalled. The leader gives the accomplice the cue with their hands. If it is the left match, they place their left hand over their right; if it is the right match, they place their right hand over their left; if it is the center match, neither hand is placed on the other.

Three matches are placed in a row on the floor and the players agree on one. The leader and the accomplice have agreed that the match to the right is to be designated by "All right," the middle one by "Ready," and the one to the left by "Come in." The leader then calls in the accomplice, using one of the three phrases, depending on which match was selected. The accomplice studies the matches and points out the right one.

Humility

A handful of beans is given to each person. Each player engages another in a conversation. A specified number of beans is lost each time the terms "me" or "I" are spoken. The person who collects the most beans after a designated time is the winner.

Deception

The leader turns their back to the people and tells someone to hold a coin in one of their hands. They tell the people to close both hands tightly with knuckles down. The person with the coin is to raise the hand holding the coin above their head for a moment, and then lower their hand as they say, "Ready!" The leader turning around quickly will notice that the hand holding the coin will be whiter than the other one because while the hand was held above the head the circulation had been limited.

S-Game

The game consists of writing a word beginning with the letter *S* in answer to the questions below. When the time limit is up (ten minutes), each player in the group is called upon to read his answer to number one. After the scores have been noted, each player reads number two, and so on.

Score your paper as follows: Ten points if no one else has your entry; Five points if one other person has the same entry; two points if three or more people have the same entry.

The player with the most points wins. And remember, the more that you "copy" your neighbor's sheet, the lower your score will be. Remind your guests that the person with the unusual words has the best chance of winning the game. Ten minutes should be allowed for writing the answers.

	Score
Something you like to do	S . . . .
Something you hate to do	S . . . .
Famous person	S . . . .
Fish	S . . . .
Vehicle	S . . . .
Title of a book	S . . . .
Inventor	S . . . .
River	S . . . .
Country	S . . . .
Animal	S . . . .
Flower	S . . . .
Author	S . . . .
College	S . . . .
Song	S . . . .
Tree	S . . . .
Color	S . . . .
Vegetable	S . . . .
Biblical character	S . . . .
Magazine	S . . . .
Household item	S . . . .

Spirit Photography

A player boasts that they have a magic spoon that when held before the face of anyone will record the picture of the person. The player leaves the room and their accomplice holds a shiny serving spoon in front of some player and then lays the spoon on the floor in the center of the seated circle of players and returns to their seat. The player is recalled and picks up the spoon and studies it intently, finally pointing out the player photographed.

They are able to do this by watching their accomplice when they enters. The accomplice indicates by a slight movement of hand or finger which side of the circle the player is on; this eliminates half of the group. Then the accomplice assumes the exact pose of the photographed player, changing their pose as the player changes their own.

It invariably happens that the accomplice is soon asked to photograph themselves. In this case the accomplice sits with their feet or legs crossed or some sign that is understood between the two.

Mysterious Message

Have some humorous "fortunes" prepared in advance, written with lemon juice on slips of paper and then dried. Pass one to each guest. The heat of a candle brings out the message.

Soul and Spirit

Have a glass filled nearly to the brim with water. Ask the guests how many single nails can be placed in the glass of water without running the water over the top. It is surprising how the answers will vary from one to one hundred. If nails are carefully dropped in the water, you can get nearly two hundred in the glass; the water will form a dome, without running over.

Barter

Give each person a slip of paper with a number on it and ten beans or counters. Make a mental note of one particular number, which is to be the lucky number: thirteen, for example. Do not tell what the number is until the end of the game. Instruct the group that they are to buy and sell numbers, using beans for "money." Numbers may never be traded for other numbers, only bought or sold for money. As an example, a person may sell his number for four beans and buy another number for two beans, thus making two beans profit. When the game is over, two people are winners, the one holding the lucky number and the one with the most beans. As no two numbers are alike, there can only be one lucky number, but there may be a tie for the number of beans.

Who Am I?

Someone goes out of the room. The crowd decides who the player is to be. It would be well to follow a given group—actors, musicians, writers, world leaders, and so on. The player comes back into the room and asks "Who am I?" The answers must be truthful and fairly relevant, but never too revealing. In the case of John Wayne they might say, "You play in many movies." "You often wear spurs." When enough light is shed on the subject, the player guesses and the one whose reply betrayed the answer must take the player's place.

Trades

Every player, except one who holds the office of reader, selects a trade or profession which they must retain throughout the game. The reader opens a book at random and reads a passage aloud. When they come to any common noun they look at one of the tradesmen, who must instantly name some article that they are supposed to have for sale, or some implement connected with the exercise of his craft. By this substitution of one noun for another, the most pathetic passage is converted into an indescribable jumble of absurdities.

Drawing in the Dark

Give each member of the group a pencil and a piece of paper. Turn out the lights and ask the players to draw a picture of a horse. They will undoubtedly be very careful the first time, expecting you to turn on the lights as soon as the horse is completed. But not yet! When they have finished their horses—and lost their places on the papers—ask them to put a rider on the horse and then a feed bag under the horse's nose, and as a final touch, have them write the word "oats" on the bag. When the lights go on, exhibit the "masterpieces" and get ready for a good laugh.

Cross Scissors

One player begins the action as the group is seated in a circle. He takes the scissors, passing them to his left, saying, "I pass the scissors crossed (or uncrossed)." The next person says, "I take the scissors crossed (or uncrossed) and I pass them uncrossed (or crossed)," depending not upon the way the scissors are held, but on the position of the player's feet at the time of taking or passing—whether the ankles or legs are crossed or uncrossed. Other players must catch on to the trick in order the pass the scissors correctly.

Magic Writing

An accomplice who knows the trick goes out of the room, while the group selects a word. The accomplice is called back in. The leader has a cane or broomstick, and pretends to write on the floor. Vowels are shown by taps (A, one; E, two; I, three; O, four; U, five), consonants by the first letter in a sentence. For example, the word selected is "hat." The leader writes saying, "Here I go," taps once, writes again and says, "There it is." Don't give the clues away. If all don't guess you can play it again another day.

Ghosts

The players are seated in a circle. The first one to start mentions a letter, and each of the other players in turn adds a letter that will form a word but not finish it. The first three letters do not count, but after that if a person adds a letter which completes a word, that player is a third of a ghost. For instance, if the first two letters are M and A, the third player may add D without being penalized, but if the fourth player adds an E and the word made is formed, they become a third of a ghost. When a player is a whole ghost they are ostracized. They may no longer add letters and the other players may not talk to them. But they can add a great deal of fun to the game by talking to the other players and haranguing them. Anyone who inadvertently replies to them becomes a third of a ghost, receiving the same penalty they would for completing a word. A player may challenge the person who preceded them if they doubt that the letter that player added doesn't form a legitimate word. If the challenger is right in their doubt, the last player becomes a third of a ghost; if not, the challenger receives the same penalty.

Famous Partnerships

Each person has a pencil and paper. At "go" all write as many partnerships, such as "coat and hat," "rain or shine," "hot or cold," and so on, as they can think of in a given time. To score, first count the number of people playing. Let us say six, for example. One reads their list slowly, pausing after every item so that the others can find out if they have the same words on their own list. All having those words, including the reader, cross them out. If two people have those words, two is subtracted from six, leaving four. This score of four is given to those two people, who mark it in the margin. When the first reader had read all his list, the second reads those not yet crossed out, others following. Those having words no one else has score highest—six in this case. If all have the same words, no point is scored.

Monkey

The players form a circle. The leader announces that he will give each in turn the name of an animal and that there will be two with the same name. They then whisper the name to each player. A circle indicated as the center of the ring has an apple in it. Those whose names are called to see who can grab the apple first. In reality the leader has given the name of monkey to each of the players and when they call "monkey," all dash for the apple. This will bring good laughs to all involved.

Malaga Grapes

Invite players to try and mimick the following task. Tapping rhythmically (as letters appear in bold) with their stick on the ground or a pencil on the table, the leader says, "**Ma**-la-ga grapes, **ma**-la-ga grapes, the **best** grapes in **town**," and challenges anyone to do the same. The trick is to clear your throat before starting.

Neighbor Hunt

As each guest/neighbor arrives they are given a piece of paper like the one below. They are to do as it tells them and write the correct answers in the blanks.

You are number . . . . . .
(Leader fills in numbers as guests arrive)
1. Find number six. Write his name . . . . . .
2. Where does number ten live? . . . . . .
3. What color of hair does number five have? . . . . . .
4. How tall is number twelve? . . . . . .
5. What color of shoes is number fifteen wearing? . . . . . .
6. What color of eyes does number thirteen have? . . . . . .
7. Find number eleven. What is their favorite food? . . . . . .
8. Find number one. What is their middle name? . . . . . .

One- or Two-Word Starters

Here is a list of words and names to use as idea starters if you want to get the group to create its own stunts or skits. Divide a large group into small ones and assign one of the idea starters below to each group to set their thoughts in motion. Allow ten to fifteen minutes, or longer if there is time, for the groups to work up a skit from their assignments.

1. Embarrassed		25. Seminary class
2. Mortgage		26. Hijackers
3. Wreck		27. Tornado
4. Mystery		28. South Seas
5. Gun		29. Stiletto
6. Missing		30. Killer loose
7. Kidnapped		31. Alarm broadcast
8. Speechless		32. Pirate chest
9. Mistaken		33. Hidden gold
10. Scream		34. Amnesia victim
11. Failing		35. Secret passage
12. Crash		36. Lost colony

13. Alarm	37. Napoleon
14. Innocent	38. George Washington
15. Sale	39. Alexander the Great
16. Explosion	40. Helen of Troy
17. Disappeared	41. Queen of Sheba
18. Hidden	42. Underworld King
19. Rural	43. Queen Elizabeth
20. Shot	44. Sir Walter Raleigh
21. Sinking	45. Pocahontas
22. Body	46. John Milton
23. Lights out	47. Caesar
24. Space men	48. Athena

Illustration: Number six: "Missing." Home scene, a couple getting ready for a party. Man puts down his glasses and pantomimes putting on a tie. He begins to look for his glasses but is unable to find them. He begins panic and asks for help. The woman helps him search and find the glasses. (Actors could ask at the end of the skit, "What did the man think had happened to his glasses?")

Silhouettes

As the guests arrive, take them individually into a room where a light is placed at the side of a chair, seat the guest, and throw a silhouette on the wall where a piece of paper has been tacked. A person draws the outline of the face. Number the sheets and put the name of the person on the back. After all the guests' pictures have been drawn, hang them around the living room and give each guest a sheet of paper and have him write down the number on the sheets and whom they think the pictures represent.

Human Lotto

Fold paper into twenty-five squares. Each person signs his name in one of the squares upon request. After a few minutes play "Lotto" (a game similar to bingo). Read out the names of those present and keep playing until someone has five in a row.

Person on Your Right

One person to be the guesser leaves the room. The game is then explained to the remaining group. The players are seated in a circle. The person who is "it" is seated on the right of each person in the circle; in other words, each person in the circle could be "it." The guesser comes back to the room and asks individual people questions about the person who is "it." The person asked answers the question as though they were the person on their right. Keep playing until the guesser catches on.

Judgment

Cut out as many pictures of important people from newspapers or magazines as you wish. After you have clipped these pictures out, cut off the names and place numbers instead. Then have a contest to see how many your players can recognize. You'll hear lots of comments and won't find many winners.

Searching

Announce that there is one person in the room who will give to the fifteenth person shaking hands with them a valuable gift. (And of course appoint the mystery person secretly, ahead of time, and supply them with the gift to be awarded.)

Taking Vows Forever

This is a fun prank to play with a group of close friends. One person is seated, representing the "ruler," and takes off one shoe and sock and places a ring on one of their toes. They place another ring on one finger. A cushion is placed in front of them. Several people that have previously been taken out of the room are brought back in, one at a time, securely blindfolded. Each person is required to kneel on the cushion and kiss the ring on the ruler's hand three times. After they have kissed the ring on the ruler's hand, the ruler hides their hand and the blindfold is removed. The player sees the ring on the toe and thinks this is what they had kissed.

One Minute to Go

The leader tells a player a letter of the alphabet and they must name as many words as they can that begin with that letter, within a minute. Give the next person a letter and keep track of the number of words each player names. The one who gets the most words wins the game.

Alphabetical Love

The players are seated in a semicircle, and the first player is asked, "According to the alphabet, how do you love your little lamb?" The player makes up an answer something like this: "I love my little lamb with an A, because his name is Arthur, and he is very artistic." The second player thinks fast and says: "I love my little lamb with a B, because her name is Bertha and she has boils." The third one says: "I love my little lamb with a *C* because her name is Cathy and she cuts cantaloupe." And so on through the alphabet, until all the letters have been exhausted. Some of the players, of course, draw easy letters; but those who have to take such letters as *Q* and *Z* may have trouble. The combinations offered by some of the players can cause much hilarity.

The Singing Lesson

The leader explains that after much study they have reduced the art of singing to a few simple exercises, the mastery of which will start anyone on the road to stardom. The three basic vocal sounds are "Oh," "Ah," and "Eee." To visualize these, use the arms in a circle above the head to represent "Oh." "Ah" is made by opening the mouth vertically as far as possible, one arm straight up and the other down. "Eee" is made by starting with both hands at the lips as if pulling a string, and straightening them out horizontally; the mouth takes the same shape, showing the teeth.

The sounds must accompany the action. The climax is reached when, after some practice, the leader says, "Now we'll have a test. You make the motions and sounds, but I'll just make the motions." The leader starts in the order "Oh," "Ah," "Eee," speeding up the "Oh," "Ah," "Eee." The leader then ends in a terrible mix-up, waving their arms around wildly with the crowd trying to follow. The leader passes them all in the test, and then they all sing.

Writing Love Letters

Divide the players into groups of from four to six and seat them at separate tables. Provide each table with a couple of old magazines, writing paper, scissors, and glue. Each group composes a love letter by clipping out phrases, sentences, and words from the magazines and inserting a maximum of six words with the pencil. A prize is given for the best letter.

Amazing Stories

The group is seated in a semicircle, and paper and pencils are handed to the person seated at one end. They are told to write the first sentence of an amazing story. For example, they might write, "Twilight was falling on the old homestead." Having written this, they fold the sentence back so that it cannot be seen, and hand the paper to the next in line, who writes the second sentence, not knowing what the opening sentence was.

The second person may write something like, "Suddenly a crash was heard, which resounded all over the glue factory." And so on, with each guest writing a sentence, folding the paper back, and handing it over to the next in line.

When each person has contributed their sentence, the paper is unfolded, and the entire story is read. In every case, the result is sure to be amazing.

Where a very large number of guests are present, this stunt may be sped up by dividing the group into smaller groups of six or eight and letting each group prepare its own story. If desired, instead of having the guests write an amazing story, they can write a love story, or a story on any other general subject that seems appropriate. But in any case, the completed efforts are sure to be good for a laugh.

Variation: Give each player a paper and pencil and have the group write their own sentences simultaneously and pass them in conjunction with one another.

Clap Seven

The players are seated in a circle. One person in each circle begins the counting, starting with the number one. The count

The LDS Game Book

continues to the right until the number seven is reached. Instead of saying "seven," the player claps their hands and the count continues but in the reverse direction. Any number that ends in seven, or is a multiple of seven, or is a number containing seven, is not spoken but clapped. The direction of the count is automatically reversed on each clap. Any time a mistake is made, the count starts over with "one."

Attention Getter

This is a great game for the whole family.

Music: Any four-beat song, such as "Pop Goes the Weasel" or "She'll Be Coming 'Round the Mountain."

Action: Teach and practice the first eight counts and then the second eight counts, and then combine. Increase the tempo and add new actions if you like.

Count 1. Slap hands on knees
2. Slap hands together
3. Snap fingers of right hand
4. Snap fingers of left hand
5. Cross right arm over left
6. Cross left arm over right
7. Jerk right thumb over right shoulder
8. Jerk left thumb over left shoulder
9. Slap hands on knees
10. Clap hands together
11 & 12. Pound right fist on top of left (twice)
13 & 14. Pound left fist on top of right (twice)
15. Wave right forefinger in air
16. Wave left forefinger in air

Adverb

The game of "Adverb" is a delightfully pleasant and funny pastime. It calls upon one's acting ability. To play it, the group appoints someone to be "it." That person withdraws from the room while the other participants select an adverb. Adverbs, as you remember, usually end in the suffix "ly," such as quickly, painfully, mysteriously, sadly, joyfully, lightly, and so on.

After the person who is "it" withdraws from the room, let us say, for example, that the adverb selected is "mysteriously." The "it" player is invited to return to the room, and they at once try to discover which adverb the others have selected by asking them to perform specific actions, or say certain sentences or words in the manner of the adverb. They may say, "John, I want you to walk across the room and shake hands with Mary in the manner of the adverb." John would then do his best to walk "mysteriously" across the room and shake hands "mysteriously" with Mary. In this case, furtive glances over the shoulder and tiptoeing across the room would add to the "mysteriousness" of the action.

Telegrams

Write out a telegram so that the first letter of each word forms a word of the telegram.

Example: President—Perhaps Roosevelt expects success in Democratic election next Tuesday.

The funniest telegram wins.

Translation

"Stepwords" are pairs of words of equal length which can be changed from one to the other by switching one letter at a time and forming a new word with each letter switch. For example, change black to white by forming these words: black-slack-stack-stalk-stale-shale-whale-while-white. The object of the game is to change one word to another with the fewest possible in-between words. The time limit is fifteen minutes.

When playing "stepwords" in competition, always be certain that the words you choose can be changed. (Some can't be.) Some sample stepwords include dry-wet, heat-cold, east-west, poor-rich, sick-well.

Advice

Provide pencils and slips of paper to all players. Instruct each player to whisper a piece of advice to the player on their right, who writes it down on their slip of paper. The papers are later redistributed, and each player in turn reads out what is on their slip.

Variation: Call out a category for the type of advice players should give.

Clap and Name

Form a circle with players either standing or sitting. The player who is "it" starts by hitting their legs twice and hitching his right thumb over his right shoulder and saying his own name; then he hitches his left thumb over his left shoulder, saying the name of someone else in the circle. That person must do the same. The rhythm is (count one) slap own knees (count two) slap own knees (count three) hitch over right shoulder (count four) hitch over left shoulder. If a person misses the rhythm or calls a name not represented in the group, they move to the end of the line.

A Fake Argument

At an appropriate time during a banquet, stunt program, or party, someone rises to protest some statement that has been made or some feature of the program. Other instructed persons take side in the ensuing argument with the intention of drawing someone into it who does not know that it is a stunt. When the argument waxes warm, one of the perpetrators rises and thanks the crowd for helping in their stunt.

Egg in a Bottle

Start with a hard-boiled egg with the shell removed. Challenge anyone in the audience to put this egg in a milk bottle or similar shaped glass bottle. Let them try. Warn them not to eat any of the egg. Some of them will try to put it through the neck of the bottle, but they won't be able to force it through. When they give up trying, show them how to perform the trick. Take a match, light it, and drop it into the bottle. You will have to remove the egg to do this, but replace it on the neck of the bottle at once. The flame of the match will consume the oxygen in the bottle, and this will create a vacuum which will suck the egg into the bottle.

Egg out of the Bottle

You have the egg in the milk bottle, but you don't want to break it to get it out. So you challenge your guests to get it out without breaking the bottle. Hand them matches to start them on the wrong track. Lighted matches won't work now. They won't be able to jiggle or shake it out. So you show them. Simply hold the bottle up, allowing the egg to fall into the neck of the bottle. Now hold the bottle mouth to your mouth and blow hard. Remove the bottle from the lips immediately and the egg will fall out. Vacuum does it.

Where Am I Going?

One player leaves the room while the other players decide what city they are going to visit. When the player who left the room is called back they ask each of the players in turn, "Where am I going?" Each person answers by giving them a clue as to their destination without divulging enough information to identify the city. When a player gives a clue that enables the questioner to name the city, that person then takes the place of the questioner.

Ten-Cent Fortune

The victim will be asked three answerable questions one at a time, such as "How many thousand will you be making when you are thirty-five? How many proposals do you expect? How many children do you expect to have by the time you are thirty-five?" The leader dips a dime in water and sticks it to the forehead of the victim. The victim then shakes their head until the dime falls off. The number of shakes it takes before the dime falls off is the answer to the question. On the third question the leader sticks the dime onto their forehead but then secretly removes it. And so the victim can shake his head but no dime will fall off.

Charades

This is an interesting contest where each player selects a word to enact and tries to stump the other members of the group. At the same time, the enactment of these charades will furnish entertainment for everybody.

Each syllable of the selected word is acted out and then the entire word. At the conclusion of each charade the family tries to guess the word. The action may be either by pantomime or conversation, but one or the other must be used by all. Practically no rehearsal or preparation is needed for charades. It is suggested that no words of more than three syllables be selected.

Here are a few good words for charades.

Antarctic (an-ark-tick)
Automat (auto-mat)
Bandage (band-age)
Decorate (deck -oar-ate)
Handkerchief (hand-cur-chief)
Handout (hand-out)
Ice Cream (eye-scream)
Knapsack (nap-sack)
Pantry (pan-tree)
Penmanship (Pen-man-ship)

Compound Word Game

To develop creativity, players draw the picture that comes to their mind from the word assigned to them from the list of objects below. When the pictures are completed, place them around the room with a number on each picture. Players may walk around looking at the pictures and try to match the list of objects with the pictures, placing the number that appears in the corner of the picture next to the correct title on the paper.

.... Butterfly
.... Football coach
.... Shoe tree
.... B-Line
.... Cow fly
.... Bottle stop
.... Walking stick
.... Pipe dream
.... Broom corn
.... Screw driver
.... Cigar box

.... King bird
.... Ice cream
.... Jumping rope
.... $5 bill
.... Sleeping tablet
.... Warm heart
.... House fly
.... June bug
.... Barn dance
.... Smoking jacket
.... Vinegar fly

.... Diving board
.... Sports fan
.... Boardwalk
.... Raising cane
.... Four o'clock
.... Snowball
.... Clock striking
.... Record player
.... Bank roll
.... Coffee plant
.... Catfish
.... Flying saucer
.... Bull dozer
.... Spelling bee

.... Saw horse
.... Blue jay
.... Tennis match
.... Watch tower
.... Watch dog
.... Deer fly
.... Road fork
.... Swimming trunks
.... Bed springs
.... Tomato patch
.... Spy glass
.... Running water
.... Ball bat

Bishop's Cat

Players sit in a circle of ten to twelve people. One player begins the game by saying, "The bishop's cat is an adorable cat." Each player must follow suit by describing the cat, using the same beginning letter on the adjective, as the first player. In this case, "The bishop's cat is an awkward cat," or "The bishop's cat is an amiable cat," could be used, and so on. Set a time limit for each person if needed. On a miss, the next player uses a different first letter.

Capital Cities

The boys are placed on one side of the room and the girls on the other. The leader stands in the center of the room and calls out the capital city of a certain state. The object is to see who can name the state first. The contest is carried on until either the boys or girls have a score of ten. The losers are required to put on a stunt, do the dishes, or some other chore.

Variation: Play the game in two teams without splitting up boys and girls.

Mix-up Story

Take two short stories like "Chicken Little" and "Red Riding Hood." Copy them sentence by sentence on separate slips of paper, one sentence to a slip. Mix them up in a hat and then have each player draw a slip or two, according to the size of the crowd. Indicate one person to begin the story. The person to the right of the starter then reads their first sentence and so on it goes around the circle. Naturally, there will be ridiculous combinations.

Balanced Writing

If you think you have a good sense of balance, try this one. Stand a quart milk bottle, or similar object, upright. Sit down on it, crossing your legs, touching the floor only with the heel of one foot. In this position hold a pad in your hand and try to write your name; or hold a candle, strike a match, and light the candle; or try threading a needle.

I Saw a Ghost

The players form a single line, all facing the same direction. The leader says, "I saw a ghost and he went like this." He makes a sound as mysterious as possible. The leader then drops down to their knees. All players follow suit, doing whatever the leader does. Again the leader makes their speech. This time they extend both hands straight out in front of them. The next time the leader suddenly shoves the next player sharply. As a result the whole crowd goes down on top of one another.

Refreshment Stunt

The refreshments are hidden somewhere near the place you eat. Couples hunt for the goodies and as soon as the food (a basket of sandwiches, plate of appetizers, the drink, and so on) is found the leader blows the whistle and calls back all the hunters. While the guests are eating the refreshments, the dessert is hidden and that too must be found.

Sewing Circle

Every alternate chair around the circle is occupied, and there are enough unoccupied chairs for all the players standing except one. The standing players walk around to the music, and when the music stops, all try to sit in one of the empty chairs. Then each begins to talk to their right-hand neighbor about a subject that has been given by the leader, such as "what they think of the new look" or "what's the best kind of car to own." If the person who didn't get a seat can discover anyone not talking, they can take that place and the guilty one must be "it."

Checkerberry

This game takes concentration and keen observation. All players stand in a circle facing the center. Each one thinks of some motion to do with his hands or feet that might be performed to the rhythm of the following little chant that they all say together: "CHECKERBERRY, CHECKERBERRY, CHECKERBERRY ON." They practice saying the words and doing the motion together. It is important that two people standing together do not have the same action. Everyone watches their own right-hand neighbor and no one else all through the game. They all begin the game by doing their own motion. Then, as soon as they all say "on" everyone takes on the motion of his right-hand neighbor. Thus, every time the group says, "CHECKERBERRY, CHECKERBERRY, CHECKERBERRY ON," all players do the motion their right-hand neighbor just completed doing. On "on," that motion is dropped and the next one is copied. No two people are ever doing the same motion at the same time. Anyone who breaks the sequence must drop out of the game.

Nursery Race

Each contestant—there should be two or more—is given milk in a nursing bottle or a soft drink bottle with a nipple on it. The first to empty their bottle is the champion (baby) of the crowd. Watch out for contestants who bite the bottle tip to make the holes larger!

The race is even funnier as a partner contest. Each contestant has a partner (mama) who holds their bottle. The contestants don bibs and sit on chairs with their backs to their partners. The partners hold the bottle while the contestants drink. The contestants may not touch the bottles.

Touch and Go

The players form in lines for relay teams. The leader names something in sight; this may be indefinite, like wood, iron, or water; or it may be a specific object, like the garage door or a certain tree. The leader may give directions, like "Hop back on the right foot." One by one the players in each line set out to touch the objects and return to their place. The line first regaining the original position wins the race.

Handful Relay

Fifteen clothespins, peanuts, checkers, or sticks are given to the first player in each team. At the starting signal they put all of them on the floor in front of the next player behind him. The player must pick them up and lay them before the next person in the line. Each person must have all of the clothespins or other objects in their hands when they pass them. The team that finishes first wins the relay.

Blackboard Relay

The teams line up in front of a blackboard, and the first player in each line is given a piece of chalk. When the whistle is blown, the first player walks to the board, writes a word, and returns to the line, giving the chalk to the next player. This is repeated until the end of the line is reached, each player adding a word to the sentence the first player started. The team that first finishes a complete sentence that each player has written a word in wins the game.

Lifesaver Relay

The players are organized into two rows facing each other, each person having a toothpick in his mouth. A lifesaver is placed on the toothpick of the first one in each row and upon a signal they must pass the lifesaver from their toothpick to the next toothpick. In this way it is passed on down the row to the last person. The first row finished wins.

Clothes Pin Relay

Players are equally divided. Each team lines up on opposite sides of a table. Each team has four clothes pins. The first player in each line places the clothes pins between the fingers on the next player's hand. This player takes them from their hand and places them between the fingers of the next in line, and so on down the line. The clothes pins are carried to the head of the table by the last player. The first team finished wins.

Fanning Relay

The group divides into even teams behind a starting line. The first player on each team is given a ping-pong paddle and a ping-pong ball. The ball is laid on the starting line. At a given signal the first player fans the ball across the room to some designated line or spot. He is not allowed to hit or touch the ball in any way, the locomotion of the ball being created solely by fanning it. If the ball is hit the player must get the ball and return it to the spot where he hit it and continue from there. After he gets it across the line he must get in front of it and fan it to get it to stop for the return trip. When he crosses the starting line again the next player repeats the performance until every player has had a turn. The first team through is the winner.

Variation: Use a broom and a feather, tissue paper, or cork.

Chair Race

Two rows face each other with at least six feet between the rows. Each team numbers off starting at the front of the row. When a number is called, the player from each team having that number leaves his chair, runs to the front of his row, around the chairs, and up the center to his own chair. The first player to be seated scores one point for his team.

Alphabetical "It"

The one who is "it" is the only one who knows who they represent. If this person decides to be Cleopatra, they say aloud, "I begin with *C*." If someone says "Are you a poet?" they reply, "No, I am not Chaucer or Coleridge." Then they go to the next person. If they cannot think of a poet's name beginning with *C*, they must challenge the questioner to name one. If the questioner does so, they are entitled to ask the one who is "it" a direct question, such as, "Are you a man or a woman?" The game continues in this way until someone guesses who the "it" player represents. Then that person becomes "it."

Nut Race

The group forms lines. One player in each line is given a nut which they put on the back of their hand. Putting their other hand behind their back, they run a prescribed course. If they drop the nut or help hold it on with other hand, they must start over. The first team finished wins.

Spoon and Beans

Each player is given a small cup or glass full of beans and a small spoon. Emptying the cup or glass on a table, each tries to fill it again with the beans by using only the spoon. If a person uses his other hand he must start over.

Judge

"Judge" is played by having someone acting as judge seated preferably with their chair elevated and a cushion on the floor in front of them. Call guests one by one (from another room) and have them tried on the cushion. The judge remarks, "I am an honest judge and must have 'honesty' for an answer." The judge asks questions such as, "How old are you?" and so on. Release the guest release only when they give "honesty" as an answer. During the game the judge will frequently repeat, "I am an honest judge and must have 'honesty' for an answer," especially if a guest hesitates in answering a question that may have been put to them.

Get Acquainted

In a large circle with name tags or in mass formation with papers, each person chooses a famous athlete, movie star, or musician with the same first or last name as their own. Everyone states their name in order in the circle, each successive person repeating the previous names given. Those missing the names or getting them out of order are eliminated. The last player remaining is the winner.

Children Indoor Party Games

Zoo Game

Participants are seated in a circle. One person in the center of the circle points to one of those seated and says, "duck." The person seated puts their hands to their mouth and makes the motion of a duck's bill. The person on their left lifts their left arm and flaps it. The person on their right lifts their right arm and flaps it. If the person in the center of the circle, "it," counts to ten before the three people do the motions, they take one of their places. This game can be more challenging by adding the motions of other animals (monkey, dog, cow, horse, chicken, elephant, and so on). This can be played by using motions of transportation, like an airplane, and also musical instruments.

Stick Hop

Each player takes their position a yard or so in front of a row of ten sticks placed within easy hopping distance from each other. If enough sticks cannot be secured, spools, clothespins or blocks may be used instead. Contestants hop on one foot down the row of sticks. They may change feet but may not touch any of the sticks in hopping over them. When the last stick has been hopped over, the player picks it up and hops back over the remaining sticks to the starting point. Dropping the stick, he again hops toward the sticks, each time picking up the stick farthest from the starting point and bringing it "home." The player getting all the sticks home first wins.

This game can be made more difficult by having the players hop on the same foot throughout the game.

Barnyard Din

Small objects, cardboard cut-outs, or pieces of candy are hidden around the room before the players arrive. For the hunt, the players are assigned to one of two teams, the Cats and the Dogs. Each team has a leader. When the signal is given to start, individual players begin hunting throughout the "barnyard" for the hidden objects. But there's a catch: only the leader may do the retrieving. When a Cat discovers an object, they meow loudly and insistently to attract the attention of the leader of their team. The Dogs bark. If the group is large, form additional teams of chickens, sheep, or donkeys. The team that recovers the most objects in five minutes wins. The losers may pay a forfeit or do a stunt.

Musical Dance

As music is played, children perform the following:

BUNNY HOP. Children squat. Hold hands behind head like bunny ears. Hop around.

WALRUS WALK. Walk by moving hands while toes drag. Body held off ground.

BEAR WALK. On all fours. Move right foot and right hand at same time and then left hand and foot.

SNAIL WALK. Like walrus walk, hitting chest with hand at each step.

CAT WALK. Hands and feet on ground, walk forward with hands, using tiny steps, as far as possible. Then arch back.

SPIDER WALK. Each player bends backwards and then walks on hands and feet.

Pencil Broad Jump

Each player toes a line, stoops, stretches forward, and sees how far he can place a pencil. He must not step over the line or lose his balance. He can use his left hand to help himself, but not the right. He must return to starting position.

Blowing Race Thumper

Everyone sits in a circle and chooses a leader. They will be number one and start off the game. Everyone picks their own sign, such as scratching his head. The game begins when the leader slaps their hands up and down on their knees in a more or less rhythmic fashion. Everyone does this for the duration of the game. The leader then says, "What's the name of this game?" The rest reply, "Thumper." The leader then asks, "How do you play it?" and the rest say "Thump." The leader immediately gives his sign and the sign of someone else. The person whose sign the leader gave must immediately give their own sign and the sign of still another person, or if they wish, the sign of the leader. This continues until someone gets out of rhythm or forgets to make a sign. The person who makes the mistake must go to the end and everyone else moves up. The leader then starts over again.

Old MacDonald's Farm

Enjoy this classic with the whole family.

"Old MacDonald had a farm" (Bob up and down, bending and straightening knees)
"E-I-E-I-O" (Place thumbs to ears and move hands up and down imitating donkey's ears)
"And on this farm he had some ducks" (Bob up and down)
"E-I-E-I-O" (Wiggle ears)
"With a quack quack here and a quack quack there; here a quack, there a quack, everywhere a quack quack," (Put palms of both hands together, holding them up to the mouth to form the beak and moving fingers open and closed, wrists stay touching. Everyone meanders and zigzags around the room as they sing and move their hands.)
"Old MacDonald had a farm" (Bob up and down)
"E-I-E-I-O" (Wiggle ears)
"And on this farm he had some chicks" (Bob up and down)
"E-I-E-I-O" (Wiggle ears)
"With a peck peck here and a peck peck there, here a peck, there a peck, everywhere a peck peck." (Use fingers to peck with)
"Old MacDonald had a farm" (Bob up and down)
"E-I-E-I-O" (Wiggle ears)

Other verses that may be used:

cow—moo moo	bell—tinkle tinkle
owl—hoot hoot	pain—moan moan
	(or groan groan)
gun—bang bang	itch—scratch scratch

133

baby—cry cry	worm—wiggle wiggle
	(or squirm squirm)
hen—cackle cackle	phone—gossip gossip
pig—oink oink	(or ring ring)
turkey—gobble gobble	train—toot toot
lamb—baa baa	dog—bow wow
cat—meow meow	bed—snore snore
bees—sting sting	tree—sway sway
(or buzz buzz)	airplane—zoom zoom
rabbit—hop hop	car—rattle rattle

Sit and Sing

Everyone leaves the room except one. This person hides a coin or other object in a secluded spot, but in plain sight. Everyone is instructed to search for the coin, and when a person finds it they must not disturb it, but must go to a chair, sit down, and start to sing. The last one down must pay a forfeit (see Forfeit section).

Run, Good Sheep, Run!

Divide into two groups, each selecting a leader or shepherd. Group One chooses a set of signals by which the leader can inform their group of the approaching Group Two. Group Two remains at base while Group One hides. After the first group is hidden, their leader returns to the base and draws a map of where they went. After the second group studies the map, they start out in search of Group One. Group One's leader can call out signals like "Ford" (searchers approaching), "Buick" (searchers close to hiding place), or "Cab" (searchers have passed hiding place). When Group two is past the hidden group, Group One's leader yells, "Run, good sheep, run!" Group One players immediately run to the base and Group Two tries to tag them. If Group One arrives at the base (or most of them arrive), then the groups swap roles and play another round. When three-fourths of one group is caught by the other, the group that caught the other wins.

Treasure Hunt

Two teams are chosen with a captain for each. One team is

designated to hide a treasure while the other team keep their eyes closed. Upon returning from hiding the treasure, the first team draws a map by which the second team must find the hidden treasure. They may refer to the map as often as they wish.

Human Tick-Tack-Toe

Nine chairs or pieces of paper are lined up in a square formation, three each way between two opposing teams. The object of the game is for one team to get three of its own players in a straight or diagonal line before the other team does—just like the old pencil and paper tick-tack-toe. Each team has a captain who calls out the next players, and of course there should be no coaching from adults on either side—that spoils the suspense.

Unlucky Spots

When the group is tired after playing active games, "Unlucky Spots" is a good rest cure. It has enough competition in it to keep the group interested, but it is not too strenuous.

The leader designates at random a number of "unlucky spots" on the floor. They may be drawn with chalk or marked with paper cutouts. Cardboard disks of different colors are suitable, but children get a bigger kick out of the game if pictures of various kinds are drawn on the floor. During the holidays the leader might quickly draw in various colors a Christmas tree, snowball, holly wreath, Santa Claus face, and a candy cane; at Halloween, a black cat, a ghost face, a witch, and a pumpkin. Or they might draw cars and give them the names of standard makes.

To start the game, the leader closes their eyes or turns their back to the group and gives the players the signal to hurry to one of the positions on or around any of the unlucky spots. Then the leader blows a whistle, and when they do all the players are standing on or near one of the objects on the floor. The leader now names one of the spots. If they call out "Snowball," all the players around it are eliminated. The game continues. The leader again turns their back, and the players scatter to new positions or remain where they are, if they prefer. The leader blows the whistle after a few moments and names an object, the same one or a different one.

Players are eliminated gradually until only a few remain. The leader now adds to the fun by asking the spectators to remain quiet while the leader listens for the footsteps of the remaining players. This makes the audience watch the game with tense interest while the leader tries to trap the other players on one of the unlucky spots.

You

Players are seated in a circle. The leader stands in the center and whispers the name of an animal to each person in the circle. Next the leader points to anyone and says, "You—1-2-3-4-5-6-7-8-9-10." The person pointed to must give the name of his animal three times before the leader counts ten, otherwise they change places. Names like rhinoceros or hippopotamus are rather a mouthful, repeated three times.

Hot Spot

Players—from fifteen to twenty is the best number—join hands in a single circle. Inside the circle are several "hot spots." These may be empty laundry baskets, empty tin cans, circles, or, outdoors during holidays, appropriate pictures drawn on the ground with chalk. When the signal to start is given, the players, keeping their hands joined, pull each other in an effort to eliminate the others from the game by forcing them to step on or knock over one of the hot spots. At the same time they are, of course, trying to avoid the hot spots themselves. The circle becomes smaller as players are forced out, but the number and the position of the hot spots do not change. After a while some of the spots are set inside the circle and some outside. Toward the end, the game requires some strength and agility as the players duck and jump and twist to avoid the hot spots.

Grab

Players sit around a table in the center of which contains a number of small objects, two less than the number of players. One player gives command such as "Hold your nose," "Thumbs up," and so on. When the commanding player says "Grab" each player grabs an object. The two players who do not get one drop out of the game. The objects are replaced, still two less than the number of players, and the game continues. The player who gets the last object is the winner.

Cat in the Corner

All players are mice except the player chosen to be "it," who is Cat. Each mouse sits on a chair. Cat goes from mouse to mouse demanding a "corner." The players refuse but by signs among themselves they change chairs. Cat tries to get a chair during these changes. The mouse whose chair is captured by Cat becomes the new Cat.

Chair-Leg Ring Toss

Turn a chair upside down so the legs lean toward the players. Make a tossing line with string, masking tape, or draw a line with chalk. Use four quoits (rings) made of rope, plastic, or rubber if you have them, or make four rings from an empty oatmeal carton by cutting off round strips about one and a half to two inches wide.

Each player in turn takes the rings and tosses them, trying to make a ringer on each of the four legs of the chair. The first ringer scores one point, and the second ringer two points, the third three points, and the fourth ten points. Two ringers on the same leg lose the player five points.

Wastebasket Toss

Use a wastebasket as the goal. Mark the tossing line with a piece of string, masking tape, or draw it with a piece of chalk. You may wish to make the tossing line closer for young children. Use a ball or beanbag for tossing. If the ball or beanbag touches the basket it counts as one point; if it goes inside and stays there it counts as five points. If the ball goes in but bounces out, it counts as two points.

Slap Catch

The players stand in a circle, with one in the center. Those in the circle bend their elbows, which should touch their sides, and extend their hands in front, with palms down. The object is for the one in the center to slap the hands of any player in the circle while thus extended. The circle players may bend their hands downward or sideways at the wrist, but may not withdraw the arms, or change the position of the elbow. Anyone slapped in this way changes places with the one in the center. The success of this game will depend on the alertness of the one who is in the center, who should dodge quickly and unexpectedly from one part of the circle to another, with feints and false moves that will keep the circle players uncertain. The circle should not be too large, or the action will be too slow to be interesting.

Spin the Platter

Number the players and seat them in a circle, except for one who stands in the center and twirls a platter, tray, or some other round object. As the center player starts it spinning they call any number they choose and the player bearing that number must spring forward and try to catch the platter before it ceases to spin and falls to the floor. If successful, they return to their place in the circle; if not, they take the place of the spinner and pay a forfeit. The forfeits are redeemed at the end of the game. This game may also be played by calling names instead of numbers.

Spans

This is a game played by snapping buttons against a wall, their landing point determining a score. Each player has a button. One of the players lays his button down on the ground near a wall or fence. The others, in turn, snap their buttons against the wall so they rebound near the first player's button. Should the button snapped drop within one hand reach or span of the button first laid down, it scores two points for the player throwing it; within two such spans of the first button, one point. Should it hit this button and bounce away within one span, it counts four points. Should it bounce within two spans, it scores three points. Should it go farther than this after bouncing off the first button, it scores only one point. The number of points in the game is twenty or thirty. The first to score the required number wins.

Shake

Form a double circle, one inside the other, moving in opposite directions. There should be musical accompaniment or a signal to stop and go. The two circles move until the music stops, and then each person shakes hands and carries on a conversation with the person or persons nearest them in the opposite circle in the manner suggested by the leader's call. The conversation and hand shaking must continue until the music starts again and the players resume their original walking directions. Useful calls are Pump Handle (very vigorous and peppy), Fish (limp and disinterested), Own Hands (shake own hands and converse with partner).

Exchange

Two lines of equal numbers face each other. The object of this game is to change places with the opposing team as quickly as possible. On a signal from the leader, each team moves to the opposite side. The first complete team to make the change is the winner. Suggested modes of changing are walking backwards, duck walk, skipping, hopping, baby stepping, and so on.

Zip and Zap

The players sit in a circle. One person is "it" in the center of the circle. The person on each player's right is "Zip" and on his left is "Zap." The center person points to someone in the circle calling "Zip" or "Zap" and counting to ten. Before the count of ten is reached, the player must have given the name of "Zip," their neighbor on the right, or "Zap," their neighbor on the left, depending on which is called. When a player can't give the name before time is up, they must become "it" and replace the player in the center.

Truth

A person is elected to leave the room. All players left in the room stand in a close circle with their hands closed. They pretend to pass a whistle around. The leader has a whistle tied to their back and, during the game, wanders around within the circle. The person is then called back into the room and told to look for a whistle in someone's hands. While the player is looking for the whistle, the leader stands in front of someone, and the person behind blows the whistle and then pretends to pass it on but really leaves it on the back of the leader.

Don't Follow the Leader

Seat players in a circle, and chose one person to start the game. All players have their hands in front of them, fingers closed. The leader says "ready" and throws their hands forward with fingers outstretched. Before their fingers are quite out, they call a number and extend the number of fingers they called. Each person extends their fingers with the leader, using any number they thought of. The object of this game is to be a "mind reader," and not to extend the same number as the leader does. All those having the number the leader calls are eliminated. The player to the right of the leader calls the next number and so on. The one remaining when the last person is eliminated is the winner.

Streets and Alleys

Form players into four lines, and choose a leader and a follower. The players in the lines, at the shout of "streets," stretch their arms so pathways are formed between them. At the shout of "alleys," they make a quarter turn to form pathways at right angles to the "streets." The leader calls out "streets" or "alleys" as they wish and the follower, who tries to catch the leader, must stay within the rows. The leader must also stay within the rows.

Finger Arithmetic

The children face each other in couples and the leader calls, "Add." Both extend any number of fingers. The first person of each couple who calls the correct total of extended fingers score a point.

Find Me!

Use a soft rubber ball for older children and a bean bag for youngsters. Players stand in an informal group. The person who is "it" stands in front of the group with his back turned. They toss the ball or bean bag over their head, and wait until they hear the signal from the group. Somebody catches the ball or bag, and then everybody puts their hands behind them and calls out, "Find me!" The "it" player turns around and tries to guess who really has the ball or bag. If they guess right, they are "it" again. If wrong, the person with the ball or bag is the new "it."

Jumping Jack

Everyone forms a circle, with one player, as "Jack," inside. Jack closes their eyes (no peeking!). The leader puts a two-inch square piece of paper or cardboard under the foot of a player. Then the leader calls out, "Jump, Jack!" Everyone jumps and Jack tries to spot the paper. If Jack sees the paper, they take another turn. If not, the player hiding the paper gets to be "Jack."

Fruit Basket

The players are seated in a circle, and count off by fours. All the number ones are lemons; the number twos, oranges; the number threes, apples; and the number fours, bananas. One player is selected to be "it" and stands in the center. The "it" player names two fruits such as "bananas and oranges," whereupon all bananas and oranges quickly exchange seats. The person who is "it" tries to get a seat in the scramble. The person left without a seat becomes "it." Any combination of fruits may be spoken. If the person in the center calls "fruit basket," everyone exchanges seats.

Poison Carton

This game is similar to Hot Spots. Place a "poison" carton in the center of a small circle. The players join hands, move back and forth around the circle, and try to force others into the circle to touch the carton. Once a person touches the carton they are eliminated.

Musical Madhouse

The players form a single circle. When the music begins all march clockwise. The leader suddenly blows a number of blasts on a whistle (for example, four blasts). Players stop marching and form small circles of four, with hands joined. Those left out of the small circles must stand in the center and sing until the next signal. The next signal may be six blasts and circles of six are formed. Vary the number of whistle blasts each time.

The Blind Musician

Blindfold one player who stands at the center of a circle of players. This player holds a wand or baton (a pencil will do). The players sit around humming some familiar tune, after disguising their voices. The blindfolded musician beats time with his baton and guesses who is humming. If they guess the hummer correctly, the two exchange places.

Penny Wise

The players are lined up in the center of the room. They are then required to guess in what hand the caller has placed a penny. Each right answer is rewarded by a move forward. Each wrong answer is penalized by a move backward. The first player to the penny holder wins.

Snootie

One player is the pointer. They stand in a circle formed by the other players. The pointer points to a player. While the pointer counts to ten, that player must hold their own nose with one hand and their own ear with the other. If they fail to do this, they become the pointer. A player who grabs their nose and ear when the pointer has merely pointed but has not started counting also becomes the pointer.

Ring around the Rosy

All children hold hands forming a circle. As they dance around in the circle, they sing, "Ring around the rosy, Pocket full of Posies, Ashes, ashes, we all fall down." As they say "we all fall down," they immediately fall to the ground. The last one down has to stand in the center as the children begin dancing around again, singing the song. The game continues until there is only one of the dancers left.

London Bridge

One pair of children joins hands and lifts them high to make an arch. The children file under one at a time as they sing, "London bridge is falling down, falling down, falling down. London bridge is falling down, my fair lady—O." As they sing the final "O," the pair with joined hands quickly bring their arms down, trapping one person and carrying them off to prison. At prison they are given a choice of two sides, each half of the "bridge" being a choice. The prisoner falls in line behind the person whose side they chose and, in the end, a tug-of-war is held between the two sides to determine the winner.

Bubble Race

Two sides are chosen (with goal lines marked or selected) and bubble pipes and soapy water are provided for each side. Each side has a bubble blower and a fanner. The two fanners stand facing one another in the center of the room, each holding a piece of cardboard or a fan. At the word "Go" the bubble blower for one side blows a bubble and the two fanners try to fan this bubble over toward their respective goals. If the bubble bursts, the two fanners start over again at the point of burst, the other bubble blower blowing the next one. The object is to get the bubble over the goal line.

Crows and Cranes

Two teams are lined up facing each other, each having a home wall or line a short distance away. One team is called the "Crows" and the other the "Cranes." If the leader calls "Crows," all the crows run to their home base while those on the other side try to tag them. A person tagged drops out of the game or, if preferred, goes over to the other team.

Grocery Store

Form the group in lines of equal numbers. The first player of each line steps forward two steps, and the leader calls out a letter. The first player to call out the name of a grocery article beginning with that letter scores one point for their team. Each player goes to the back of their line when they have completed their turn, and the next player steps forward two steps. If any player calls a name out of turn to help their teammate, they cause their team to lose one point.

Blindman's Bluff

Blindfold the player who is "it." The other players clasp hands, forming a circle around the blindfolded player. When the "it" player says, "Go!" the other players begin to move in a circle. At the command, "Halt!" the other players stop. The "it" player then points in the direction of a player. The player pointed to goes into the circle and the person who is "it" must catch him. When they catch the player, they must name them. If the "it" player is right, that player becomes "it." If not, the game continues with the same person as "it."

Animal Blindman's Bluff

This game is played the same as Blindman's Bluff except that the person whom the "it" player points out steps into the circle and imitates an animal (chosen by the group previously). The person who is "it" then guesses the name of the player but does not have to catch them.

Stir the Broth

One player stands in the center of the room with a cane, umbrella, or stick. There is a chair for every player except one. The players walk around the one in the center, saying, "Stir the broth! Stir the broth!" The center player stirs with the stick. Suddenly they rap the stick on the floor three times and dash for a chair. The others try to get to their chairs first. If the center player gets a chair, the player who fails to do so becomes the next stirrer.

Bandit

The player chosen to be "it" points to one of the players in the circle and says, "Stick 'em up!" The player pointed to must put up both hands. The person to the right must put up their left hand while the person on the left puts up their right hand. The last to do so is eliminated, stands back from their chair, and calls the next "Stick 'em up!" The last two persons to remain seated are the winners.

Black Magic

This fun game requires the leader and guesser to know the secret before starting. Seat the players in a circle. Chose one to be sent from the room (the guesser) while the others select an object for them to guess. When the object is selected, the leader tells the guesser to come back. The leader then asks the guesser a question. For example, "Is it Mary's dress?" The guesser says, "No," and the leader asks another question. The secret is that when the leader refers the guesser to a black object, the guesser knows that the next object mentioned will be the thing the group chose.

String Spoons

Play this game when you serve refreshments. Tie two teaspoons together with twine so that they are about eighteen inches apart and pair off the guests so that a girl has one spoon and a boy another. At the word "Go," they eat the ice cream. The first couple to finish wins and is entitled to eat the next portion with no strings attached.

Riddles, Puzzles, and Jokes for Indoor Party Games

Flower Riddles

What flower . . .

do ladies tread under foot?	(Lady Slipper)
is most used by cooks?	(Buttercup)
tells how a man may get rich quick?	(Marigold)
indicates late afternoon?	(Four O'Clock)
tells what father says when he wants an errand run?	(Johnny Jump Up)
is a parting remark to a friend?	(Forget-Me-Not)
do people get up early to enjoy?	(Morning Glory)

do men often handle?	(Lady Finger)
reminds one of church?	(Jack in the Pulpit)
describes a beautiful specimen of an animal?	(Dandelion)

Tree Riddles

What shall we wear to keep us warm?	(Fir)
What do ships prefer in a storm?	(Beech)
Which tree do we offer friends when we meet?	(Palm)
Which tree shows what lovelorn maidens do?	(Pine)
Which is the Egyptian plague tree?	(Locust)
Which tree is left in men's pipes?	(Ash)
Which is it bad boys dislike to see?	(Willow)
Which is a girl, both young and sweet?	(Peach)
Which is like a man, bright, dapper, and neat?	(Spruce)
Which tree is never seen alone?	(Pear)
And which is a bright warm tone?	(Redwood)
And which is an office held in a church?	(Elder)
Which tree do you find on calendars?	(Date)
What kind of tree do we use in a storm?	(Hat)
And on our feet we wear what tree?	(Rubber)
And which our heroes crown will be?	(Myrtle)
For this one do not look far, it tells what charming people are?	(Poplar)
The carpenter uses which tree to make his walls straight as can be?	(Plum)

Berry Riddles

What berry is . . .

employed by Mark Twain?	(Huckleberry)
on the grass?	(Dewberry)
irritating?	(Raspberry)
a dunce?	(Gooseberry)
used for hats?	(Strawberry)
respected because of its age?	(Elderberry)
a beverage?	(Teaberry)
melancholy?	(Blueberry)
a reminder of news?	(Newberry)

Guess What!

1. What is full of holes yet holds water? (Sponge)
2. Why is a proud girl like a music book? (Full of airs)
3. Why is a philanthropist like a lazy horse? (Both are arrested by every cry of woe [whoa].)
4. What turns without moving? (Milk)
5. What word contains the vowels in their proper order? (Facetiously)
6. What goes around all day with its head down? (Nail in a horseshoe)
7. Why is the nose in the middle of the face? (Because it is the scenter)
8. What is the cheapest sheet music? (Snoring)
9. Why is an Irishman trying to kiss a tall girl like a traveler climbing Mount Vesuvius? (Trying to get to the crater's mouth)
10. Why is a schoolroom like a Ford? (Crank in front and noise all around)
11. What two flowers should decorate a menagerie? (Dandelion and tiger lily)
12. What occurs once in a minute, twice in a moment, but not at all in a thousand years? (The letter m)
13. Why is the heart of a tree like a dog's tail? (Farthest from the bark)

Cake Walk

What cake did the lover buy? (Sugar)
What cake did the moocher buy? (Sponge)
What cake did the tramp buy? (Loaf)
What cake did the dairyman buy? (Cream)
What cake did the champion buy? (Cup)
What cake did the shoemaker buy? (The last)
What cake did the sculptor buy? (Marble)
What cake did the gossip buy? (Spice)
What cake did the jeweler buy? (Gems)
What cake did the pugilist (boxer) buy? (Pound cake)

Gates

What gate proclaims and publishes? (Promulgate)
A gate of inquiring turn? (Interrogate)
A gate full of wrinkles? (Corrugate)
A gate which travels by water? (Navigate)
A gate which increases by length? (Elongate)
A gate which conquers? (Subjugate)
A gate which acts as a representative? (Delegate)
A gate which cleanses? (Fumigate)
A gate which waters the land? (Irrigate)
A gate which assembles? (Congregate)

The Bishop's Riddles

Once there was a bishop who claimed that wherever he went, night or day, he was accompanied by (see if you can guess them)

Two playful animals.	Calves
A number of animals of the rodent family.	Hares (hairs)
A member of the deer family.	Hart (heart)
Some whips.	Lashes
Two military weapons.	Arms
Two hotel steps.	Inn steps (insteps)
The senate, when it takes a vote on a hotly contested issue.	Ayes & noes (eyes & nose)
Ten Spanish gentlemen.	Ten dons (tendons)
Two places of worship.	Temples
Two students.	Pupils
Two coverings for kettles.	Lids
What the king leaves for his offspring.	Crown
Two percussion instruments.	Drums
Two established measures.	Hands & feet
Two head coverings.	Caps (kneecaps)
What a carpenter needs.	Nails
A couple of fish;	Soles
Some shellfish.	Mussels (muscles)
Two lofty trees.	Palms
Two kinds of flowers.	Tulips & iris (two lips)

More Riddles

Which is the largest room in the world?
   The room for improvement.
What is the difference between a hill and a pill?
   One is hard to get up, and the other is hard to get down.
What is the difference between a greedy man and a hungry
   man? One eats too long, the other longs to eat.
What is the difference between a man who is broke and a
   pillow? One is hard up, the other is soft down.
What is the surest way to keep water from coming into your
   house? Don't pay your water bill.
Why is a room full of married people like an empty room?
   Because there is not a single person in it.
Why is a kiss over a telephone like a straw hat?
   Because it's not felt.
Why is a quarrel like a bargain?
   It takes two to make it.

Graveyard Riddles

If you lived in a graveyard,
   With what would you open the gate? (With a skeleton key)
   What would you do if you got a bad cold that settled in your
      throat? Start coffin.
   How would you identify in three letters a plaintive poem?
      L-E-G, elegy.
   What kind of jewels would you wear? Tombstones.
   Where would you keep them? In a casket.
   How would you get money? Urn it.
   What would you eat? Pyre cake or buries.
   How would you move things about? By carrion them.
   What would you do getting ready for a play? Rehearse.
   What would protect you from the sun? The shades.
   Suppose a woman told you she was going to call?
      You would specter.
   What would be your disposition? Grave.

Mystery Story

A man gets into an elevator in his apartment and descends twelve floors, gets out, and goes to work. He returns in the evening, gets into the elevator, but only goes up seven floors. He gets out and walks the remaining five floors. Why?

Answer: He's a very short person and can only reach the bottom buttons in the elevator.

Trust

This is a good prank to play with a close group of friends. Call for two volunteers, and line them up one on each side of a shallow pan of water placed on a table. Lay a match on the water and tell each player to try to blow it across the pan when you count to three and say "Go!" Faces should be down close to the water. Count to three, slap the pan of water with the palm of your hand, splashing water in the faces of each player, and then bring out the towels.

Variation: You can skip the prank portion and let the players actually play the game, making it a tournament to see which player wins the most games.

Riddles

Read these riddles to the group and give a candy kiss to the first person who answers correctly.

1. For what man should you always take off your hat?
2. When can three fat women go out under one little umbrella and not get wet?
3. A hen can lay an egg four inches long. Can you beat that?
4. When will a net hold water?
5. What is the best way to keep a skunk from smelling?
6. What is the best way to make pants last?
7. What is white, has just one horn, and gives milk?
8. What is the best way to catch a fish?
9. What kind of animal eats with his tail?
10. What sings, has four legs, is yellow and weighs one thousand pounds?
11. What is the best thing to put into a pie?
12. Why does a giraffe eat so little?

13. Why does a cook always put on a high, white hat?
14. When should you give elephant milk to a baby?
15. Which will burn longer, the candles on the birthday cake of a boy, or the candles on the birthday cake of a girl?
16. In America, black horses eat more than white horses. Why?
17. Do you know why they are not making matches any longer?
18. Where can happiness always be found?
19. There is one thing you always overlook; what is it?
20. Why do we all go to bed?
21. If a blue stone fell into the Red Sea, what would happen?
22. What is the easiest thing to part with in hot weather?
23. What did Paul Revere say when he finished his famous ride?
24. What has a bed but never sleeps?
25. On which side does a chicken have more feathers?
26. Why does a milkman have a white horse?
27. Do you know why the Lone Ranger and Tonto broke up?
28. What is a favorite word with women?
29. What is the best material for kites?
30. How do you pronounce the capital of Kentucky, "Louisville" or "Louee-ville"?
31. How many animals of each kind did Moses take on his ark?

ANSWERS

1. The barber.
2. When it is not raining.
3. Yes, with an egg beater.
4. When the water is frozen.
5. Hold his nose.
6. Make the coat first.
7. A milk truck.
8. Have someone throw it to you.
9. All kinds—they can't take them off.
10. Two five-hundred-pound canaries.
11. Your teeth.
12. He can make a little go a long way.
13. To cover his head.
14. When it is a baby elephant.
15. Neither. They both burn shorter.
16. Because there are more black horses.
17. Because they are long enough.
18. In the dictionary.

19. Your nose.
20. Because the bed will not come to us.
21. It would get wet.
22. A comb.
23. "Whoa!"
24. A river.
25. The outside.
26. To pull his wagon.
27. The Lone Ranger found out what "Kemosabe" meant.
28. The last one.
29. Fly paper.
30. The capital of Kentucky is pronounced "Frankfort."
31. It wasn't Moses—it was Noah!

Animal Game

We often compare people with different kinds of animals. The following are some common comparisons. Write in the name of the correct animal or bird.

As sly as a . . . . . .   As stubborn as a . . . . . .
As happy as a . . . . . .   As busy as a . . . . . .
As black as a . . . . . .   As crazy as a . . . . . .
As mad as a wet . . . . . .   As strong as an . . . . . .
As wise as an . . . . . .   As bold as a . . . . . .

Answers: fox, lark, crow, hen, owl, mule, bee, loon, ox, lion

Doodles

Give each person as many pieces of paper as there are people playing the game. On each piece the players make a doodle, any combination of lines and circles, but the same doodle on each paper. These papers are exchanged until each person has a complete set of varying drawings, out of which they makes a picture. It's interesting to see the different ideas which emerge from the same doodle.

Decode

Decipher the code to form an old proverb.
Z ILOORMT HGLMV TZGSVIH ML NLHH. (Reverse each letter—Z becomes A, and so on.) A ROLLING STONE GATHERS NO MOSS.

Puzzle

Make only one word out of the following letters:
DENORWOLYNO
Answer: Only one word

Tree Quiz

What tree suggests . . .

the hand?	(Palm)
the seaside?	(Beech)
history?	(Date)
neat appearance?	(Spruce)
a winter coat?	(Fir)
a valuable oil?	(Olive)
a well-worn joke?	(Chestnut)
a good-looking girl?	(Peach)
the color black?	(Ebony)
a carpenter's tool?	(Plane)
in high favor?	(Poplar)
a parent?	(PawPaw)
an inlet of the sea?	(Bay)
a Church official?	(Elder)
syrup?	(Maple)
a dead fire?	(Ash)
sadness?	(Weeping Willow)
of a bottle?	(Cork)
of a bouncing ball?	(Rubber)
two?	(Pear)
a kind of grasshopper?	(Locust)

Clues

During a war, I watched a friend of mine who was flying alone on an observation flight above the lines. When he had completed his mission and was thinking to himself how lucky he was not to have seen an enemy plane on his way home, an Austrian aviator suddenly swooped upon him from above a cloud bank, and shot him to the ground. He was dead when the first person reached him.

What is the fallacy in the story?

Answer: Who could know what the aviator was thinking to himself?

Riddles

1. At what time of the day was Adam born? A little before Eve.
2. Who first introduced walking sticks? Eve gave Adam a little Cain (cane).
3. When was tennis first mentioned in the Bible? When Joseph first served in Pharaoh's court.
4. What is longest word in the English language? Smiles, because it has a mile between its first and last letter.
5. Why is a good story like a church bell? Because it is often tolled (told).
6. Why did Noah object to the letter D? Because it makes the ark dark.
7. How many of the forbidden fruit were eaten in the Garden of Eden? Eve ate, and Adam, too, and the devil won—eleven in all. (Add the figures [8,2, 1].)
8. When was Rome built? At night—because it wasn't built in a day.
9. Why was Moses the most wicked man that ever lived? Because he broke all the Ten Commandments at once.
10. Who is your greatest friend? Your nose, because it will run for you till it drops.
11. When did the boy stop bragging about his family tree? When he was told that he was the only sap.
12. How were Adam and Eve prevented from gambling? Their pair o' dice (Paradise) was taken away from them.
13. What do ladies look for when they go to church?
    The hymns (hims).
14. Who may marry many a wife, and yet live single all his life? A clergyman.
15. How long did Cain hate his brother? As long as he was Abel.
16. Why was Goliath astonished when David hit him with a stone? Because such a thing had never entered his head before.
17. How did the whale that swallowed Jonah obey the divine law? Jonah was a stranger and he took him in.
18. What man had no father? Joshua, the son of Nun.
19. What did Adam and Eve do when they were expelled from Eden? They "raised Cain."
20. Who first introduced salt pork into the Navy? Noah, he took

Ham into the Ark.

21. How did Jonah feel when the whale swallowed him? Down in the mouth.
22. Why was Adam the happiest man in the world? He had no mother-in-law.

Riddles

Have a sheet of paper for each member of the group with the following questions. Set an alarm clock and when it rings give a prize to the one with the most right answers.

What is always behind time? (Back of the clock)

When is a clock dangerous? (When it strikes)

What is time and yet a fruit? (A date)

What does the proverb say time is? (Money)

When the clock strikes thirteen, what time is it? (Time to have it repaired)

I have hands but no fingers, no bed but lots of ticks. What am I? (Clock)

What month of the year is a command to go forward? (March)

Which Man Was Right?

Three men on the bank of a river argued about who first knew of the discharge of a rifle on the opposite side. Number one heard the report; number two saw the smoke of the discharge, and number three saw the bullet strike in the river at his feet. Who knew first?

Answer: Number two, then number three, then number one.

Harry's Allowance

Harry has three times as many nickels as dimes. If the value of his money is $3.75, how many coins of each kind does he have?

Answer: fifteen dimes and forty-five nickels.

Punch Glasses

You have six glasses lined up in a row; the odd ones are full, the even ones are empty. Move only one glass, and by so doing line up three full glasses next to three empty ones.

Answer: Pour the contents of glass number five into glass number two and replace number five.

How Many Pages?

A set of books is arranged in orderly fashion on a shelf. Each book has five hundred pages, making one thousand pages in all. A worm starting on the first page of the first book eats his way through the last page of the last book. How many pages has he eaten through?

Answer: Two pages. He bored through only one page of each of the two books.

Hello, There!

A man met an old friend he hadn't seen in ten years. The old friend said, "I've married someone you don't know, and this is my little girl." The man asked the girl what her name was. She replied that it was the same as her mother's. How would the man have known that the little girl's name was Ann?

Answer: The old friend was the girl's mother, so he would know the girl's name.

Brothers and Sisters

Brother and sister have I none, but that man's father is my father's son. What relation is that man to me?

Answer: My son.

How Old Is B?

A is thirty-six and twice as old as B was when A was twenty-seven. How old is B now?

Answer: B is twenty-seven. When A was twenty-seven, B was eighteen; therefore, A is nine years older than twenty-seven (which is thirty-six) and B is nine years older than eighteen (which is twenty-seven).

Catching the Train

I have two minutes in which to catch a train and two miles to go.

If I go the first mile at the rate of thirty miles per hour, at what rate must I go the second mile in order to catch the train?

Answer: The train has gone—two minutes were spent in the first mile.

Outdoor Games
Relay and Running Games

String Winding Relay

Give the first player of each team a ball of string. At the signal, the first player wraps the string around their body, hands it to the second who wraps it around their own body, and so on. When the last player has wrapped it around their body, they unwrap it, wind the string on the ball again, and hand the ball to the next player who repeats the action. The winner is the team that has its ball wound up again first.

Gorilla Relay Race

Each player spreads his feet shoulder width apart, bends down, and grasps his ankles. He walks forward, keeping his knees extended and his legs straight, to a prescribed goal.

Barefoot Marble Relay

The players are barefoot. The first player runs to a line fifteen feet away. He grasps and carries one marble with the toes of each foot and returns to tag the next person. The second person does the same, and the game continues until all the players on one team have completed their run in this way.

Crab Relay Race

Players crawl crab-style to a line fifteen feet away, stand up, and return to tag the next player, who repeats the performance and tags player number three. The first team to complete the course wins.

Thirty-Yard Dash

Ready, go! They're off! Pick first, second, and third places for the players that run the distance fastest.

Cracker Race

The first player in each line runs to their team's chair on the "goal" line and eats a cracker. As soon as the second in line can hear them whistle, they run to the chair and eat their cracker and whistle. This continues until one line gets all its players through eating and whistling.

Hopping Relay Race

One at a time the players from each team hop twenty-five feet on the left foot to a marker and then hop back on the right foot to tag the next player.

Foot and Nose Relay

The first runner in each line must hold their right ankle with their right hand and their nose with their left hand. In this position they hop to the turning line and then run back and tag the next runner. If a player lets go of their nose or ankle, they must return to the starting point and begin again.

Ball Relay

Have the group line up facing each other with arms bent. Each person holds the elbows of the person opposite. A ball is started down the line, being passed from one set of arms to the next. When the end pair get the ball, they race to the front of the line carrying the ball on their arms and start the ball down the line again. If the ball falls, the runners must pick it up, still holding arms, and start over.

Variation: Play the game with multiple groups or against a certain time limit.

Steal the Bacon with Poles

The object of the contest is to pick up "the flag" on the end of a pole and get it back to your goal line before the other team gets it back to theirs. The players are divided into equal numbers for two teams and given a number. Each player on each team has a number corresponding with a person on the other team. Goal lines are set up thirty yards apart. Each team is given a pole that lays on the ground on its respective goal line between plays. The flag, which is a piece of cloth, is placed between them in the middle. The leader calls a number and the player who has that number picks up their pole and runs to the flag and tries to race back to the finish line with it before the other team's member gets it. It is legal to take the flag from the other player on your pole before they get to their goal line.

Dizzy Dizzy Relay

Teams are equally divided and placed in lines with each team having a long pole. At the command "Go," the first person in each line places the pole above their head and, while watching the top end of the pole, spins ten times. They then run to a goal and return handing the pole to the next person, who then does the same thing. The game is completed when the last person in a team's line has completed their turn.

Bean Bag Relay

Equally divide the teams and place them in lines parallel to each other. The teams are given an equal amount of bean bags that are placed in front of the first member of each team. On the command "Go," the first person in each line places a bean bag on their head and the second person takes it from them and places it on their own head. Each person in the line takes the bags off the head of the person in front of them until the last person in the line has all of the bags on their head. The first team to have all its bean bags on the head of the last person in line is the winner.

Pour the Water

Form two lines of players sitting cross-legged. A bucket of water is placed at the front of each line and an empty bucket is placed at the end of each line. Each player is given an empty cup. The first player of each line dips their cup into the water and places it on their heads. The object is to pass the water down the line and empty it in the provided bucket. However, apart from the first player filling their cup, all players must hold their cups on their heads and tip their heads forward and back to pass the water. The game is over when the water is gone from the first buckets. The team with the most water in their end bucket wins.

Balloon Kick

Divide players into equal teams and give them one balloon per team (or if played outside, one ball per team). On the command "Go," the first player of each team kicks his balloon to a goal line and then picks it up and runs back to his team and gives it to the next person in line, who does the same thing. The first team to finish is the winner.

A variation of the balloon kick is for two players on each team to kick the balloon, not letting go of each other's hands during their turn.

Crawl-through-the-Hoop Relay

Teams are equally divided. A hoop is placed about twenty feet in front of each line. On the command "Go," the first person in each line runs to the hoop, crawls through it, and then returns, and the next in line does the same thing. The first team to have everyone through wins.

One variation is to have two teammates try to crawl through the hoop at the same time with a leg of each of them tied to the other's. Another variation is to have three players try to crawl through the hoop at the same time.

Handkerchief-Tying Relay

Seat the players in rows. Give the first player a large handkerchief. At the signal they tie it, using one hand, around the left arm of the next player, between the elbow and shoulder. The second player unties it with their right hand and then with one hand ties it on the arm of the third player, and so on. The last player runs with the handkerchief to the first player to end the contest.

Tire Change

A number of old car or bicycle tires (or other material made into circles) are scattered around the lawn in a rough circle. There should be a tire for each pair present minus one. A pair stands in each tire, and another pair, "it," stands in the center.

The pair who is "it" calls, "Change," and all the pairs leave their tires and attempt to get into another tire. In the exchange, the pair who is "it" tries to get into a tire. The pair left without a tire is "it."

Variation: pair boys with girls.

Help Your Neighbor

Divide the group into teams and have the team members pair off. Each pair in each team, in turn, race to a chair at the head of a line where there are a needle, thread, patches, and a large piece of fabric. The first person threads the needle held by the second person. Then the two sew a patch on the piece of fabric, alternating who sews with each stitch. This done, they run back and tag the next pair, who repeat the process with a new patch. The team finishing first wins.

Two Deep

A group of players in single circle formation stand arm's length apart and face the center. Select one player as a runner and another as a chaser. The chaser attempts to tag the runner, who tries to escape by running around the outside of the circle and jumping in front of a player standing in the circle, and that person becomes the runner. If the chaser catches the runner, the two exchange roles and the game continues.

Third Man

All of the players but two take partners and scatter in an irregular way. The players forming each couple stand facing each other, with the distance of a long step between them. To make the game a success, the distance should be considerable between the various couples. Of the two odd players, one is the runner and the other the chaser, the object of the latter being to tag the runner. The runner may take refuge between any two players who are standing as a couple.

The moment he does so, the one toward whom his back is turned becomes the runner, and must in turn try to escape being tagged by the chaser. Should the chaser tag the runner, they exchange places, the runner immediately becoming the chaser and the former being liable to tagging instantly.

Partner Tag

All of the players but two hook arms in couples. Of the two who are free, one is the chaser and the other the runner. The runner may save themselves by locking arms with any couple they choose. Whenever they do so, the third party of that group becomes the runner and must save themselves in like manner. If the runner is tagged at any time, they become the chaser and the chaser becomes the runner. The couples should run and twist and resort to any reasonable maneuver to elude the runner, who is liable at any time to lock arms with one of them and so make the other a runner. For large groups, there should be more than one runner and tagger.

Statues

This game is similar to "Red Light! Green Light!" Arrange players along a starting line. The leader, with their back toward the players, stands some distance in front on a finishing line. When the leader says, "Come," the players advance, but when the leader gives a signal and then suddenly turns and faces the players, all must remain still, like statues. Those caught moving at this point must return to the starting line and advance as before. Continue playing until half the players have crossed the finishing line. The player crossing the finishing line first becomes leader for a new game. The game may be varied by having players advance by different methods, such as hopping on one foot or jumping with both feet.

Tommy Tiddler's Ground

The ground is divided by a line into two equal parts. One of these belongs to the player chosen to be "Tommy Tiddler," who stands on their side of the line and may not cross it. All of the other players are on the other side of the line and venture across into Tommy Tiddler's ground, taunting Tommy with the remark, "I'm on Tommy Tiddler's ground, picking up gold and silver." Tommy may tag anyone on his ground, and anyone tagged changes places with Tommy. The players can venture as near Tommy Tiddler as possible and encourage him to run after them. Tommy Tiddler can trick the others in order to tag them, such as devoting all his time to one player and then turning quickly on another.

Slap Jack

The players stand in a circle, clasping hands. One player runs around the outside of the circle and tags another person as they run. The player tagged immediately leaves their place and runs in the opposite direction. The object of both runners is to get back first to the vacant spot. The winner stays in that spot, and the one left out becomes the tagger.

Snake in a Circle

A large circle is made on the ground or floor. One player, who is "Snake," stands in the center of the circle; the other players stand outside of the circle, surrounding it. These players may be tagged by Snake whenever they have a foot inside the circle. They step in and out of the circle, teasing Snake in every possible way to tag them. Anyone whom Snake touches becomes a prisoner and is another Snake, joining the first one in the circle to help tag the others. The last one left is the winner of the game.

Shoe Relay

Players form in lines of equal numbers. At a signal, the first player on each team runs to a given point and takes off one shoe and leaves it there, hopping back and keeping the shoeless foot off the ground. They tag the next player and then go to the end of the line. As soon as all the players on the team have left one shoe at the given point, all race down, find their own shoe, put it on, and return to starting position. The first team to resume the starting position is the winner.

The Family Takes a Walk

The whole group is divided into teams, or "families," to take part in this relay. Each team is composed of a "father," "mother," and as many "children" as are left for all teams to have an equal number. The first player of each team, the father, starts walking as fast as they can up to and around a designated goal, which may be a box, stool, or chair. They return to the starting line, take the mother's hand, and walk with them around the goal. They return to the starting line and one of the children joins them, linking hands with the mother. The trip to the goal and back continues until the whole family is walking.

As the line increases, the first players have to take only a few steps in each direction and swing their lines around in order to pick up the rest of the family. The object of the game is to see which team is quickest in getting around the goal.

Variations: Walk cross-legged; skip; hop; walk backwards.

Ways of Getting There

In this relay players travel across a prescribed area, using any form of locomotion they wish, but no two players on the same team may use the same method. They may walk, run, somersault, walk backwards, or use any method to get there as long as it is different from the methods used by the other players on the team. The second player does not start until the first reaches the finish line.

Balloon Tap Relay

The group is divided into two teams and paired off into pairs (boy/girl). Each pair holds hands. Each team is given a balloon. Each pair taps the balloon to the goal line with the two free hands and return. If they let go of hands, they must start over.

Variation: Girls tap the balloon, boys kick it.

Slap Tag

Players in two equal lines stand facing each other about fifteen feet apart. Each player holds one hand outstretched, the arm bent at the elbow and the palm up. To start the game, a player from one line goes across to the opposite side and, walking along in front, he slaps the palm of each player in the line. When he comes to the one he wishes to tag, he quickly slaps the player's palm and also the back of their hand from below and dashes for their own line. The player who was tagged tries to catch the first player. If caught before they reach their own side, the first player joins the opponent's team. The chaser then goes across, and after slapping several palms along the line, they slap the back of someone's hand and dash for home. The side with the largest number of players at the end of ten minutes wins.

Circle Tag

Players form a circle, standing about three feet away from each other. At a signal from the leader, all start running in the same direction around the circle, trying to tag the person in front and also trying to avoid being tagged by the person behind. When the leader blows the whistle again, everyone reverses and chases the person who was chasing them. Players drop out quickly as they are tagged. The circle must be maintained in size as the players drop out.

How Do You Measure Up?

A predetermined, premarked course is laid out with chalk or masking tape. Each team member, with a yard stick, measures the "course line" (the chalk markings or tape). The leader writes down each person's measurements of the total distance. Team winners are determined by speed of measuring (one point), total accuracy of measurement (four points), and individual accuracy of measurement (six points).

Obedience

All players stand side by side at the starting line and race to a goal. Each player starts with their right foot. They put their left heel in front of their right foot so that it touches their right toe and then place their right foot in front of their left in the same way and so on. All players must race to the goal in this manner.

Handicap Relay

The players are lined up in relay teams. The person at the beginning of each line is given a plate to put on their head, a knife with a bean on it to hold, a pillow to be placed between their knees, and a coin to be held in the eye, like an eye piece. The object is for the teams to run a prescribed distance in this manner. The first team finished wins.

Suitcase Relay

The players are lined up in relay teams. A suitcase for each team is at the goal line filled with an article of clothing for each player. The players must run to the suitcase, open it, and put on some article of clothing, and run back to their place.

A follow-up to this would be to have each player run back to the suitcase, take off their article of clothing, put it back in the suitcase, and run back to their place.

Catch the Cane

Use a section of a broomstick about thirty inches long. Assign each player a number. A player chosen to be "it" sets the stick on it's end on the ground, as near vertical as possible, holds it with a finger placed on the top, and calls a number, quickly removing their finger. The stick must be caught before hitting the ground by the one whose number the player called. If the one called fails to do this, then they become "it."

Skip Tag

All players but one form a circle. The one left out, "it," skips around on the outside of the circle and tags another player. The one tagged skips after the tagger, trying to catch them. If they are caught, they must be "it" again, but if they reach the vacant place first, they are safe, and the other player becomes "it" and skips around the circle to tag someone else.

Variation: Use this setup to play the popular game "Duck, Duck, Goose." Have the "it" player walk around the circle, touching each player's head and saying, "duck." When the player chooses to tag someone, they tap them on the head and say, "Goose." The tagged player chases after the tagger, who tries to steal the vacant spot.

Back to Back Race

Two couples race each other. The two partners stand back to back at the starting line and link elbows. At the signal, the front player bends forward and lifts the back player from the ground and carries them to the turning line. On reaching it, the supporting player drops the rider, and the rider immediately leans forward, lifting the former supporting player, and races back to the starting line.

Heel Hold Race

Each of the two contestants bends down and grasps their left heel with their left hand and their right heel with their right hand. At the signal, they race across the lawn or room to the turning line and then back to the starting line.

Parlor Tilting

Two contestants stand on stools, each holding an ordinary dust mop. The stools should be just far enough apart so that the players can touch each other easily with their mops. At the signal they try to push each other off the stools.

The following are fouls and give the match to the opponent: (1) grabbing the opponent's mop handle, (2) hitting the opponent above the neck or below the knees, (3) dropping the mop.

Bicycle Tire Relay

The players run in couples, so there should be an equal number of players on each team. Arrange into two teams in file. Give the first couple of each team an old bicycle tire. At the signal, the first couple of each team slips the tire down over their heads to their waists, and when it is thus placed, they run to a predetermined line and back inside the tire. On crossing the starting line, they remove the tire and give it to the second couple, who repeat the action, and so on until all of one team have run.

Variation: Make each couple pairs of boys and girls.

Rubber Band Contest

Establish two lines, one on each side of a play area. Give the first two contestants in each line an inch-wide rubber band, either regular rubber bands or obtain by cutting cross sections from an old inner tube. At the signal they run to the opposite line and back. As they run they go through the rubber band by passing it over the head and working it down. The first player hands the band to the next one at the starting line, and so on. The side finishing first wins.

Plus-and-Minus Snatch the Handkerchief

Arrange and number players in two lines facing each other and designate one team as "plus" and the other team as "minus." A handkerchief is placed on the ground, centered between the lines. The leader calls two numbers—"nine and four," for example. The players in the "plus" team add the two numbers to see who runs, and the players in the "minus" team subtract the numbers to determine the runner. Thus, in the "plus" team, number thirteen would run, and in the "minus" team, number five. The runners go to the handkerchief and watch for a chance to snatch it and return it to their place before being tagged by the other. The player who gets to their own place with the handkerchief without being tagged scores one point for their side, but if they are tagged, one point is scored for the tagger's side.

Siamese Twins Race

Two broomsticks, four feet long, are needed. Two pairs of contestants race each other. The partners stand back to back at the starting line, place the stick between their legs, and grasp in front with both hands. At the signal, they run to the turning line, one running forward and the other running backward. On reaching the turning line they stop and, without turning around, race back to the starting line.

Dizzy-Izzy Relay

Divide the players into equal-numbered teams in lines. Give the front player of each team a baseball bat. Station an official at the front of each team. At the signal, the first player holds the bat vertically, placing the end of the bat on the ground and placing their forehead on the upper end. They then run around the bat five times, pass the bat to the next player, and so on. The game continues until a team finishes.

Match Box Relay

Teams are in lines. Place a small matchbox cover over the nose of the first player of each team. At the signal they run to the turning line, return, and push the matchbox cover over the nose of the next player without the use of hands. The rest of the players do the same in turn. If a box cover falls off a nose, the runner may set it on again with their hands. A box that falls off while being transferred between noses must be returned to the nose of the one transferring.

Keeping It Up

Each team forms a small standing circle, the players placing their arms around each others' waists. A balloon is given to each team. The object is to keep it in the air as long as possible, using only the players' breath. The entire team works together. The circle cannot be broken and touching the balloon is not allowed.

Ostrich Tag

Players all stand in different places in a designated area and the person chosen to be "it" says, "Ready." Then the players run to get away from "it." They can save themselves from being tagged and made "it" by holding their right foot in their left hand and holding their noses with their right hand. If the "it" player has a certain person whom they wish to tag, they try to make that person lose their balance, drop their foot, or take the hand from their nose. The tagger is not allowed to touch anyone in an effort to make them lose position.

Bean Balance Relay

Divide the group into three or four evenly numbered rows and have them stand in a line facing forward. The first person in each row will be given a bean and a knife. Each first person places the bean on the knife and at the starter's signal races through obstacles (chairs and so on). These obstacles are arranged in a zigzag fashion. When the runner reaches the last obstacle (perhaps twenty-five feet ahead), they run straight home backward. When they reach home base, the next person runs the course in the same way, and so on until one of the lines finishes. If a person drops their bean, that person has to go back home and begin zigzagging all over.

Seats for the Ladies

Teams of equal numbers of men and women pair off and line up within their teams. The first couple in each line runs to the turning line, the man carrying a folding chair. When they get to the line, the man unfolds the chair, the woman sits on it, raises her feet, and clicks her heels. She gets off and the man picks up the chair and runs back to the second couple. This couple repeats the action, and so on until one team finishes.

All in Order

At a goal line in front of several teams, place the following objects on the ground, one set per team: a foldable chair, an umbrella, bottle with a screwable cap, and a whistle that goes inside the bottle. The first player on each team runs to the goal line, unfolds the chair, sits down, puts up the umbrella, unscrews the bottle cap, takes out a whistle, blows on it, puts it back in the bottle, screws on the cap, lets down the umbrella, folds up the chair, and runs back to tag the next player. Each player repeats these actions in turn.

Active Games

Sky Ball

This is a simple game. One player throws a ball up in the air as high as they can. The ball must be caught by another player on the other side. If the ball is not caught, the throwing team scores one point. Play continues until each thrower on one team has had one throw. The other team then becomes the throwing team and may score points. No interference is permitted. Play may continue for as many rounds as desired. It may be well to select some mark, like the second-story window, and require that the ball be thrown at least above this height.

Throwing-Drive

Each team stands on its own half of a field (two hundred feet by one hundred feet). One team has the ball at about the center of its half of the field. One player throws the ball as far as they can into the other team's field. The opponents try to get to the ball as soon as possible, or if possible, catch it. Then they must throw the ball back from the point at which it was touched. If a player catches the ball on the fly, they may take three running steps toward the thrower's, or opponent's, side. They then throw the ball onto the thrower's side as far as they can. The object of the game is to throw the ball over the end line of the field without it being caught by an opponent. The team that does so earns a point. Play may continue as long as desired.

Elbow Tug of War

Draw two parallel lines ten feet apart. Divide the group into two teams of even numbers. Arrange one team parallel to, and midway between the lines facing one of them, with players standing at intervals of about two feet. Place the second team in intervals in the ranks of the first team and facing the opposite direction. We now have the two teams standing in a single line with players alternating, the two teams facing in opposite directions. Instruct all of the players to link elbows. At a signal, each team tries to pull their opponents across the line. The team successful in pulling all of the opposing team across the base line wins.

Spud

Children play this game with a soft rubber ball. Everyone has a different number and one person throws the ball up in the air to start the game. As the player throws the ball up, they call out a number.

The person whose number they call chases the ball and, when the player catches it, yells, "Stop!" They then throw the ball at the closest player near them. If they hit the other player, that player has an "S." The game is continued until one player has "spud" and is out of the game.

Round Up

Three children are designated cowboys; the rest are steers. The cowboys must capture the steers by encircling them and holding hands. The steers are brought back to the corral (a designated area).

Gathering of Israel

One child is chosen as "it" while the others hide. "It" then hunts out the others; as the "it" player finds them, they march in single file behind the leader and help find the others.

Croquet Golf

Lay a course out on a section of lawn, with tin cans six inches in diameter as cups. Sink the cans to ground level. A hole may vary from thirty to a hundred feet, and hazards should be added or the course laid out to include natural hazards such as trees, shrubs, and so on. Use croquet mallets and balls, and the general rules of golf apply. Set the par for each hole at approximately par two for thirty-five feet and under, par three for thirty-six to seventy feet, and par four for seventy-one to a hundred feet.

Clock Golf

Draw a circle twenty to twenty-four feet in diameter on a level, closely mowed area of yard. Place markers around the circle representing the twelve hours of the clock. Sink a can for a putting hole somewhere within the circle but not in the center. Using a putter, each player putts from the one o'clock marker to the hole, from the two o'clock to the hole, and so on around the clock face. The object is to "hole out" from each marker in the fewest number of total putts.

Grab Ball

Divide the group into two or three teams. Assign a number to each team member. Line all teams up at a common starting line. About twenty feet away place balls one less than the number of teams. Call a number and the team member from each team with that number races out and returns with a ball. The player failing to get a ball scores a point. The team with the lowest score wins when the play ceases.

Hand Baseball

Lay out a small baseball diamond with base lines not exceeding thirty-five feet and a pitching distance of about fifteen feet. Use a large rubber ball (as used in kickball or dodgeball) or volleyball. Divide players into two teams. The pitcher tosses the ball under-handed and the batter bats it with their fist or open hand. Basic baseball rules apply except that the runner may be put out by being hit with the thrown ball. (No hunting or base stealing allowed.)

Keep Away

Divide into two teams. One team starts with a basketball or football, passing the ball among its members to prevent the other team from getting it. The ball cannot be held longer than five seconds by any one player at a time. There is no scoring or goals, but play area limitations and types of passes may be designated.

Paddle Tennis

Play on a smooth, firm lawn with paddles, net, and rubber sponge ball or tennis ball. Two or four people can play. Basically the rules of tennis apply, although only one serve is allowed on each point. Players alternate serves at the end of each game (four points). The server hits the ball from behind his baseline diagonally across the net to the opposite court. After the serve, the entire court is used. Returns must be made on one bounce. The object is to win a set of six games.

Basketball Shoot

Draw a line twenty feet from the basketball backboard. The first throw must start behind this line. The first player throws for the basket and follows up with a short shot. If they score with a basket, the long shot counts two points and the short shot one point. Players take turns and the player scoring twenty-one points first wins.

Bucket Ball

This basketball game is suited to yard play because court size, type of ball, and style of basket may vary with available equipment. Two metal buckets or bushel baskets are placed on the ground for the goals. Players must dribble the ball, and the general rules of basketball apply. Two points are scored each time the ball is put into the basket. If ball does not remain in the basket, or if the bucket falls over, no points are scored.

Japanese Tag

One player is the chaser or "it" and tries to tag any of the other players. The one tagged then becomes chaser. Whenever a player is tagged, they must place one hand on the spot tagged and, in that position, must chase the other players. They are relieved of this position only when they succeed in tagging someone else.

Dodgeball

Divide into two groups. One group forms a large circle, the others scatter inside it. The circle players throw a volleyball or soft sport ball (as used in kickball) at the inside players. The center players dodge but cannot leave the circle. When hit by the ball they join the players in the circle. The winner is the last man in the center.

Can Cricket

Place two cans on the lawn less than sixty feet apart. The pitcher and runner stand by one can, the batter by the other. Other players scatter as fielders. The pitcher bowls a softball to knock the can over and the batter attempts to hit the ball. If the can is knocked over, the batter is out. If the ball is hit, the batter runs to the other can and the runner runs to the batter's can, when they become batter. They continue until one is put out. A runner is out when someone catches a fly ball or when someone knocks the can over with the ball before the runner or batter reaches it. When a batter is out, all fielders move up and the catcher becomes batter. Adapt scoring from normal cricket.

Bowling

Play this game on a smooth, closely cut lawn. Use wooden balls made especially for this game, but substitute croquet balls as needed. Each player has two of these balls called "bowls." A smaller ball is called the "jack." The first player rolls the jack out on the lawn and then rolls the bowls at it in turn. The jack as well as the other bowls may be hit in play. A bowl touching the jack scores three points. The nearest bowl to the jack scores one point. If two bowls by the same player are nearest the jack, two points are scored.

Tin Can Bowling

Punch holes in the bottom of six one-quart cans and sink them into the ground level with the surface. Sink one in the center with the remaining five in an eighteen-inch-radius circle. Bowl from a line twenty feet away using croquet balls. Players take turns bowling two balls each turn. The center can counts five points. The other cans count one point each. Twenty-one points makes a game.

Skittles

Five pins or sticks are needed, 5½ inches long and 1½ to 2 inches thick, and three throwing sticks, 14 inches long and 2 inches thick. Draw a thirty-inch square on the ground and place a pin on end at each corner and one in the center. At a spot sixty feet from the point of the nearest corner of the square mark a throwing line. The pin nearest the throwing line scores one point, the one to the right two points, the one to the left three points, the farthest one four points, and the center pin ten points. The players take turns, each throwing all three sticks each turn. The game is won by the player reaching a hundred points first.

Soccer Bowling

Set up ten Indian clubs, bowling pins, or blocks of wood in

bowling pin order. Kick a soccer ball or rubber ball at them from a line twenty-five to thirty-five feet away. Keep score as in bowling.

Tetherball

The equipment needed for this game are a tetherball, a rope, and a ten-foot pole. Attach one end of the rope to the top of the pole with a permanent, stationary hook. Attach the ball to the other end of the rope to hang three feet from the ground. (It is recommended that the pole be permanently installed. It has been found that, once the tetherball equipment is put to use, it receives constant, hard usage. One method is to cement the pole inside a car tire.)

The game is usually played with one individual against another. It may be played with two members on each side, either alternating turns at the ball (as in table tennis) or hitting by opportunity (as in tennis).

The ball is put into play by the first player's hitting the ball around the pole. His opponent must allow the ball to make an entire revolution before hitting it back in the other direction. The game continues with exchanges of the ball until one player winds the ball completely around the pole, or a foul is committed.

Inner Tube Games

1. Lay several inflated inner tubes in a row and take turns jumping from rim to rim without touching the ground. Then jump from center to center without touching the tubes. Rearrange the inner tubes zigzag fashion and try these jumps again. They take balance and skill and appeal to all ages, but younger children especially like them.

2. Straddle an inner tube that is standing upright, feet resting on the bottom inside, and jump like a kangaroo. Take turns or all do it together if you have enough inner tubes, seeing who can stay on the longest. Then see who can arrive first at a marker placed several yards away. Acquire a few smaller inner tubes so small children can participate.

3. The person first in line is the leader. This person rolls an inner tube toward the line, and each person must jump over the tube

without touching it. Those whose long legs make jumping over the tube too easy, must jump sideways. Whoever touches the tube must go to the end of the line, while the others move forward. The first person to jump free three times replaces the leader.

4. Put Mom and Dad inside an inner tube, back to back, holding the tube around their waists, and set up two children the same way. A race across the lawn will usually find the youngsters way ahead, and after they have won, they will enjoy watching their parents struggling along.

5. Tie several inner tubes together into a funnel. Games can entail crawling through for speed, taking turns lying in the middle and being rolled around the lawn, diving through one tube and landing on top of the rest, walking along the top of the tubes without falling, and a variety of tumbling stunts that youngsters find more fun on inner tubes than on mats. An old quilt or small mattress stuffed into the funnel will give it more body for these last activities.

6. If you are in an area with large trees, make a "mass production swing" by stringing a cotton-based rope, which is easier on the hands than regular manila rope, between two trees about forty feet apart. The center of the rope should be about five feet lower than the ends. String enough inner tubes on the rope for the entire family. You will find that children love to play above the ground, hanging with their hands, and throwing their feet up over the rope while Dad gives them a push. This is good exercise. By attaching a short rope to the swing, Dad or Mom can pull the whole family at once. Even without the inner tubes, these ropes are fun to play on and swing from.

7. Less active games might include rolling inner tubes for accuracy, or taping down their valves and then pitching a ringer over the head of someone while they run around the lawn.

Pillow Fight

Lay an inner tube on the ground. Let a member of the family stand on either side of the tube and try to knock each other off balance by hitting them with pillows. With the younger children, make a rule: no hitting above the shoulders. Extra pillows can be made easily by filling pillowcases with blankets.

Bar Kick Baseball

Don't have the equipment for baseball or kickball? Here's a baseball game without a ball or bat! The diamond should be nearly standard size as space permits. Place a block of wood on each side of the home plate. Lay across the blocks a "bar" of folded newspaper or a section of hose. Form two teams, one to be the fielders and the other the batters or kickers. The first person at bat kicks the bar across the line and runs for base. The fielders try to recover the bar and replace it on the two blocks while the batter is off base. A batter is out if a fielder succeeds in replacing the bar while the batter is between bases, or if they kick a foul that lands outside the field of play. Other players progressing from base to base also are out if the bar is replaced while they are off base, but they may return to their last base if the batter kicks a foul. Three outs retire a side.

Capture the Flag

This is a war game in which the group is divided into two armies, each army with one or more flags to defend. Mark a line dividing the territory and establish boundaries that the game must be played within. After a signal is given for the start of the game, any person caught in hostile territory becomes a prisoner, but they may be released if, with one hand on their capturer's flagstaff or prison tree, they are touched by one of their teammates who is uncaught. Released prisoners and their rescuers are free to return to their own side without being caught again, but may not run off with the flag. The game is played either for an agreed time, or until one side has captured the other's flag. Sometimes a score is kept through a series of games, allowing one point for each prisoner held at the end of each game, and five or ten points for each flag captured.

Throw Around

A baseball field with thirty-five-foot baselines should be laid out. One team lines up at home plate. The other team takes the place of the team in the field with one player at each base. One man starts at home plate and runs around the bases. At the instant the runner starts, the catcher, who has the ball, throws it to first base, the first baseman throws it to second base, and so on around the diamond. The object of the game is for the base runner to complete one circle of the bases while the team in the field is throwing the ball around the bases twice. If the base runner comes out ahead, one point is scored for their team. If the team in the field gets the ball around twice before the base runner completes one circle of the bases, they score a point. When each player on the team at bat has had a chance to run, the team takes the field and the other team goes to bat. After both teams have had a chance to run, the team with the highest number of points is declared the winner.

Swimming Games

Piggyback Wrestling Contest

The water should be up to the armpits for this contest. Two players stand in the water, each having a lighter player astride their neck. The top partners endeavor to unhorse each other, while the bottom partners try to maintain a firm balance by active footwork and judgment. The top partner will lock their feet behind their partner's back. The bottom partner will also wrap their arms around the top partner's shins.

Note: This game may be prohibited from public pools.

Water Basketball

Have goals the length of the pool apart, or shorter according to the playing area. All play should be in deep water. Play the game by adapting regular basketball rules. This also is a good game for non-swimmers playing across the shallow end of the pool.

Goldfish-Catching Contest

If a small wading pool is available, liberate a number of goldfish and offer a glass bowl as a prize to the one who catches the most fish with their hands.

Walking Underwater

This game may be prohibited from public pools. This is a fine stunt when carried out correctly. Four performers are needed. Two people, each with another person astride their shoulders, walk out from the shallow end of the pool toward the deep end, the object being to see who can stay down the longest.

Tunnel Swim

There are two teams of four to ten players each. The members of each team stand in single file in the shallow end of the pool. The players, with the exception of the last person in each line, stand with feet spread wide apart. At the word "go," the last player in each line swims underwater, between the knees of the other players, to the head of the line. When they reach the head of the line, they stand and spread their feet apart. The player who is now last in line watches carefully, and when the first swimmer's head appears above the water at the front of the line, they begin their underwater swim. Each player has their turn. The team finished first wins.

Cross Dive Relay

Equal teams line up at each side of the pool. At "go" one player from each team dives across the pool, gets out on the opposite side, and then dives back. As soon as they touch the next person, that player dives in, and so on. The team finished first wins.

Scramble Ball

Twelve floating balls or corks are required. Players are divided into two teams, Team A on one side of the pool, Team B on the other. The players are in the water, hanging from the side of the pool. The director stands on a spring board and tosses the balls into the water. At the command "go," players try to get as many balls for their team as possible. Balls are then collected and teams are credited with the number of balls obtained. The game continues until one of the teams has secured fifty balls or any other number previously decided upon.

Object Recovery Race

Competitors line up and on a signal throw their sinkable objects ahead into the water. They dive immediately for the objects, come up, and throw ahead again. They repeat until three surface dives and recoveries have been made successfully and then swim with their objects to the end of the pool. They place their objects on the edge of the pool and race back to the starting point. The first one there wins.

Dog Race

At a signal, all dive in at the deep end and swim dog-paddle style the length of the pool toward the shallow water. They then stand in the shallow water, bark three times, touch the end of the pool, and dog-paddle back to the starting point. The first swimmer to finish wins.

Polo Ball Swimming

Players swim freestyle (crawl), pushing a water polo ball ahead of them. They must keep the ball in front of their heads and between their arms.

Walk across Pool

At the deepest end of the pool, swimmers submerge, then with a breast stroke or an alternate upper-cut movement of the arms, they walk to the other side. Their feet must be on the bottom at each step as they endeavor to walk across.

Balloon Race

Swimmers must swim across the pool and back pushing a balloon. However, they may push only with their faces.

Run across Tank

All line up on one side of the pool (tank) and run across to the other side at the signal "Go." They may not swim. The one reaching the opposite side first wins.

Water Ball

The entire pool is used as a playing area. The teams line up at opposite ends of the pool and change sides after each score. The ball is tossed into the center of the pool and may be advanced by any means while players and the ball remain in the pool. A score is made by placing the ball in the trough or in a container at the opposing end of the pool. A game consists of two halves of ten minutes with a two-minute intermission.

Treasure Dive

Two teams line up on opposite sides of the pool. Throw a coin into the center of the pool. One player from each team dives at the same time and the one who brings up the coin scores for their team. Continue until all players have tried. The team with the most points wins.

Cork Retrieve

Assign a small area of the poolside to each player. Scatter a dozen or more small corks or blocks of wood or other floating items on the water close to the far side of the pool. At a signal each player dives into the pool and brings back corks, one at a time, and places them in their assigned area. The player who retrieves the most corks wins.

Water Log

Players line up at either end of the pool or establish goals about sixty feet apart in open water. One player acts as the log and floats on their back midway between the goals. The other players swim around the log. Suddenly the log rolls over and gives chase. The players attempt to reach their goals before being tagged. Those tagged become logs and float in the center with the first log. The last one caught is the first log in the next game.

Kitty in the Water

Players in the water hang on to the side of the pool. Each player chooses some mark or spot for his base. A player chosen to be "it" is stationed near the center of the pool and tries to tag players as they exchange places with one another. If the "it" player succeeds, the player tagged becomes "it."

Take Away

The swimmers choose sides and may play in the shallow or deep end of the pool. The object is for one side to take the ball away from the other and retain it.

Ball Tag

This game is played in a limited area, in water waist deep for nonswimmers, or in deep water for swimmers. A player chosen to be "it" tries to tag someone by hitting them with the ball; the one tagged then becomes "it."

Japanese Water Tag

The leader announces a certain part of the body that must be tagged by the player chosen to be "it," for example, head, right shoulder, left hand, and so on. Those who are tagged must join the "it" player and try to tag the remaining players.

Stunt Ball

The leader calls a certain part of the body that must be out of the water to secure immunity. The person who is "it" may tag any player not thus immunized. Body parts such as "one foot," "head submerged and hand out," "both feet out," and so on may be called.

Tread Tag

One player is selected to be the tagger. The other players swim about the pool. To escape being tagged, a player must tread water. The tagger tries to touch a player before they can stop swimming and begin to tread. When a player is tagged, they changes places with the tagger.

Handicap Tag

One player is "it" and tries to tag the other players as they swim about the pool. He must tag them on the arm or leg. When a player is tagged they continue to swim but do not use the arm or leg that was tagged. When a player has been tagged several times and can no longer swim at all, they are out of the game. The player keeping in motion longest wins.

Black and White

Beginning swimmers can play this in waist-deep water, while the more skilled swimmers can play in deeper water. Two teams equal in number line up facing each other, with the lines about fifteen feet apart. One team is designated as the white team, the other as the black team. Each team should be assigned a home base equally distant from the starting lines. The leader throws a block of wood (one side of which has been painted white and one side painted black) into the area between the teams. If the white side turns up, the white team chases the black team to its home position. Players tagged before reaching home are eliminated and a new round begins. The team with the most players remaining at the end wins the game.

Touch

Two teams equal in number line up in an assigned home position. The leader names an object equally distant from the two teams. Every player of each team must touch the object and return home. The team that has all its players home first wins the point. The game may be played for time or points. Vary the objects, but be sure that the teams are at an equal advantage for each object selected.

Space Formation

This game may be played with one small group or as a contest with several small groups competing as teams. The following instructions are for a team contest. Each group has a home base. The leader calls out a formation. For beginners in shallow water, circles, columns, lines, squares, and the like are suitable. For advanced swimmers in deep water, these plus letters or numbers may be used, with the swimmers treading water. As soon as the formation is announced, the teams move into the designated formation. The team that assumes the correct formation first wins a point. After the point has been awarded, the teams return to home base. This game may be played for a certain number of points or for a certain amount of time.

Tag

One player is "it" and the others try to keep out of reach by swimming and diving into the water.

Over and Under

In chest-deep water, teams form columns all facing in the same direction. On the starting signal the last person in each team leap-frogs over the person directly in front of them and then goes between the legs of the next person in line. They continue this way till they reach the front of the line. The person who is last in line then starts. The team that lines up in its starting position first wins.

Underwater Tag

One player is "it" and starts chasing the rest. A player must be underwater when they are tagged. The player tagging also must be underwater before the player they tag is "it."

Cross Tag

The player who is "it" names one of the players and starts chasing them. The player being chased must keep out of the "it" player's way, for if they are tagged they become "it." If another player comes between the person chased and the chaser, then that player becomes the one to be chased.

Water Ostrich Tag

The players are all grouped together at one end of the pool, preferably the shallow end. One player is designated to be "it." This person starts chasing the others until someone is caught. To avoid being caught, a player must have one of their arms under one of their legs and with that hand hold their nose between their thumb and fingers. The player tagged becomes "it" and the game proceeds.

Follow the Leader

One player acts as a leader and the rest follow. The leader demonstrates all kinds of strokes, and so on. The players following must do everything the leader sets for them to do. The crowd that can stay to the finish in a match of this sort can be rated in the class of "human fish."

Water Baseball

The diamond may be all deep water, all shallow water, or only outfielders in deep water. Use an indoor baseball and bat.

Fox and Ducks

Choose a player to be the fox and another to be the mother duck. The other players are little ducks; these form in a line behind the mother duck, each one holding the waist of the one in front of them. The fox attempts to catch the last duck. The line led by the mother duck turns in various ways to protect the last little duck from being caught by the fox. When the last duck is tagged, that player becomes the fox and the fox becomes the mother duck. Similar to Coyote and the Sheep (p. 22).

Water Poison

Form a ring by joining hands, or grasp a rope tied together to form a ring. Poison is some floating object anchored in the center of the group. The object of the game is to pull others so that they touch poison, but keep from touching it yourself. Anyone who touches poison is eliminated from the ring until one person is left.

Swimming Spill Down

The leader calls out a stunt. Swimmers who perform the stunt remain in the game; the others are eliminated, like a spelling match, until a champion is left. Start with easy stunts to prevent players from being eliminated too fast, and gradually make stunts more difficult.

Water Simon Says

The players stand in waist- or chest-deep water facing the leader. The leader calls out skills to perform, prefacing some commands with "Simon says" and calling out others without "Simon says." The players perform only those skills that "Simon says" they must do. Players moving at the wrong time may be out of the game or may acquire points against them. In the latter case, the highest number of points loses, and the lowest number of points wins. Suggested skills for "Simon says" include blowing bubbles, jellyfish float, treading water, ducking the head and touching the bottom, and so on.

Number Retrieve

Beginners can play Number Retrieve in waist-deep water, while more skilled swimmers can play in deeper water. The players form a circle and number off so that each player has a number. The leader calls a number and simultaneously throws a slow-sinking object into the center of the circle. The player whose number is called must retrieve the object before it reaches the bottom. This game can be played for points or for a specified time.

Number Change

Assign each member of the group a number and have the group form a circle in chest-deep water. One player, who is "it," stands in the center of the circle and calls out two numbers. Players assigned to these numbers exchange places. The "it" player attempts to take one of the vacated places before the swimmer whose number has been called gets there. The player left out of the circle becomes "it."

Pom, Pom, Pull Away

The abilities of the players should determine the depth of water and the size of playing area used. All players except one designated as "it" line up on one side of the pool or swimming area. The "it" player is in the center of the swimming area. They call, "Pom, pom, pull away," whereupon all the players must cross to the other side while the "it" player attempts to tag them. A player who is tagged becomes "it" as well and tags the remaining players on succeeding attempts to cross the swimming area. The player who is the last to be tagged wins.

SPECIAL
OCCASIONS

A. Family Reunion Games

B. Father-Son Outing Games

C. Youth Conference and Convention Activities

D. Seminary and Church Activities

E. Holiday Games

F. Teaching the Play Way

Introduction

This final section consists of a great variety of games ideas and suggestions for use on various occasions. The games in the "Family Reunions" division are geared toward use with adults, teens, and children. Under "Party Games," you will be able to find more games that are applicable for teens, adults, and children, especially if you plan your reunion so that the three groups are divided according to ages. The games in "Father-Son Outings Games" consist mostly of rougher games geared toward fathers and sons, though girls and women may enjoy them as well. "Youth Conferences and Convention Activities" contains most of the dances in the book and also those games and activities that are designed especially for getting people acquainted with one another. The games and activities in

"Seminary and Church Activities" can be used in the seminary classroom, Young Men and Young Women, and Sunday School. Some of the games obviously are for younger ages while older students will enjoy others. There are games that can also be used at dances, seminary, and Church functions. You can also find more gospel-oriented games under the "Games for Family Home Evening" division in the "Family Recreation" section. The "Holiday Games" division lists games and activities that add special fun to Christmas, Thanksgiving, and other holidays, for your family as well as for neighborhood parties. Our final division, "Teaching the Play Way," is a special section devised mainly to give ideas to grade-school teachers who wish to teach principles to students with a new flair. We firmly believe that these games of teaching will make learning more enjoyable for students. These games can also be played in the home.

Family Reunion Games

Places for Reunions

Places for reunions can be as varied as there are nationalities. Always check ahead, make reservations, and find a clean place close to where family lives. The heat of summer makes mountains exceptionally appealing. Canyon picnic areas, beaches, and campgrounds in forests also are good places for families to get together.

A good place that is seldom thought of it a church cultural hall. This is the members' second home and can be used to an advantage for this type of occasion. Find a church that has plenty of lawn and trees for outdoor games and eating places. If including a focus on family history, make sure there is a place inside with blackboards and tables for it and other programs. Many homes also have backyards large enough for family reunions and places to roll out sleeping bags.

Why a Theme?

A theme is an essential part of the family reunion because it gives the reunion a purpose or a central idea. It makes for more successful reunions because all things are related. One could say that a theme at a reunion is like a topic sentence in writing. It is the skeleton that the decorations, invitations, dress, music, games, and activities are based around. It is the glue that binds the reunion together, and can make the difference between a successful and an unsuccessful family get-together. Without a theme, a reunion may have no related sequence. It is a known fact that people learn more effectively through participation, and with a theme you learn the same thing over and over again in different ways. Thus, you not only have fun but also participate in a learning experience.

There are as many themes as there are ideas. Themes such as seasons, cultures, periods of time, other countries, generations, and family history are always good ones, and the list can go on and on. Picking a theme is probably the hardest part of all. From there on everything is much easier. A theme acts as a guide for your planning and will make your reunion and activities much more enjoyable and successful.

Things to Do at Reunions

1. Have each family report on the past year's activity. Each family entertains during the program.
2. Involve the whole family in family history work, telling stories about grandparents to primary-aged kids while teens and adults work on the family history.
3. Have free time allotted just to visit and reminisce.
4. Plan for next reunion.
5. Have a program with a good Master of Ceremonies.
6. Have stories told about relatives. Have stories told about ancestors.
7. Get addresses of all relatives, both those at the reunion as well as those not present.
8. Have a theme for next year's reunion announced.
9. Have a big bonfire at night with a family sing-along.
10. Have different games for different age groups.
11. Have some children's games that entertain adults.
12. Have someone give a toast to the grandparents.
13. Give prizes for the largest family, oldest person, youngest married, and so on.
14. Show family movies that would be interesting to the whole group.
15. Have the reunion at Thanksgiving or Christmas so that it could be planned and groups could meet twice a year.
16. Make a remembrance book display.
17. Have grandparents share their stories and romances with the younger group.
18. Place a big family tree made out of paper prominently for all to study.

19. Take pictures of group activities with all included.
20. Organize a family band for dancing at night.
21. Have a talent program.
22. Have a three-day reunion well planned in advance.
23. Have initiations of newlyweds into the family.
24. Have a baby's parade.
25. Show movies of past reunions.

Nobility

Divide the group into two teams and have several judges and scorekeepers for each team. Give each team fifty points to start. Every time a player makes a mistake they lose a point for their team. The leader calls out the characters. Players must impersonate each character immediately and correctly and must not change their pose until the judges have counted the score. Characters and poses are as follows:

Cruel King—Left hand on hip, right holds imaginary knife with blade up as a scepter; head high.

Cringing Queen—Left hand over heart, right holds fork to plate as if eating, head low.

Pretty Princess—Left hand in lap, drinks from imaginary glass or cup with right hand, little finger crooked gracefully; head tilted.

Proud Prince—Arms folded on chest, head thrown back.

Captain of the Guards—Left hand at hip on imaginary scabbard; right hand as if drawing sword, head high, very arrogant.

The team having the most points left at the end wins. If the leader drawls the c in "cruel," "cringing," and "captain," and the pr in "pretty" and "proud," they will add to the confusion and fun.

Scavenger Hunt

As the members arrive at the meeting place, give each person a copy of these individuals to find. They must obtain the signature of some person who answers the given requirements under each item listed. It is entertaining to have the individuals stand when the answers are read. The winners will be determined by speed and accuracy.

A high school teacher . . . .
An auxiliary board member . . . .

A Young Women teacher . . . .

A Sunday School teacher . . . .

An executive . . . .

A member of a bishopric . . . .

An aunt . . . .

A second cousin . . . .

A grandparent . . . .

A great-grandparent . . . .

A third cousin . . . .

A veteran . . . .

A couple married in the temple . . . .

A convert to the Church . . . .

A returned missionary . . . .

An uncle . . . .

A secretary . . . .

A Democrat . . . .

A Republican . . . .

The oldest person . . . .

The person who has traveled the farthest . . . .

The person with the largest family . . . .

The newest bride . . . .

The person married the longest . . . .

The couple married the longest . . . .

The oldest person with the youngest child . . . .

Little-Known Facts about Well-Known People

Write up facts about the family and use as a pre-opener or send to each family before the reunion. Give a prize to the person having the most correct answers. Here are a few example facts.

1. . . . . Lived in Tahiti when he was 8 years old.
2. . . . . Boxed in a match refereed by Jack Dempsey.
3. . . . . Was student body president at BYU.
4. . . . . Lined his future wife up on a blind date with someone else.
5. . . . . Was born in Oklahoma and drilled for oil in Texas.
6. . . . . Two brothers married sisters.
7. . . . . His wife is due to have a baby the day of our reunion.
8. . . . . Was in charge of a German prisoner-of-war camp during World War II.

9. . . . . Late for his wedding.
10. . . . . Met his wife when he knocked her over with a door. (She really fell for him!)

Adjective Story

As each person arrives, ask them for an adjective and write the adjective in sequence in the blank spaces. Read this story during the entertainment. The following story is an example of one family:

THIS IS A .... STORY ABOUT A .... FAMILY OF .... COXES

Once upon a time there was a .... family of .... Coxes. There were .... males and .... females, ... uncles and aunts, ... cousins, and .... grandparents. One spring they all went to a .... reunion, something about .... meeting .... relatives, they said. Great-great grandpa was a .... Cox. He was converted to this .... Church in England. He was such a .... guy. Some of the .... family thought he was ...., while others thought he was .... Now this .... family started on a .... morning. A few of the .... grandparents pulled their .... trailers. Others took their .... campers, but most of them rode in the comfort of their .... cars. They held the .... reunion in the .... park where their .... president greeted them. .... pre-openers were planned to get them acquainted and to keep this .... group of relatives from forming .... cliques. There were also .... stunts, ... entertainment, ... songs, and too many other .... things to remember.

This special group of .... descendants were different from other .... family groups. They were so smart; they had a special talent—whole one of the .... uncles was explaining .... game for the children, the .... president of this .... family organization had gone through the family history ten times. All at once some .... great uncle shouted, "Let's have a .... family history meeting," he said. He was such a .... fellow. I hated to claim him for my .... relative.

Well, that finished all the .... fun. The .... old folks were so pleased with themselves that they forgot all about their .... children, which goes to prove there is no moral in this .... story.

Setting-Up Exercises and Getting-Up Exercises

Everyone stands and follows the leader as he repeats the following verses and performs the indicated actions:

> (1) Hands on your hips,
> Hands on your knees,
> Put them behind you,
> If you please.

> (2) Touch your shoulders,
> Touch your nose,
> Touch your ears,
> And touch your toes.

> (3) Raise your hands high in the air,
> At your side, on your hair.
> Raise your hands as before,
> While you clap 1-2-3-4.

> (4) My hands upon my head I place,
> On my shoulders, on my face,
> Then I raise them up on high,
> Make my fingers quickly fly.
> Then place them out in front of me,
> And gently clamp them 1-2-3.
> (Be seated)

Descriptive Initials

Seat everyone in a circle. Ask each person to introduce to the group the person on their right and describe that person with words starting with their initials. For example, "On my right is Amelia

Printly, who is awfully pretty." "On my right is Vern Rainy, who is very rambunctious."

The Noise Machine

The leader assigns a certain phrase to each of three groups and asks everybody to control the volume by means of the leader's aim that acts as a noise-machine switch. As the leader raises their arm the noise gets louder, and as the leader lowers it the noise dies down to a whisper. The leader starts with their arm down. One group says, "Rhubarb, rhubarb." A second group says, "Says you, says you." The third group says, "Hi babe, hi babe." With a rather fast up-and-down motion of the arm switch, some unusual effects will be produced.

Cousins-Cousins-Cousins

The audience is given a moment for each person to learn the names of their neighbors on either side. A person chosen to be "it" points to or calls the name of a person and says, "Right—cousin-cousin-cousin," and the player pointed to must instantly respond with the name of the person on their right. If they fail to respond before the "it" player says "cousin-cousin-cousin," they change places with the "it" player who pointed to them. "Left—cousin-cousin-cousin," may also be used.

Completing the Analogy

The players are seated in a compact group, and the leader reads an analogy such as "Father is to son as mother is to . . . ." The first player calling "daughter" gets a candy. The leader then reads other analogies rapidly. The following list provides suggestions of types, and leaders can quickly compile a long list of others:

Father is to son as mother is to . . . . (daughter).
Foot is to shoe as hand is to . . . . (glove).
Dog is to pup as bear is to . . . . (cub).
Cow is to calf as deer is to . . . . (fawn).
Sheep is to lamb as frog is to . . . (tadpole [pollywog]).
Hen is to chick as fish is to . . . . (fry).
Hat is to head as coat is to . . . . (back).
Coat is to vest as shoe is to . . . . (sock).
Pencil is to paper as chalk is to . . . . . (blackboard).

Balloon is to gas as football is to . . . . (air).
Scissors are to cloth as razor is to . . . . (whiskers).
Sailboat is to sail as canoe is to . . . . (paddle).
Bow is to arrow as shotgun is to . . . . (shell).
Baseball is to bat as tennis ball is to . . . . (racket).
Pen is to ink as brush is to . . . . (paint).
Horse is to halter as dog is to . . . . (leash).

Introducing the Family

This mixer is very efficient in familiarizing everyone with the names in each family. For example, the Master of Ceremonies calls for the Alma Heaton family. The father arises and says, "It's a pleasure to meet you all. My name is Alma." The next family member stands and says, "Hi Dad, my name is Randel." The third stands and says, "Hi Dad and Randel. My name is Hal." The fourth says, "Hi Dad, Randel, and Hal. My name is Rochelle." Each person must mention the names in turn of all who have already introduced themselves, until all the family are introduced.

Variation: The leader calls the Allen Cox family. The family arises and the father calls each of their names. Each bows as their name is called. Allen Cox then calls another family to stand.

Left-Handed Cousins

The relatives are notified upon entering that all handshaking must be done with the left hand. Give each person a large autograph card and pen, and announce a prize for the greatest number of autographs secured in twenty minutes. All autographs, however, must be written with the left hand.

Relative Mixer

Prepare beforehand a sheet of paper for each guest, marked out into twenty-five squares, five squares in each row. The squares should be about an inch in size. Give each person a paper as they arrive and ask them to introduce themselves to twenty-five relatives and write their names in each of the squares. When all have their twenty-five squares filled, assemble the guests, and have each person in turn read one name from their sheet. As a name is read, each guest checks the square in their sheet that that name appears in. The first person to have five checks in a row, either horizontally, vertically, or diagonally, calls out "relatives." As the player reads the names of the five relatives on their card they stand. If they all stand, the player wins the prize.

Solemnity

This is a duel contest. The two players stand back to back. At the signal, the two face each other and try to make each other laugh. They may use any device except to touch one another. The one laughing first is eliminated, and someone else challenges the winner.

Meet the Relatives

The leader announces that they are going to give each person a number and then call on them to stand and recite a little poem about their family. Allow about five minutes for the family to compose their rhymes.

Examples:

> My number is four
> And my name is Stone.
> I've been here before
> And I'd rather stay home.

> My name is Bill Stokes
> And my number is one.
> I do not mind jokes
> If they lead to fun.

> My number is four
> And my name is Jones.
> My favorite sport
> Is rolling the bones.

> I never was a lucky soul,
> Good fortune ne'er was mine
> For what will rhyme with Davidson
> Or even with number nine?

People of all ages will contribute many clever rhymes.

Yes or No

As each family member enters they are given ten candy chews or grains of corn. The relatives are then told to ask questions of each other, collecting a chew from everyone who answers a question with the words "yes" and "no." A prize is awarded to the one having the largest number of chews when time is called.

Laughing Uncles

The leader stands where all can see them (on a stage). They toss a handkerchief in the air and while it is in the air everyone laughs, but when it touches the floor all must have stopped laughing and assumed a long face. Those who laugh when the handkerchief is not in the air are eliminated and stand where they may assist in attempting to make those who are still competing laugh. Likewise those who do not laugh when the handkerchief is in the air have to stand up and help make others laugh. The leader will need an assistant to stand by them and help pick out those who laugh. The height to which the handkerchief is thrown should be varied so that the players are confused as to the length of the laughing spell. Humorous remarks by the leader between throws makes the long face difficult to maintain.

Pat and Rub

Men stand, and the leader instructs all to rub their stomachs with their right hand and pat the top of their heads with the left. When the leader calls "Change" they attempt to pat their stomachs and rub their heads. As soon as they can do this they sit down. Girls are judges. Those left standing demonstrate for the crowd.

After this has been done, the leader may ask the players to start as before and then reverse the position of their hands, rubbing their stomachs with their left hands and patting their heads with their right hands.

Smiling Aunts

All stand up. Girls are named "heads" and the men "tails." The leader tosses a coin and calls out the side that turned up. If it comes up heads, the heads laugh and smile while the tails must keep a straight and sober face. The heads, of course, attempt to make the tails laugh. All who laugh must sit down. The coin is then tossed again. The last one left standing is the winner.

The Frog Pond

Divide the family into three groups. Have the first group says in high treble voices, "Tomatoes, tomatoes, tomatoes." The second group in a slower tempo and deeper voices says, "Potatoes, potatoes, potatoes." The third group says in deep bass voices, "Fried bacon, fried bacon, fried bacon." When you have rehearsed each group, turn them all loose at once, to continue until you give them a prearranged signal to silence.

Long Whistle

The contestants stand side by side, take a long breath, and at the signal begin a long sustained whistle. A judge stands by each person and signals when their player's whistle becomes inaudible. The one whistling the longest wins.

In order to save breath the whistlers usually whistle so faintly the sound is scarcely audible to the spectators. The judge should stand at least three feet distant and when the sound cannot be heard, gives the signal that the player is through. If there is the slightest break in the whistle, the whistle is considered ended.

Whistling Fest

Players stand back to back, and at the signal they turn, face each other, and whistle, both together and any tune they choose. The result is that they usually whistle different tunes. Time is called at the end of thirty seconds. Judges select the winner, or the leader may ask for applause for each in turn and the one receiving the most applause wins.

Dog-Calling Contest

The contestants stand back to back, and at the signal turn and begin calling a "dog." Whistling is also allowed. Both call at the same time, pretending that the other players are the dogs. Time is called at the end of thirty seconds. The judges pick the winner or the crowd picks them by applauding first one, then the other.

Dog Barking Contest

Each contestant is given twenty seconds to bark like a dog. The judges pick the winner, or the crowd picks them by applauding first one, then the other.

Bumblebee Buzz

The Master of Ceremonies calls for each family to send its busiest bees to the stand. Stand the contestants back to back. At the signal they take a long breath, turn to face each other, and begin to buzz like bees. The winner is whoever buzzes the longest with one breath without stopping. If one starts laughing and thus stops buzzing, they lose. Continue until a champion is determined.

The Lion Hunt

(Adapt this title to carry out the reunion theme.)

Story:

Wanna' go on a lion hunt? I do! Let's walk. Wh'da ya' see? Grass. Tall grass! Shall we go through? Let's. Wh'da ya' see? A river. Should we swim it? Yes! Have to dry off. Shall we run? Let's. Wh'da ya' see? A tree. A big tree! Let's climb it. Have to be careful. This limb's narrow. Wh'da ya' see? A cave. Shall we go in? Scared? I'm not! Shh, let's tip-toe. Did you hear something? I did. What's that? It's big! It's furry! It's a lion! Scared? I am! Safe at last!

Directions:

Have the group follow the leader's actions and repeat everything they say. Hands and feet should be used together in all walking movements. Voice and expression should be used in telling this story.

Actions:

Wanna' go on a lion hunt? (Group repeat.) I do! (Point to self while saying this.) (Here leader makes reaching motion with hand for key above door; opens door, and closes it; locks door, and puts key under door mat.) Let's walk. (Starts walking motion for a few seconds, then stops.) Wh'da ya see? (As this is said, make looking motion with hand above eyes.) Grass. Tall grass! Shall we go through? Let's. (Here make the motion of parting grass and walking for a few seconds, then stop.) Wh'da ya' see. (Here make looking motion.) A river. Should we swim it? Let's. (Here make a swimming motion for a few seconds, then stop.) Have to dry off! (Here make a drying motion.) Shall we run? Let's. (Here make a running motion with both hands and feet, then stop.) Wh'da ya' see? A tree. A big tree! Let's climb it! (Put arms in a round formation and begin to make climbing motions.) Have to be careful! This branch is narrow. (Here make the climbing movement very slow; after a few seconds stop.) Wh'da ya' see? (Here make looking motion.) A cave! Shall we go in? Scared? I'm not! (Here make the climbing movement going down the tree.) Shh, let's tiptoe in. (Here use a moderately quiet voice and tiptoe action that replaces the walking action.) Did you hear something? (Here put hand up to ear and make listening action.) I did! What's that? (This is said while pointing to middle of room.) It's big! (Pause.) It's furry! (Pause.) It's a lion! (This is said in almost a whisper.) Scared? I am! (Here use motions to run out of cave, hurriedly climb up and down tree, run a bit, swim the river, run some more, hurriedly part grass while running, run for a little, pick up mat, take up key, drop mat, unlock door, open and close door, put key over door with a sigh.) Safe at last.

This story can be varied any way the leader wishes. It can be made more complex and difficult, or it can be used this way, depending on the age level and group of players.

In Days of Old

As the leader recites the following poem, they give an arm signal that the audience responds to as follows:

hand up in air (fist)	Hurrah
move hand up slowly (palm)	Ah-h-h
move hand down	Boo-o-o
move hand across body	Sh-h-h-h

In days of old when knights were bold (Hurrah)
And barons held their sway, (Ah)

A warrior bold with spurs of gold	
Sang his merry way	(Hurrah)
My love is young and fair!	(Ah)
My love has golden hair.	(Ah)
With eyes so blue and heart so true	(Ah)
That none with her compare.	(Hurrah)
So what care I tho' death be nigh,	(Boo-o)
I'll live for love or die!	(Sh-h-h)
So what care I tho' death be nigh,	(Boo-o)
I'll live for love or die!	(Sh-h-h)
So this brave knight with armor bright	(Ah)
Went gaily to the fray!	(Hurrah)
He fought the fight, but ere the night	
His soul had passed away.	(Sh-h-h)
Yet ere he died he bravely cried,	
"I've kept the vow I swore!"	(Hurrah)
So what care I tho' death be nigh,	(Ah)
I've lived for love and died!	(Sh-h-h)
So what care I tho' death be nigh	(Ah)
I've lived for love,	(Hurrah)
For love!	(Bigger hurrah)
For love!	(Tremendous hurrah)
And died.	(Boo-o-o)

Hat Stunt

This is a hilarious game for family reunions. If your family reunion group is more than twenty people, use this game as a stunt to play on a few good sports and entertain the rest. Beforehand collect enough hats of various sizes and shapes for each player to have one. Women's hats or old fatigue hats from army surplus stores are good. Have players stand in a circle facing inward, put on the hats, and place their right hands on their right-hand neighbors' hats and their left hands on their left-hand neighbors' hats. When the leader calls "left," all players move hats from the person on the left to their own head with their left hand. If "right" is called, they reverse the motion and move the hats from the person's head on the right to their own head, using the right hand. Have the players practice a little, and then tell them that anyone caught at any time without a hat will be eliminated from the circle and will have to entertain by reciting a poem, give a reading, dance, or tell a joke. Call the shift quickly. This game is bound to bring a laugh, especially with a mixed group.

Audience Action Stunt

The Master of Ceremonies begins, "Sometimes I think we don't really appreciate the efforts of the mothers whose work makes this reunion possible. Take that delicious chocolate cake that Mrs. [Blank] (use name of actual person) brought tonight. She had quite a time baking it this morning; in fact I understand it was the second cake she made today. I'd like to tell you the sad story of what happened to the first one. In order for you really to sympathize with her, I think you'd better stand up and go through just what she did. Watch me carefully, so you can follow my actions. When I make a noise or make a motion you repeat it, too. (Everyone stands up.)

So here we are in Mrs. [Blank]'s kitchen. First she started lit the oven (strike match on shoe, bend down, and light oven). Then she took down the mixing bowl (take down the bowl), set the sifter in it (place sifter) and poured in the flour, sugar, the baking powder, and the salt (pour in each item, one at a time). She sifted them together (turn handle). She turned around to get the eggs (turn around), but she turned back (turn back) when she heard a loud crash (clap hands). Some cans had fallen from the shelf. One of them was the pepper and she began to sneeze (sneeze three times). She was so busy sneezing she didn't notice that a lot of extra baking powder had fallen in the bowl too.

She took the eggs from the refrigerator (open door, take out eggs) and set them on the table (place on table). One by one, she broke three eggs into the bowl, one, two, three (break eggs). The fourth egg fell to the floor with a squish! Before she could mop it up, the baby began to cry (waah). She picked up the baby and rocked the baby with her left arm (rock with left arm), while she stirred the cake with her right (stir cake). At the back door, the dog barked (arf, arf) to come in. She opened the door (open) and shut it (shut) behind him with a bang (stamp foot). She tried to go back to rockin' and stirrin' (rock and stir), but the dog smelled the cake and tried to jump up to the table. All the poor woman could do was hold out her foot to keep him back, still rockin' and stirrin', mind you. (Do all motions at once.) Finally, he got the idea and went away.

Now she was ready for the milk. She opened the refrigerator door (open), reached in, grabbed the milk (take milk), and closed the door with her elbow (close door). Of course, it was a bit awkward, what with holding the baby, and the bottle slipped from her hand with a crash (stamp foot). The cat meowed and came running. The dog began to bark.

Well, I tell you friend, Mrs. [Blank] had really had it! She plunked the baby in the play pen (waah), threw the dog in the base-ment (bark, open door, shove dog in), and tossed the cat out the back door (meow, throw out cat). She got a new bottle of milk and poured the milk (pour), beat the cake a bit more (stir), poured it in the pan (pour), and set it in the oven (place in oven).

Then she gave a great sigh and collapsed in a chair. (Everybody sit down). (Pause) Suddenly she heard a noise. She jumped up. (Everybody stand up.) It went bang, bang, bang (three stamps with feet)! The oven door blew open, and the cake went all over the room. (Look around, say "aah!") Remember that extra baking powder that fell in? Mrs. [Blank] collapsed back in the chair and muttered, "nuts!"

Of course, it was actually just as well that the cake blew up. Did you notice that in all the excitement she forgot to put in the choco-late? Well, that's why Mrs. [Blank] had to bake that cake all over again. And for her trouble and all the mothers who are always baking for our reunions and parties, I think we should give a loud hurrah (hurrah). Come on, louder! (Hurrah!) Once more, now! (Hurrah!!!)

Friends, Friends, Friends

Sing as a round to the tune of "Row, Row, Row Your Boat," with group in two lines facing each other.

Song:
Friends, Friends, Friends ya say, (Do action #1 below)
All along the way (Do action #2)
Smile, Smile, Smile, Smiles, (Do action #3)
Every single day. (Do action #4)

Formation:
4 Parallel lines

Actions:

1. Walk forward four steps, shaking hands as you go with people in the opposite line.
2. Walk backward four steps.
3. Slide to the right four steps with hands over head moving hands and fingers.
4. Slide to the left four steps.

Father-Son Outing Games

Ball Throwing Contest

Ball throwing contests between fathers and sons for distance or for accuracy are always an interest getter. Make sure there are different sizes of balls, even one as large as an old basketball.

Archery Contest

There are usually archery enthusiasts within each family, and most father and son outings are held in the woods, which make for an ideal target range. Besides the usual ring targets, have plenty of cardboard deer, rabbits, and crows nailed to the trees. Give prizes to the best hunters.

Chin-up Contest

Many boys can do more chin-ups than their fathers. Give a prize to the best father and son team. Pushups and other physical endurance activities also are exciting.

Horse and Rider

Each father places his son on his shoulders. The pairs all must stay within a ring marked on the ground. Only the boys may grab opponents to force them down off other fathers' shoulders. If one boy can pull another boy off, the fallen father and son team must leave the ring. Give a prize to the last team remaining.

Bubble Gum Contests

Sons can usually blow larger bubbles than their fathers, but it's interesting to see how many fathers cannot blow a bubble of any size. A prize can also be given to the person that can pop his gum the loudest.

Entertainments

Announce that the entertainment will be a contest between father and son teams. This may be in music, stunts, skits, or some special skill in sports, drama, speech, or dance. The best time for this activity is around the evening campfire.

Bean Bag Basketball

A human "goal" holds a wastebasket or large pan at each end of the court. The game is played as in basketball, except that it is all passing; that is, no one can run while in possession of the bean bag. The "goal" may move any part of the body except the feet, to help the bean bag go in. Score as in regular basketball.

Bronco Tag

All the players but two form bronco teams. A bronco team is composed of three or more players who stand behind each other, grasping the waist of the person in front. The first player in the line is the head. His arms are free. The last player is the tail. Of the two extra players one is the runner and the other the chaser. The chaser pursues the runner who tries to hook on to the tail of one of the broncos. If he succeeds, the head of that bronco becomes the runner. The broncos must stay intact as they run and twist to keep their tails away from the runner. If the chaser tags the runner before he can hook on to one of the broncos, they exchange places and the game continues as before.

Are You There, Mike?

The contestants are blindfolded, and each one has a folded newspaper or something similar. They hold on to opposite corners of a neckerchief or similar cloth. One says, "Are you there, Mike?" The other one takes a swing at him. This goes on for three tries. Next the positions are reversed, and the former talker has three swings. Keep score with the number of successful hits.

Toe-to-Toe Balance

Two contestants face each other. Each man has his left foot in back of his right one, heel to toe. Both feet must be in a straight line. Indoors this may be done by standing on a crack in the floor. The contestants try to upset each other or cause a "spill" by slapping each other's hand, palm to palm.

Four-Way Tug of War

Four boys about the same size and weight stand back to back, in the form of a small open square outside a rope. An eight-foot length of ¾-inch rope is suggested. This is tied together at the ends, and each player holds the rope with one hand only. They gradually pull on the rope until it is taut, forming a square with a boy on each corner. Now a paper drinking cup or a bean bag is placed about three feet in front of each player. The leader says, "Take the strain—go!" Each player tries to pick up the cup or bean bag, the first one to do this being the winner.

How's Your Grip?

Hold a horizontal staff as high as possible. Two players facing each other grip the staff as tightly as they can. Now, with arms straight, they bring the staff down to waist height. Because the staff turns, obviously someone must release his grip.

Balloon Bursting

A contestant is blindfolded and equipped with a club of rolled-up newspaper. The balloon is suspended on a cord, which hangs from a light (preferably bamboo) pole. A nonparticipating person holds the balloon in front of the player and says "Here." The player is allowed three swings, and the person holding the pole does nothing to prevent him from connecting. The player, or the team he represents, loses one point for each unsuccessful swing.

Kangaroo Pillow Fight

Tie the ankles of each contestant together, using a neckerchief, rubber band, or similar heavy cloth, as it will be subjected to some strain. The toes should point straight forward. The contestants then start beating each other with pillows. One point is lost by a contestant whenever he takes a fall. Two falls out of three can be the losing score. The ground should be free from stumps and stones. Pushing with a pillow is allowable. This is a stunt with plenty of action that everyone, even the busy contestants, will enjoy.

Circle and Staff

Holding a horizontal staff chest-high and gripped with both hands, players try to push each other out of a circle.

Tails

The tails are neckerchiefs, or something similar, tucked under the rear of the belt with at least two-thirds left hanging down. Tying the neckerchief to the belt or giving it a twist is not allowed. The idea is to get the tail off the other fellow's belt. This stunt is better with three or more contestants. Place them in a circle and disqualify anyone who steps out.

Rope Jumping

This effective arm and leg builder can be used whenever you have extra time. All that is required is a rope, six to eight feet long. Try jumping with both feet together and elbows close to the sides of the body or the alternate foot jump for speed.

Gorilla Relay Race

Boys spread their feet shoulder width, bend down, and grasp their ankles. They walk forward, keeping knees extended and legs straight.

Grasshopper Race

Line up teams single file. Mark a turning spot twenty-five feet away for each team. Give each leader a small ball of wadded paper. On signal, the first in each team hops to the turning spot with the paper ball between his knees. He returns and hands off to the next player. If the ball is dropped, the player replaces it and carries on. The first team to finish wins.

Chariot Fight

This game is loaded with action. Form teams of three with the first two boys linking arms. They are "horses." The third boy is the "driver." He holds onto the belts of the two horses. The driver has a section of a rolled newspaper tucked into the back of his shirt to form a horse's tail. The object of this game is for a team to steal the newspaper tail of the other teams without losing their driver's tail. Only the horses may grab tails. When a team loses a tail, the game leader issues another. The team gaining the largest collection of tails wins.

Father and Son Race

This event for father and son is a great source of fun for the spectators. Blindfold both the fathers and sons. The fathers drop to their hands and knees and the sons mount their backs. At the signal they race to the finish line about one hundred feet distant. The first ones to reach the line (if anyone gets there) are the winners.

King of the Walk

Lay a two-by-four board on the grass; place a boy (king) on one end of the board with a pillow. All other boys line up at the other end of the board with their pillows to take their turns at trying to knock the king off. The one lone boy is the king. The boy who knocks him off becomes king.

Blind Shot

Draw a large bull's-eye by making a series of concentric circles on a blackboard or wall, and number the circles from the center out. Stand each player in turn about fifteen feet away, and let him study the bull's-eye, and then blindfold him. He turns around three or four times, and then approaches the bull's-eye and attempts to put his finger on it. He may feel along the wall or the edge of the blackboard before placing his finger. Each player scores the number of the circle he touches.

Tug of War

At many father and son outings the preponderance of sons balances out a good tug of war. Two twelve-year-old boys are a good, even match for an average father. A good-sized soft cotton rope is the easiest on the hands. It's more exciting if the tug of war is held across a stream of water. There should be two out of three tries with plenty of prizes for the winners.

Medicine Ball Throw

Father and son can work as a team, throwing the ball for speed. The first team to catch the medicine ball ten times wins the prize. Substitute any sort of ball, the heavier the better, if a medicine ball is unavailable.

Hammer Throw

Tie a rope on the end of a stack of sawdust and let the boys throw for distance. An old basketball or punching bag filled with cloth will also serve the purpose well.

Pillow Fight

Place a pole over two sawhorses or on two barrels so that when two boys straddle the pole their feet will not touch the ground. Use materials to make pillows for the occasion (pillows made out of old pant legs filled with feathers or cotton). The boys sit on the pole face to face and try to knock each other off the pole with the pillows. When a boy loses his balance he usually just turns and grabs the pole with his hands and does not fall to the ground.

Egg Throwing Contest

Fathers and sons stand about five feet apart. On a signal, a raw egg is tossed back and forth between father and son until it is broken.

With each throw the father and son back up one step. The father and son team that is standing the farthest apart when the egg breaks wins the prize.

A balloon filled with water may serve the same purpose as a raw egg.

Climbing a Rope Ladder

Place a dollar bill at the top of a ten-foot rope ladder that is tied with one rope at the top and bottom. The ladder is tied diagonally from the bottom of one tree to the top of another tree. About half way up, the ladder will turn and the boy will probably fall to the ground. It's a good idea to have a mattress or soft grass under the ladder. The boy who gets the money can keep it.

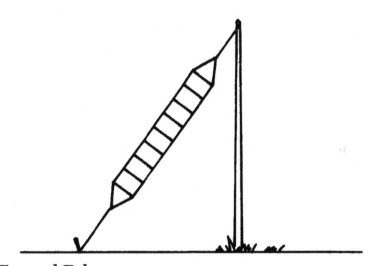

Greased Pole

Place a dollar bill on top of a greased steel pole and give it to the boy who can climb up the pole and get the money. Those who get to the top will usually slide back down when they let go of the pole with one hand to get the money. If none succeed, place a five dollar bill on top and let several boys stand on each other's shoulders.

Variation: Let a boy stand on his father's shoulders or let the father push his son up the greased pole.

Sawdust Scramble

Place several pennies, candy chews, or gum in a pile of sawdust. All boys of the same age line up fifty feet away. At the starting signal, they run to the sawdust and hunt for the candy. They may keep all they can find.

Each age takes their turn with more candy and more sawdust added with each age. Last of all, the fathers take their turn. All will climb over each other to get to the sawdust. The boys get a laugh watching their fathers act like boys.

Nail Driving Contest

With the father on one end of the plank and the son on the other, a big nail is started in the board. On the signal to start the father and son take turns hitting the big nail with a small hammer. If the nail bends, they have to straighten it up. The team with the best time wins the prize. All fathers and sons can start at the same time if enough hammers are provided.

Variation: Start ten shingle nails in a board and have the father compete with his son to see who can drive the most in the board without bending the nails.

Wood Sawing Contest

This game takes coordination as well as cooperation. With a log resting over a saw horse or another log, the father stands at one end of a big timber saw and son on the other. The father and son groups are timed to see which group and saw through their log the fastest.

Usually the fathers and sons try to push instead of pull the big timber saw. The saw bends, and there is a lot of coaching from the sidelines before the block of wood falls to the ground.

Blind Alley

Each father is blindfolded and lined up on all fours at a starting point with his son on his back. At a distance of fifty to one hundred feet away is the goal line or a sack of candy. The only directions the fathers receive to direct them to the candy are the verbal directions their boys give them. The boy may say, "Turn left (right, or east, or west)." It is fun to see how much wandering the fathers do while traveling on hands and knees to the goal line.

Bronco Riding

Each father has a son on his back and they all stand in a circle facing the center. At a whistle blow each boy jumps down and runs around the circle and jumps back on his father's back, raising his hand. The first son to raise his hand is declared the winner.

This may also be used as an elimination game; the last one around on each try is eliminated.

Wheelbarrow Race

A rod through a tricycle wheel axle makes a good wheelbarrow wheel, especially if a bicycle handle grip is placed over the rod. The sons hold onto the handles and the fathers pick them up by the ankles. It is a good idea to have the race go to a marker and back to the starting point. Usually on the turn, the boys tip over and watching the boys try to get back on the wheel creates a good laugh.

If stakes are driven in the grass so the boys have to weave in and out, then more skill is required, and it is a lot more exciting for the spectators.

Variation: On the signal "Go," two players race to a turning point in wheelbarrow fashion (one holding the legs of the other who walks on his hands). They reverse positions and race back to the starting line.

King of the Mountain

The top of a hill or haystack serves as the battleground and players try to gain it. When one player gains it, he says, "I'm king of the mountain," and the other players try to knock him off, while each tries to gain it for himself. The winner is the one who controls the top of the hill and maintains this position for a certain length of time. Sometimes the boys can form teams long enough to knock the larger boys off, but after that, it is every man for himself.

Kangaroo Hop Race

Players assume a semisquat position. Keeping their feet together, they spring forward to cover a set distance.

Calf Roping

This may be played as a contest between individuals or between teams. Each player is equipped with a yard or two of stout rope. The object is to tie the other person's feet without letting your own be tied. If playing as a team, the team whose member is the last one standing wins.

Rooster Flight

In a circle, two players hop, each on one leg and holding the other with his hands. To win, a player must make his opponent lose balance or step out of the circle by bumping his shoulders.

British Bulldog

One or two older people are chosen as the first "bulldogs." Standing in the center of the playing area, they face the group. On the signal "Go," the entire group charges from one end of the field to the other, everyone trying not to be caught by a bulldog. To catch someone, bulldogs must tackle the player and hold him down while counting to five. Victims become bulldogs for the next charge. No more than two bulldogs can tackle a player. If a bulldog does not hold his victim down on the ground while counting to five, the victim is free for another charge. Play until all have been caught. The winner is the last man to be "grounded."

Arm Wrestle

Players grip each other's hand while resting their elbows on a flat surface. Each player tries to force his opponent's hand to the ground or raise his elbow without moving his own elbow. Try alternating hands.

Elephant Roll

Count off in twos. Have all players line up, alternating ones and twos. Number one players face one way and number two players face the opposite direction. All get down on hands and knees to form an "elephant." One is named the "rider." On a signal, those forming the elephant move their bodies backward and forward. Each moves in an opposite direction from his neighbor. The rider attempts to crawl along their backs from one end to the other. The rider has two tries to go all the way without stopping, and if he fails he goes to the end of the line and the first elephant becomes the rider.

Three-Legged Soccer

Set up your outdoor meeting place for this game by designating field boundaries on each side and two improvised goals at opposite ends of the field. Organize the group into two teams. Each team pairs up and ties the inside legs of each couple together with neckerchiefs or a similar cloth. One pair in each team acts as goal tender. Place a ball in the center of the area. Both teams take positions in front of their goals. On signal, each team runs to the center of the field and tries to kick the ball through the opponent's goal, using the untied legs only. After a score is made, place the ball in the center and kick off the next play. The team with the most goals in five minutes wins.

Stick Fight

Two players grip a broomstick firmly with both hands. Each tries to force the left hand of his opponent to the ground. Repeat several times.

Pull Apart

A couple sit foot to foot with hands locked and legs spread wide apart. Each tries to pull his buddy hard enough so that he himself can lie on his back at the end.

Fireman's Drag

A father ties together the wrists of his son, who is lying on the ground, with a neckerchief or similar cloth and kneels above his head. The father puts his head through the victim's arms and drags him to safety.

Back Pull

Two players stand back to back, locking hands over shoulders. Each person tries to pull his opponent off his feet and to carry him to the finish line.

Hand Pull

Two contestants sit on the ground, facing each other with the soles of their shoes braced each other's and their hands clasped. The winner must pull his opponent forward to his feet.

Belt Tug

Boys fasten their belts together and place the loops around their heads. They kneel face to face on all fours. Each tries to pull the belt off his opponent's head without his knees or hands leaving the ground.

Hand Tussle

Two boys face each other and clasp hands. Each tries to get his opponent out of position. The first to move his feet is the loser. A quick thrust forward or backward may do it.

Push Back

Two boys stand back to back with their arms linked. Conduct the contest between two lines, twenty feet apart. The winner is the one who pushes his opponent over the line.

Shoulder Push

A couple face each other five feet apart. They lean forward with hands on each other's shoulders. Each tries to push his opponent back at least three steps.

Human Burden Race

Count off two teams with the even numbers of each team lined up on one side of a line thirty feet away and the odd numbers on the other side. Upon the command "Go," number one from each team runs across the course, allows number two to jump on his back, and immediately starts back to his original side. Arriving at the starting line, number two quickly dismounts, takes number three on his back, and races across to the other side. Here number four mounts on number three, and so on until the last number has been carried across. The first team through wins the race.

Tire Pull

Use an old bicycle tire to play this more rugged version of "Steal the Bacon." Divide into two equal teams. Teams line up twenty feet apart facing each other. Place the tire on a center line marked on the ground. Count off by team, from one to the total number in each team. On a signal, the leader calls a number. The numbers called run to the center and grab the tire. Each tries to pull the tire to his side and score for his team. The team with the most points in a given time wins.

Jump the Shot

A long rope with a soft knot on the end is held by the leader. Players must jump as he swings it around in a circle below their knees. If they are hit, they are penalized one point. The player with the least number of penalties wins.

Obstacle Race

Lay out an obstacle course including things like a horizontal pole to climb over, a rope suspended from a tree branch to swing over, an eight-foot mock ditch, a low-level bar to crawl under, a six-foot wide area to jump over, a four-inch board to walk on, a zigzag row of tires to step in, and an empty barrel to crawl through. Add a muscle builder. Players complete each obstacle before they move on. The one who finishes in the shortest time wins.

Elastic Rope

Army surplus stores usually sell elastic rope. Get a half-inch for children and three-quarters- to one-inch for adults. Fasten between two trees. Use a folded inner tube for a seat and a belt to tie around the individual and the rope. The rope may go up and down or forward and back.

Youth Conference and Convention Activities

Youth Convention Workshops

Planned workshops with a specialist for each group work well for youth conferences and conventions. As pertinent, divide the group into six equal parts with both males and females in each group, making the activities will be more successful. Allow youth to select the classes they would like to attend, this will generate more interest in the classes.

Advertise dances beforehand so youth will know what to expect.

Musical Rounds

Row, Row, Row Your Boat

Row, row, row your boat
Underneath the stream.
Ha, ha, fooled you all.
It's a submarine.

Hey, Ho

Hey, ho; nobody at home.
Meat nor drink nor money
have I none.
Still I will be happy!

John Brown's Chevy

John Brown's Chevy had a puncture in it's tire.

(Repeat twice)

And he patched it up with chewing gum.

Actions:

Chevy—make a motion for cranking or going over bumps

Puncture—make a sound for hissing or whistling

Tire—form a loop with arms

Chewing gum—make a motion or sound for pulling, snapping, or chewing

Come A-Hunting (to the tune of "Are You Sleeping?")

Come a-hunting, come a-hunting,

Wolf cubs all, wolf cubs all;

Out into the jungle, out into the jungle

Hear the call, hear the call.

The Three Fishermen

There were three jolly fishermen,

There were three jolly fishermen,

Fisher, fisher, men, men, men.

There were three jolly fishermen.

The first one's name was Abraham,

The second one's name was Isaac,

The third one's name was Jacob.

They all went up to Amster-shush,

You should not say that naughty word.

This Old Man

This old man, he played one, he played knick-knack on my thumb.

Knick-knack, paddy-wack, Give your dog a bone. This old man came rolling home.

He played knick-knack on my shoe (tap shoe with knuckles)

On my knee (tap the knee)

On the floor (bend and beat time on the floor)

On my hive (both hands as if brushing bees away from ears)

On my sticks (tap knuckles on fingers of other hand)

Up to heaven (points toward the sky)

On my pate (tap top of head)

On my spine (drum knuckles on backbone)

Now and then (hands raised shoulder-high; beat in rhythm, twice with closed fists and third time with open hands)

Wooden Cow Milking Contest

In a board, cut four holes the size of the bottom of a gallon can. Punch a few holes in the bottom of each can being used. Stretch a rubber glove over one end of each can and place it in one of the holes. Fill the can with white-colored water or powdered milk. In each finger of the glove, stick a hole the size of a little pin. Give the contestants a cup to hold in one hand. The other hand is used to "milk" the fingers of the glove. They may milk as many fingers at once as they can put in one hand. The contestant who fills the cup first wins.

Find a Partner

Boys are lined up on one side of the room and girls on the other. Everyone is blindfolded and walks across the room to find a partner to dance with or for some other activity.

Color Groups

Use this game to set up for Track Meet. Divide the group into color groups. (Chairs are already set up around the hall in groups and a group leader has been appointed and instructed beforehand.) Each color group makes up a team name (for example, Green Beret or Blue Bonnets). The groups also choose cheerleaders and make up yells for their team. They also choose the members they want to participate in Track Meet.

Track Meet

Judges are selected from among the adults to measure, keep score, and help run the meet. The following events are used:

Javelin throw (use a drinking straw), one from each team.
Shot put (use a balloon), one from each team.
Discus throw (paper plate), one from each team.
Weight lift (judged by facial expression—two balloons on a stick), one from each team.
Balloon break (form a circle and interlock arms. Five balloons

are dropped to the floor and the contestants must break them by stepping on them with their feet. Twelve or so participate in each group.)

Balloon blow (keep the balloon in the air by blowing; it cannot touch a person, wall, or floor.)

The points awarded for Track Meet are first place, five points, second place, three points; third place, one point. The team with the most points goes to the meal first. The losing teams compete in another game to determine who goes to lunch next.

Get Acquainted List

(This can be used as part of the dance program.)

Name . . . . District or Stake . . . .

Find a person from outside your district or stake who will qualify for the following and obtain his or her signature. Always go to a member of the opposite gender for your answers.

1. Find someone whose birthday is in the same month as yours. . . . .

2. Find someone whose parents drive the same make of car that yours drive. . . . .

3. Find someone who wears the equivalent size shoe as you. . . . .

4. Find someone who has had private lessons in music, drama, dance, and so on, and write their talents and name down. . . . .

5. Find someone whose group leader has the same last initial as your group leader. . . . .

6. Find a member of the opposite gender whose first and last initials are the same as yours. . . . .

7. Find a member of the opposite gender who is one inch taller than you. . . . .

8. Find two members of the opposite gender whose first names are the same. . . . .

9. Find a member of the opposite gender whose last initial is the same as yours and who traveled from another city to this youth conference. (May be from your own stake.) . . . .

10. Find a member of the opposite gender with the same color of

eyes as yours who traveled less than three miles to the youth conference. . . . .

The Era Match Game

This is a question-and-answer contest to stimulate the youth to read the *New Era*. There will be four members on each team, preferably two boys and two girls. Each district or stake can enter one team only. Members can be chosen from the district or stake at large. There will be a double elimination tournament that will compete one team against another.

A moderator asks the two teams questions that will require specific answers taken from articles in The New Eras during a designated period of time. The members of each team answer each question without consulting one another. They write their answer on a piece of paper. Their answers are compared with the specific answers shown by the moderator.

Each match counts tens points. The maximum a team could get on one question would be forty points. The first team to reach a hundred points, or the team that is ahead at the end of five questions, is the winner and advances to the next round. If at the end of the five questions the two teams are tied, the team to get the most matches on the next question will be the winner. Questions will be asked until one team is ahead. Prizes will be given to each team entering and for first, second, and third place.

Blindfold Dance

The boys are lined against one wall and the girls against another. There is one extra boy; all players are blindfolded. Make sure there are no objects in the room that the players can bump into. At the signal the music is started and both boys and girls start walking to the center until they meet. With eyes still blindfolded, they walk till they bump into someone of the opposite gender and begin to dance. Then an extra boy wanders around till he bumps into a dancing couple and then tags in. The tagged boy has to wander until he bumps into another couple and tags this couple, and so on until the music stops.

Broom Dance

Each boy picks a partner for the dance, except one who is given a broom to dance with. As the dance music begins and the couples start dancing, the extra boy with the broom tags in on someone who then dances with the broom. This is continued until all the couples are mixed up and the record ends. This is a good icebreaker at parties.

Entrance Exam

Give each player a copy of this sheet, without the answers, and have him find the special message.

(H) 1. If blackberries are green when they are red, write *H* on the right-hand side of this test. If not, write *X*.

(A) 2. If black cows give white milk that makes yellow butter, write *A* on the right-hand side. If not, write *Y*.

(V) 3. If a regulation football field is ninety yards long from goal to goal, write *Z* to the right. If not, write *V*.

(E) 4. If paper is made out of wood, write *E* to the right. If not, write a zero.

(A) 5. If an airplane can travel faster than an automobile, write *A*. If not, write *R*.

(G) 6. If the summer is warmer than winter, write *G* in the margin. If not, write *R*.

(O) 7. If Longfellow wrote "Twinkle, Twinkle, Little Star," write *S* in the margin. If not, write *O*.

(O) 8. If candy is sweeter than lemons, write *O* in the margin. If not, write *B*.

(D) 9. If Beethoven wrote "Moonlight Sonata," write *D* in the margin. If not, write *E*.

(T) 10. If the climate in Siberia is warmer than it is in Florida, write *X* in the margin. If not, write *T*.

(I) 11. If the printing press was first invented by an American, write *Z* in the margin. If not, write *I*.

(M) 12. If New York City is the capital of New York State, write *A* in the margin. If not, write *M*.

(E) 13. If baseball is a major sport, write *E* in the margin. If not, write *O*.

Freeze Dance

A moderately fast song is put on and couples dance in their usual style, but when the music is stopped they must stop also. If they move in any way after the song is stopped, they must leave the dance floor. The song is started again, and the dance continues in this way until there remains only one couple, who become the winners.

Get-Acquainted Name Game

Give the following to each player as they arrive. They must find other players who meet the qualifications and spend some time getting to know them. They should try to avoid using the names of players they already know.

1. Someone with same color of eyes as yours.
   . . . .
2. Someone with same last name initial as yours.
   . . . .
3. Someone with same color shoes. . . . .
4. Someone wearing fingernail polish. . . . .
5. Someone wearing dark rim glasses. . . . .
6. Someone wearing argyles . . . .
7. Someone wearing a hair ribbon or ornament of some kind in their hair. . . . .
8. Someone in the same church organization as you.
   . . . .
9. Someone from a state different than yours.
   . . . .
10. Someone who drives the same make of car as yours.
    . . . .

Seminary and Church Activities

Tic-Tac-Toe

Divide the class into two teams. Make a tic-tac-toe outline on the board and put in the numbers of different questions (questions that are created before the game). Each team member, in turn, may choose a question. If they answer it correctly, their team's mark is placed over that question's number in the outline. The first team to make a tic-tac-toe wins. The game may be repeated until the questions are all used. Have several free questions that players may choose the numbers of and receive a free mark.

Service

Players divide into teams and form two lines. Each girl ties a tie on her partner, and he, in turn, ties a scarf on her. When this is accomplished, both go to a prescribed goal and return to serve the next couple and the team by giving up their tie and scarf. The next couple repeats the performance and the team completed first wins.

Gospel Application: Progress is happiness and results from cooperation and service.

Prophets

Give each class member a small card and a pencil and tell them to write their first and last name vertically down the card. Instruct each to name as many prophets or Bible characters as they can by using the letters in their name as initials.

The Ten Commandments

Underline the answer you think is best.

1. The first and second commandments emphasize which attribute? kindness, honor, love of God, or honesty.
2. The fourth commandment emphasizes which attribute? reverence, respect for others, kindness, or responsibility.
3. The fifth commandment emphasizes which attribute? self-control, responsibility, honor, or honesty.
4. The sixth and seventh commandments emphasize which attribute? loyalty, courage, faith, or self-control.
5. The eighth and tenth commandments emphasize which attribute? cooperation, honesty, generosity, or sincerity.

Fill in the blank.

1. Which commandment speaks of the Sabbath day?
   . . . .
2. The Ten Commandments were given on Mount
   . . . .
3. Which one tells us not to steal? . . . .
4. To whom did the Lord give the Ten Commandments?
   . . . .
5. What were the children of Israel doing when the prophet came back from receiving the Ten Commandments? . . . . . .
   . . . .

Answers: fourth, Sinai, eighth, Moses, worshiping an idol

Book of Mormon

Seat the group in a circle. The first person starts out by saying, "I'm Nephi, the son of Lehi." The second person refers to the first, "He's Nephi, the son of Lehi. I'm Moroni, the son of Mormon." This continues around the circle, each one going back to the first and repeating everyone's name and designation and adding another.

Untwist the Twister

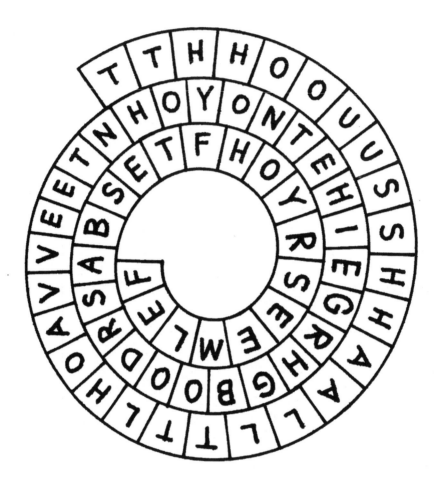

Two very important rules for living are wound up here. To unwind them, start with the first letter *T* and jot down in the margin every other letter. To find the second rule, start with the second letter *T* on the outside and write down every other letter.

Answers: 1. Thou shalt love thy neighbor as thyself. 2. Thou shalt have no other gods before me.

Sharing

Provide one set of alphabet cards for each team, with a few extra vowels and letters often used twice. The leader calls out a sharing word such as give, cooperate, receive, and so on. The first team holding the letters in line to form the word wins a point. Teams are to compete to see who can formulate the most words.

The Bible Association

Fill in the blanks on the left with the numbers on the right.

(19) A burning bush	1. Solomon
(18) A smooth, round stone	2. Joseph
(17) Long hair	3. Daniel
(16) A dove	4. Ten virgins
(15) Mess of pottage	5. Cain and Abel
(9) Mother-in-law	6. Abraham
(8) A ladder to heaven	7. Jesus
(4) Lamps	8. Jacob
(3) Lions	9. Naomi
(1) Great wisdom	10. Ruth
(2) A loud coat	11. Isaac
(5) Murder	12. Prodigal son
(7) Raging tempest	13. Satan
(6) Numerous posterity	14. Jezebel
(10) Daughter-in-law	15. Esau
(11) Ram in a thicket	16. Noah
(12) Fatted calf	17. Samson & Delilah
(13) Serpent	18. David
(14) Wicked queen	19. Moses
(23) Great patience	20. Jonah
(22) A shipwreck	21. Joshua
(21) Walls of Jericho	22. Paul
(20) A big fish	23. Job

Match Up

Place letters from the column on the left in the blanks on the right. (Answers are in parentheses.) Score: eighteen to twenty, excellent; fifteen to seventeen, good; thirteen to fourteen, fair; under twelve, review the Book of Mormon.

(S) One of the eight witnesses to the Book of Mormon	A. Zoram
(E) Who cut Laban's head off?	B. Gospel
(I) Eldest son of Lehi	C. Benjamin
(Q) Lehi's wife	D. Celestial
(N) Place where Nephi built a ship	E. Nephi
(H) Who slew Gideon?	F. Red
(T) One of the three witnesses to the Book of Mormon	G. Moroni
(P) Name sometimes applied to nonmembers	H. Nehor
(B) Rod of Iron	I. Laman
(A) Servant to Laban	J. Cumorah
(L) Who killed Abel?	K. Genesis
(C) An Israelite tribe	L. Cain
(G) Angel who revealed plates to Joseph Smith	M. Seth
(M) Adam's son	N. Bountiful
(K) First Book of Moses?	O. Lucifer
(F) Name of the sea near where Lehi traveled	P. Gentile
(J) Place where plates were buried	Q. Sariah
(O) Another name for Satan	R. Joseph
(R) One of the twelve tribes	S. Hyrum Page
(D) Highest degree of glory	T. Oliver Cowdery

Song Scramble

Copy the lines of several gospel songs (depending on how many people) on separate pieces of paper (one line on each piece) and let each person draw one out of a hat. All members sing their lines at the same time and try to find the people who have the other lines. The first group to get all the lines together sings the song and wins.

Men and Women of the Bible

Listed below are thirty famous men and women of the Bible. Match the appropriate modern term from the column to the right.

(5) 1. Ruth	1. Businesswoman
(6) 2. Hannah	2. Conscientious housekeeper
(1) 3. Lydia	3. Seamstress
(7) 4. Deborah	4. Adulteress
(11) 5. Leah	5. Ideal daughter-in-law
(13) 6. Jael	6. Unselfish mother
(14) 7. Sarah	7. Judge
(12) 8. Naomi	8. Week-end guest
(15) 9. Esther	9. Betrayer
(3) 10. Dorcas	10. Knowing wife
(4) 11. Bathsheba	11. Contributing mother of nations
(10) 12. Eve	12. Nail driver
(2) 14. Martha	14. Mother of nations
(8) 15. Queen of Sheba	15. Liberator

(6) 1. Abraham	1. Perfect man
(13) 2. Elijah	2. Hermit
(11) 3. Matthew	3. Miracle worker
(12) 4. David	4. Soldier
(2) 5. John the Baptist	5. Shipwright
(14) 6. Samson	6. Stockman
(4) 7. Gideon	7. Doctor
(8) 8. Melchizedek	8. Priest
(15) 9. Jonah	9. Tentmaker
(1) 10. Job	10. Dirt farmer
(5) 11. Noah	11. Tax collector
(9) 12. Paul	12. Musician
(10) 13. Cain	13. Nature boy
(7) 14. Luke	14. Lawbreaker
(3) 15. Moses	15. Deep-sea diver

Gospel Football

Layout a football field on a piece of cardboard. Using a quarter as the ball, asking gospel questions valued at a different number of points, and using points as yards, see who scores the most touchdowns. You lose ten yards if you miss a question and the other team gets the next question.

Bible Questions

The leader stands in front of the class and reads a question. Throw a candy to the person who first gives the correct answer.

Which of David's sons was killed when in rebellion against his father? (Absalom)

Which of Solomon's sons succeeded him as king? (Rehoboam)

What woman threatened the life of Elijah so that he fled? (Jezebel)

To whom did Jehovah speak with a still small voice? (Elijah)

Who asked for a double portion of Elijah's spirit and became his successor? (Elisha)

What king of Israel was noted for his furious driving? (Jehu)

What two books of the Old Testament are named after women? (Ruth and Esther)

Who was Ruth's mother-in-law? (Naomi)

Who was noted for his patience? (Job)

Whom did God send to preach to the people of Nineveh? (Jonah)

Which queen risked her life to save her people? (Esther)

Which king captured Jerusalem and carried the Hebrews into exile? (Nebuchadnezzar)

Which woman was named by her husband? (Eve)

Who asked, "Am I my brother's keeper?" (Cain)

Which man is first said to have "walked with God"? (Enoch)

With whom did God make the covenant of the rainbow? (Noah)

Name three sons of Noah. (Shem, Ham, and Japheth)

Who is described as "a mighty hunter before the Lord"? (Nimrod)

Which son did Abraham prepare to offer as a sacrifice to God? (Isaac)

Whose wife "looked back" and became a pillar of salt? (Lot's)

Who was Isaac's wife? (Rebekah)

Who sold his birthright for a mess of pottage? (Esau)

Who was Rebekah's favorite son? (Jacob)

Who served fourteen years for his wife? (Jacob)

What Hebrew became a high government official in Egypt? (Joseph)

Who was found in an ark of bulrushes by Pharaoh's daughter? (Moses)

Who watched the ark of bulrushes where her brother was laid? (Miriam)

Who was the first great law-giver of the Hebrew people? (Moses)

To what mountain did Moses lead his people? (Mt. Sinai)

Who succeeded Moses as leader of the Hebrew people? (Joshua)

What city in Canaan did Joshua and his men capture and destroy? (Jericho)

Which woman was a judge in Israel? (Deborah)

Which leader armed his soldiers with trumpets, lamps, and pitchers? (Gideon)

Which child was taken by his mother Hannah to serve Jehovah? (Samuel)

Who was the first king of Israel? (Saul)

Which musician was brought to court to play for Saul? (David)

With whom did David form a lasting friendship? (Jonathan)

What Philistine champion did David kill? (Goliath)

Who succeeded Saul as king of Israel? (David)

Honesty

Pass out the following story on sheets of paper and ask questions for a discussion.

A king, wishing to get rid of his prime minister, puts two pieces of paper in a hat. He tells a judge present that if the prime minister draws out the paper marked "stay" he may remain in the kingdom, but if he draws out the paper marked "go" he must leave.

The trick is that the king had written "go" on both pieces of paper.

How did the prime minister outwit the king?

After some have given answers to the question, ask, "Was someone dishonest?" (There will be some disagreement in the group.)

Who? And why?

How honest is your life? Is it like the king's?

Offer a reward to the first person who reaches a correct solution to the story problem and to others who have good ideas or comments about the topic.

Answer: The prime minister drew one piece of paper from the hat. Without looking at it he destroyed it and asked the judge to read the other one. If it said "go" the one the prime minister destroyed must have said "stay."

Men of God

Cut one or two pictures of present-day Apostles of the Church into pieces. As each piece is placed on a board, read statements about the apostle to the group to see who can first recognize him. Points are given to the winner on a decreasing scale as more and more of the pieces of the picture are placed on the board. The one with the most points at the end of the game wins a prize.

Love Thy Neighbor

Arrange the teams in parallel lines facing the front in the pattern girl, boy, girl, boy, and so on. A boy and girl hold hands. Place a box or wastepaper basket a short distance in front of each team. Place a pile of paper bags in front of each line. At the signal, the first player (a girl) picks up a bag and runs to the basket, blowing it up as the boy behind her runs as well. He kneels down at the basket. She bursts the bag on his head and throws it in the basket, and they return to tag the next players. Continue until all have run. The team finishing first wins.

Scriptural Questions

Prepare a large number of index cards each containing a question and an answer. As the students arrive give each person three or four cards. Instruct them as follows: Introduce yourself to a person and ask them a question from one of your cards. If they answer the question correctly, give them the card. If they cannot answer the question tell them the answer and collect a card from them. The person you questioned must now ask you a question to give you a chance to win a card from them or to lose one. Each of you will then move to another person.

The object of this game is to collect as many cards as possible. Questions may be prepared on any scriptural subject.

Question Draw

Put enough questions in a box to accommodate the class. Divide the class into teams. Choose a member of team A by number and draw a question out of the question box. If the player answers it, they get five points and draw a second time. If they answer the second question, they get ten points. For a third question they can earn fifteen points. Then give team B a chance. Keep track of points and score by teams.

Judge and Conductor

Questions for this game may be written and arranged beforehand so that appropriate questions are assured. Select or elect a "judge" and a "conductor." The conductor reads a question. All who can answer it stand. The judge then calls upon one of these and the others sit. At the end of the answer, those who are not satisfied may rise and give additional information, explanation, opinion, or ask the "answerer" any appropriate question. The judge or conductor may rule out any questions or remarks that seem inappropriate. Disagreements, when not settled by the speakers, should be settled by the judge or the teacher.

A variation which stimulates interest consists in having those who rise remain standing until they can no longer make any corrections or add any significant fact. This device usually improves in effectiveness with continued use.

Spelling Baseball

Divide the group into two teams. The pitcher (leader) "pitches" a Bible word to the batter. If the batter spells it correctly, they go to first base. If they fail, they are out. Base runners may advance only by the movement of succeeding runners. When three are out, change sides. Play for nine innings and keep score.

A Written Game

This game applies well to the meridian of time, the time when the Savior dwelt among men. If students follow the instructions and read accurately, they get the answer that goes in the fourteen blanks. Use this game as a pre-opener into the study of the meridian of time.

1. In blank one write the first letter of the last word in John 12:44.

2. If in reading John 13, you think Jesus knew his hour was come before the hour of the Passover, fill in blank fourteen with the letter *H*; if not, fill it in with the letter *S*.

3. If Jesus is speaking in John 14:2, write the letter *O* in blank nine; if someone else is speaking, write the letter *I*.

4. Read Acts 2:17. Does this refer to the last days? If your answer is yes, put *F* in blank ten. If no, put *R* in blank two.

5. Read Acts 4:10. Put in blank eleven the seventh letter of the town Jesus is from.

6. If you think Peter was full of the Holy Ghost in Acts 5:3, cross out the letter on blank fourteen and put *E*. If not put an *S* over blank eleven.

7. If Gamaliel was a Pharisee but showed fairness to Peter in Acts 5:34–35, put in the letter *I* in blanks four, six, and twelve; if not, use the letter *A* in those blanks.

8. If Stephen in Acts 7:55–56 had a vision before his death, put the letter *R* in blank three; if not, put an *N* in blank three.

9. Read Acts 8:17–18. Put the last letter of the name of the man who wanted to purchase the Holy Ghost with money in blank eight.

10. After reading Acts 10:1–6, if you feel that Cornelius was a good man even though he was wealthy, fill in blank thirteen with the third letter of the first name of the man whom Cornelius had been directed to find. If not, fill blank ten with the letter *R*.

11. In Acts 5:1–5 if Ananias was guilty of practicing dishonesty, put the letter *A* in blank seven. If you think Ananias died due to a heart seizure, leave the blank as it is.

12. If Peter and Paul were blood brothers, write *M* in blank five. If they were brothers only in the gospel setting, write *E* in blank two.

13. See D&C 20:26. If Peter is the one referred to, record the letter *A* over the letter in blank one. If Jesus Christ is the one being referred to, put the letter *D* in blank five.

1 2 3 4 5 6 7 8   9 10   11 12 13 14

... ...

The Rod

This is a creative way to create two teams randomly. Choose two team captains. Call one side the Nephites and the other group the Ammonites. Have the captains march around the room while the group sings only the chorus to " The Iron Rod." When the group sings the word "rod," the captains grab the person closest to them. This person becomes a member of the team that chose them. The second time they sing the word "rod" both captains and crew grab others in a snowballing effect. The chorus is repeated until the teams are evenly divided and everyone is on their feet.

The Savior's Principles

Form the class into small circles of teams. A leader is appointed for each group and has a paper with the word "principles" written vertically on it. From this word each team is to make up sentences showing a principle the Savior taught during his ministry.

Togetherness

Set aside a certain number of students to be judges. Divide the rest of the class into four groups and give each group a set of alphabet cards. The cards should be three by four inches in size, with the letters *J*, *Q*, *X*, and *Z* omitted and an extra set of vowels added. At a starting signal, each player looks for letters that will form a word of three or four letters as called for. If the group is large, form five-letter instead of three- or four-letter words. Suppose the leader calls for a five-letter gospel word. The group decides on faith. They all hunt for the letters. Five arrange themselves so that the letters are in the correct order and then run to one of the judges who writes the word on the blackboard. Five minutes are allowed to see which team can get the most words.

Socializing

Give each class member four or five pieces of wrapped candy, small nuts, dried peas, or beans. Announce that everyone is to introduce themselves to everyone else, shaking hands and giving their name. Each time two people shake hands the one who first gives their name claims a nut from the other person. The same individuals may greet each other any number of times, but never twice in succession.

There will be pandemonium for a few minutes as each one tries to tell another "I'm so-and-so." This is especially good when there are newcomers in the group. You can be sure that at the end of five minutes any awkwardness that may have been in the atmosphere will be gone.

Variation: Play the game while dancing. The only time one can talk is when the music stops.

Jaredite Jump Relay

Members of two equally-numbered teams pair up. Give a ruler or a stick to the first pair of each team. Each takes hold of an end. At a given signal, the pair lowers the stick and all their teammates must jump over the stick and return to their position. When everyone has jumped over the stick it is handed to the next pair who takes it to the starting position, and the first pair run to the end of the line. The relay continues until everyone has had a turn. The team who finishes first wins.

Hold to the Rod Relay

There is a rope stretched from starting line to finish line. The first person in each line puts a quarter in their eye, a book on their head, and a balloon between their knees. While in this awkward position the player must grab the rope, walk to the finish line, remove the quarter, balloon, and book, run back, and give the three items to the next person. The relay proceeds in this manner.

Gadianton Run-Around Relay

Divide players into teams. Give players Book of Mormon names. Give the same set of names to each team's players. When the leader calls out a name, each person with that name must run around their entire team and end up back in the same spot. The first one back wins. Points are scored for each victory.

Hold to the Rod

Improvise a rod by tying a bamboo pole, broomstick, or mop-stick between two chairs. Instruct players to always hold to the rod to receive a blessing. Blindfold each player when their turn comes. By grasping the rod and walking carefully the player is guided by the rod to tiny jars or baskets at the end of it that hold slips of paper. The player picks one slip and returns to the group by the rod. Have slips of paper on the left and right hand. If the player lets go of the rod they receive a slip with a penalty. If the player holds on and takes the slip with their free hand they get a blessing. If you prefer you may use a heavy cord tied to a chair and leading to the next room to represent the rod.

Authority

The leader of a group tells the group they want three items brought to them. The first person to give the leader the three items has the authority to call out the next orders. Items may include a 1952 penny, a watch, a shoe, a belt, and so on.

Articles of Faith

Have two or more lines with six to eight people in each one. The purpose of the game is for each person to say one word of an article of faith. When a person doesn't know the next word the rest of the team acts it out.

Religious Password

Give a clue word that may describe or in some way lead the other person to say the password that the first person is holding.

For example, for the password "Noah," the clue could be "flood." Only one-word clues are allowed. If it only takes one clue word for a player to guess correctly, the password is worth ten points; with each clue given it becomes worth one point less. This can be played in teams or just by two individuals. The one scoring the most points wins the game.

Word Game

The word "seminary" is placed on a board or cardboard.

Players attempt to select as many names of Bible characters as possible with names beginning with each letter used in the word "seminary." Each row can be given one of the letters, and groups can compete if this is desired.

Gospel Word Scramble

Here are gospel names whose letters have been scrambled. See how many you can unscramble.

eklme = (Melek)

mazor = (Zoram)

elamhis = (Ishmael)

lyonbab = (Babylon)

shanba = (Bashan)

majinben = (Benjamin)

zaob = (Boaz)

untobiulf = (Bountiful)

zamocer = (Cezoram)

esredet = (Deseret)

orhen = (Nehor)

ipneh = (Nephi)

isamnatle = (Lamanites)

domnir = (Nimrod)

nitam = (Manti)

umtrirean = (Irreantum)

ablan = (Laban)

ailshmeties = (Ishmaelites)

liglag = (Gilgal)

ominla = (Lamoni)

namal = (Laman)

leulem = (Lemuel)

mas = (Sam)

honlaia = (Liahona)

dig = (Gid)

isarah = (Sariah)

hilim = (Limhi)

honleti = (Lehonti)

ahon = (Noah)

sesmo = (Moses)

edingo = (Gideon)

mada = (Adam)

ilicma = (Amlici)

tihenpes = (Nephites)

Unscramble the Book of Mormon Prophets

1. Hpeni   (Nephi)
2. Mealahn   (Helaman)
3. Rehte   (Ether)
4. Ionorm   (Moroni)
5. Ornmom   (Mormon)
6. Hisamo   (Mosiah)
7. Laam   (Alma)
8. Bajoc   (Jacob)

9. Seno   (Enos)
10. Roajm   (Jarom)
11. Niom   (Omni)

Books-of-the-Bible Hunt

Form small groups of any number up to ten. Have one Bible for each group. The groups form a semicircle in front of the leader, or in a circle around the leader, and count off by numbers one to ten. Place the Bibles in front of the leader. The leader calls out a number and a scripture reference, and those in each group that have that number race for the Bibles and see who can find the reference first.

False Prophets

Select one person to be blindfolded and three to be "prophets." Blindfold the player and then mix up the desks into a maze with several dead ends. Hide an object such as a book in some portion of the room. The prophets, two false and one true, then start shouting instructions to the blindfolded player who does not know which is the true prophet. The player must select one voice to follow, then follow it until he either is led into a dead end or is led to the object.

Gospel Application: Throughout this life there are many people who would like to tell us where to go or what to do, but we must select the voice of the true prophet in order to find the truth.

Savior

The class is divided into small circles with a leader for each group. He is given a pencil and paper with "Savior" written vertically on it. The teacher then says, "The teams will use each letter on their paper to start words that will form into sentences. These sentences must show a principle Christ taught in His ministry. The first team to finish will be the winning group." When the first group finishes, the leader of that group is asked to read the sentences they constructed.

Nephi Crossword

2 Nephi Chapters 1 and 2

Across

2. Because of Christ we are . . . . forever from the Fall.
4. If iniquity abounds in America, the land will be . . . .
5. Christ's redemption.
7. Redeemed mankind from the Fall.
10. Blessing of those who keep the commandments of God in America.
12. Satan desires us to be . . . .
13. Lehi counsels his sons to arise from the . . . . and be men.
14. Atonement.
17. Choose eternal life, according to the will of his . . . . Spirit.
18. If Adam and Eve had not partaken of the forbidden fruit, they could have had no . . . .
20. Adam's transgression is known as the . . . . of man
21. None have come to America except those guided here by the hand of the . . . .
22. If Americans keep the commandments, America will always be a land of . . . .
24. Cause of curse to come upon America

Down

1. Cause of affliction and sorrow to Jacob in the wilderness.
3. Because of Christ's Atonement, we are free to . . . . for ourselves.
6. There must needs be . . . . in all things.
8. Adam's wife.
9. Lehi is encircled about eternally in the . . . . of Christ's love.
11. What would have happened to Lehi's family if they had remained in Jerusalem.
15. When Adam partook of the fruit, he knew good from evil. This is known as the . . . .
16. . . . . fell that men might be.
17. Place reserved for the wicked.
19. . . . . seeks to make all people miserable.
23. God desires that we have . . . .

246

Clue

Give clues about some famous battle in the Book of Mormon while students try to guess the battle.

Priesthood

Arrange nine books in the center of the room, and place chairs around the walls. The books are arranged according to the illustration below. Place the beginning letter of the name of each priesthood office on the end books and place the words "Aaronic," "Service," and "Melchizedek" on the center books.

The person who is "it" must know the game before they are sent from the room. When they are out of sight and hearing, the leader has the class choose one of the books, such as the "Deacon" as illustrated by the figure below. The "it" player is ushered back in, and the leader touches any book in the corner corresponding to the "Deacon" in the overall pattern as illustrated by the figure below. Example: He touches the "High Priest" in the lower left-hand corner and asks, "Is it High Priest?" The "it" player will say, "No." When his pointer touches the "Deacon" in the lower left hand corner, the player must answer "Yes." The fun comes when other members of the class try to figure out how the "it" player can be so smart.

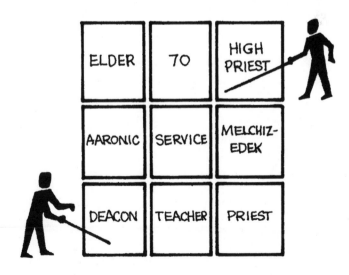

A What?

Each class row is a team, with each team leader having a pair of scissors. The leader of each row says, "I have a pair of sharp, shiny, silvery scissors," and turns to the next in line and says, "I have a pair of sharp, shiny, silvery scissors." The second person says, "A what?" The leader repeats and hands the next player the shears. Number two turns to number three and says, "I have a pair of sharp, shiny, silvery shears." Number three says, "A what?" Number two turns to the leader and says, "A what?" The leader tells number two, number two tells number three, and so on to the end of the line. The first team completed wins.

Family History Relay

Divide the group into teams and organize each team into a line. The first person in each line walks ten steps forward from their line to a chair that has a card containing a name, birth date, date of marriage, and date of death.

When the first person memorizes this information they lay the card on the chair and run to the next person in line. They take the next person by the hand and start walking back to the chair. On the way to the chair the first person teaches the second person the information that was written on the card. As soon as the second person thinks they have the information memorized, player number one remains by the chair, and player number two runs back to the line to pick up player number three. The game continues in this way.

Should anyone forget the information on the card, they must start over by running back to the chair and looking at the card. The first line through wins, providing the last person can quote the information on the card correctly to the class.

Gospel Application: This game is a good introduction to family history work.

Standard Works

The leader names one of the standard works and the rest of the players start to name books one by one. Each player takes his turn around the circle. When a mistake is made, that person goes to the bottom spot in the circle.

Variation: When the leader calls a book in one of the standard works, they point to another person and start counting to ten. If the leader counts to ten before the person pointed to can name another book in the same book of scripture, that person has to go to the end; if not, the leader points to another person and starts counting again. No book can be repeated.

Shake Hands Blindfolded

Line the boys against one wall and the girls against the opposite wall. Blindfold the first boy and the first girl and tell them to walk toward each other across the room and shake hands. No one must help them or make a sound while they are trying to do so. If either of them reaches anyone else in the room and starts to shake hands they must pay a penalty. As soon as they have succeeded in reaching each other and shaking hands, the next two start.

How Much Do You Know about Your Brother or Sister?

Pair off the group. Give players a specified length of time to find out all they can about one another. At the close of the given time, give each person fifteen seconds to tell all they can about their partner. For each thing they mention the leader of the game attaches a clothespin on their clothing. When all players have finished presenting, the one with the most clothespins is the winner.

Saints Get Acquainted

Each person takes a pencil and numbered paper and goes around the group having individuals sign their names until the numbers are all filled. Then they must identify each person on their paper. The person who can identify all of them is the winner.

Seminary Basketball

Divide the class into two teams and number them. (If there is one student left over after the division into teams, they could be the timer, or if not, the teacher could time.) Choose one side to start ,and give the topic to be discussed. Let the first person on the team chosen to start give a pertinent fact on the topic given to them from a previously prepared list. They must do it within ten seconds. If they supply a correct fact within the ten seconds, give the next person on their team an opportunity to do the same, and so on down the line as long as they are able to supply the facts within the time limit. (This is similar to passing the ball.)

If a person is unable to supply a fact within the prescribed time limit the other side "intercepts" the ball and in regular order give its members the chance to do the answer in the prescribed time. They can keep adding pertinent facts down the line until another miss. The side that is holding the ball or has given the last answer at the end of one minute scores two points. When one side scores, the other side is given the ball to start with on a new topic. Be sure to keep the teams in numbered order so that everyone gets an equal chance to answer a question.

This game is applicable to any class in seminary. Topics like "The Ten Commandments" will get facts such as (1) Moses received them on Mt. Sinai. (2) They also are known as the Decalogue. (3) They were written on stone. And so on. "Baptism" may get (1) Must be by immersion. (2) Pattern for process was given by Christ. (3) Must be performed by one who has authority.

This game moves along very fast and is unpredictable, therefore the students will enjoy it very much. If they get unruly or if they try to help team members, award the other team a "foul shot" in the form of a question to answer for one point.

Scripture-Character Relays

Divide the group into teams. Then follow these instructions for a variety of relays. In any of the relays, the team that finishes first gains a point:

a. The first player on each team goes to the board and writes a name of some Old Testament (New Testament, Church history) character. When that person returns to the line, the last person of each line goes to the board and writes a short complete sentence about the name written there. If a player cannot write a sentence or name they must write their own name accompanied by the phrase "I don't know." Avoid duplications.

b. The teacher or leader announces the name of some character. The first person in each line places the first word of a sentence on the board; number two places the next word, and so on.

c. The leader announces or writes on the board the name of some character. Each member of each team writes a complete sentence about the character. No writer should duplicate the sentence written by any other member of either team.

d. The first person on each team writes a sentence on the board about some character the class has studied. The opposite ends of the lines write the name about whom the sentence is written.

Partner Pairing

(1) Each boy has a different flag, and all the flags are put in a pile on the floor. Each girl picks a flag and finds the owner. He becomes her partner.

(2) The boys are given names of presidents of the Church and the girls are given themes of those presidents. The girls find their statesmen and the boys find their statements, and thus they find their partners.

Telegraph

The group is seated in a circle with one person standing in the center. The designated starter sends a message to someone across the circle. (This person must be indicated.) The message is sent by squeezing hands along the circle until the message is received. The person in the center tries to intercept the message along its track. If the message is intercepted the person in the center takes the place of the person caught sending the message and another message is sent. When the message is received the receiver calls, "I got it!"

Gospel Application: Heavenly Father answers our prayers, but sometimes we are not in tune to receive the message He sends and Satan can distract us from receiving the message.

Seek and Find

Form a circle of seated people (not too large a circle). One person in the middle must be blindfolded. Each player is assigned a different gospel word, for example, honesty, faith, and so on. The blindfolded person then calls out two words and tries to touch the players as they exchange seats. Anyone caught is then blindfolded and joins the blindfolded person in the center.

Gospel Application: When you are instrumental in bringing the gospel to a person, they help you as a missionary.

Give

Each person takes an article (assigned by the leader) to the center of the room. The first one there with the article gets a point. Personal and interesting things may be called for.

Gospel Application: Learn the joy of giving and sharing.

Who's the Leader?

Players stand in a circle. One player leaves the room. A leader is selected, and the whole group of players begins to clap. This is the signal for the player who left the room to return. This player goes to the center of the circle and tries to find out which player is leading the group in its action. In the meantime the leader changes from clapping to jumping, hopping, patting his head, and so on, and the players immediately do the same thing. Sometimes it takes quite a while for the player in the center to discover who the leader is, especially if the group members do not watch the leader. They can watch others in the circle and get the next action as quickly as watching the leader. This game is good when played to music.

Gospel Application: Discernment is necessary to tell the difference between true and false prophets. Or, prophets can delegate authority, and we should follow our priesthood leaders.

Sincerity

Each player is given five beans. Any player may approach another player and say something like, "I have three beans in my hand." If the person approached thinks the other is sincere, they say, "I believe you." If they think the person is insincere, they say, "You're not sincere." If they guess right, they take the beans from the other person; if they guess wrong, they must give the other player the same number of beans as the player had in their hand. The player with the most beans at the end of a given time wins.

Fellowshipping

Three or four boys and girls are tappers. Others put their heads down on desks. The tappers walk quietly around the room and tap a head. The person tapped raises their hand to show they were tapped. When each tapper has tapped someone and all have returned to the front of the room, the leader says, "Heads up." Those tapped stand and, in turn, try to guess who tapped them. If successful, they became a tapper.

Gospel Application: Everyone can have the opportunity to participate through Church activity. Seek to fellowship others so they can also participate and enjoy the blessings of Church service.

How Do You Like Your Counselors?

The players are seated in a circle with the player chosen to be "it" standing in the center. There are just enough chairs for those seated but not one for the "it" player. This person approaches one of the players and asks, "How do you like your counselors?" If the player says, "All right," everyone shifts one seat to the right; if the player replies, "All righteous," they shift to the left; if the reply is "just fine," everyone moves to the other side of the circle; if the person answers by saying "Not at all," the "it" player asks, "Whom do you like?" The person then gives the names of any two persons in the circle, for example, "I like May and Jay." May and Jay must then change places with those next to the one being questioned. The "it" player tries to occupy one of the chairs vacated by the players as they move.

Family Ties

The object of this relay is for each team to try to tie themselves into a bundle before the opposing team does. The first player in each line is given a ball of string. At the signal this player passes it to the next in line behind them, but holds the end. The ball is passed from player to player, being unrolled as it goes. When it arrives at the end of the line it is passed up the line behind the backs of the players until it reaches the first player again. The line that first wraps itself into such a bundle is the winner. In the sequel to the race the bundle is untied by passing the string through each player's hands back to the first player again, winding it into a ball as it goes.

Gospel Application: Each family member is important, and each must cooperate with the other to make a happy and successful family.

Human Hurdle Relay

Arrange the players in two lines facing each other. Have them sit with legs extended. The captain of each team rises and hops over the extended legs of their teammates to the end of the line. After hopping over the last players, they return to their original place by running around behind the line, tagging the second person in the row and sitting down. The second player then hops over the third player and down to the end of the line, runs to the head of the line and hops over the first player, tags the third player, and sits down. The race proceeds, each player in turn hopping, running, tagging, and sitting.

Gospel Application: We must face each problem in life as it comes, overcoming it before going on to the next.

Cooperation

Players are in lines as teams. Each person, in turn, tries to bat a balloon in the air up to the goal line. When the player reaches the goal line they grab the balloon, run back, and tag the next player, who repeats the process.

The game is played again but this time two players put the balloon between their foreheads and run to the goal line and back to tag the next couple. The first team finished is the winner.

Gospel Application: We must work with our brothers and sisters to reach our gospel goals. We cannot do it alone.

Jacob and Rachel

A circle is formed, players holding hands. "Jacob" and "Rachel" are on the inside. Jacob is blindfolded. He asks, "Rachel, where art thou?" As she endeavors to evade him, by ducking under his arms, slipping past him, or walking on tip-toe just behind him, she replies in any quality of voice she chooses, "Here I am, Jacob." Each time he asks the questions she must answer. If he catches her, a new Jacob is chosen. She may become "Jacob," or different players may be selected for both parts.

Holiday Games

Christmas Bell Trade

Each player is given a small paper bell. Give one player a gold bell, the others red ones. Each player walks about with closed hands, one of which must be holding their bell, and introduces themselves to other players. As they do so they extend their closed fists and tap one of the fists of the other player. If the player happens to have their bell in the hand tapped they must trade with the player who introduced themselves. At the end of three minutes the player holding the gold bell is rewarded.

Christmas Gifts

Couples are placed back to back while one describes a Christmas gift and the other draws it on a piece of paper. At the end of ten minutes the drawings are passed around with the name written under the article for inspection.

Debate

"Resolved; that there is not a Santa Claus." Appoint debaters a week or so in advance. Limit each one to five minutes.

The House Where Santa Claus Lives

If Santa cannot memorize this, he can direct the actions while someone else reads this story. While everyone is singing carols, one of the dads, dressed as Santa Claus, enters from the rear of the room.

He says "Merry Christmas, Merry Christmas" and throws candy or unshelled peanuts or something similar to the crowd.

When Santa reaches the front of the room he tells the following story:

"Old Santa has traveled many a mile to be with you. He's been impressed with your preparations for the Christmas season and he's had a look into all your homes. Tonight Santa would like to tell you about a house you have never seen before. It is the house where Santa Claus lives.

"While telling this story, Old Santa will need your help for certain words. Every time these words are spoken, I want you to make certain signs. Let's all practice them before we start the story.

House (hands over head in an inverted *V*)
Shed (hands in front of chest in inverted *V*)
Sled (hands together in waving motion from left to right)
Reindeer (one hand, palm out, at each side of head)
Pack (both hands over right shoulder as if carrying a sack of potatoes)
Little boys (all boys, young and older, stand up)
Little girls (all girls, young and older, stand up)
Box (show dimensions—length and width—with hands)
Doll (both hands at right side of head with head slightly bent)
Lion (extend both hands and give deep growl)
Soldier (give a salute while at attention)
Train (make figure eight with right hand)
Santa Claus (pat stomach with both hands and say, "Ho, ho, ho")

"Now let's begin our story (dashes indicate signs).

"This is the house -- where Santa Claus lives --. This is the shed -- behind the house -- where Santa Claus lives --. These are the reindeer -- that pull the sled -- that is kept in the shed -- behind the house -- where Santa Claus lives --.

"This is the pack -- all filled with toys for good little girls -- and good little boys -- that is carried by old Santa Claus -- who guides the reindeer -- that pull the sled -that is kept in the shed -- that is behind the house -- where Santa Clause lives --.

"This is the doll -- that is in the box -- that is in the pack -- all filled with toys for good little girls -- and good little boys -- that is carried by old Santa Claus -- who guides the reindeer -- that pull the sled -- that is behind the house -- where Santa Claus lives --.

"This is the lion -- that frightened the doll -- that is in the pack -- all filled with toys for good little girls -and good little boys -- that is carried by old Santa Claus -- who guides the reindeer -- that pull the sled -- that is kept in the shed -- that is behind the house -- where Santa Claus lives --.

"This is the soldier -- that shot the lion -- that frightened the doll -- that is in the box -- that is in the pack -- all filled with toys for good little girls -- and good little boys -- that is carried by old Santa Claus -- who guides the reindeer -- that pull the sled -- that is kept in the shed -- that is behind the house -- where Santa Claus lives --.

"This is the train -- that runs on the track and carries the soldier -- forward and back, who shot the lion -- that frightened the doll -- that was in the pack -- all filled with toys for good little girls -- and good little boys -- that is carried by old Santa Claus -- who guides the reindeer -- that pull the sled -- that is kept in the shed -- that is behind the house -- where old Santa Claus lives --.

"Now old Santa must be on his way. He has a few parting thoughts. Parents, work hard at this job we call parenthood. By doing so, you can make it Christmas every day of the year for your youngsters. Kids, obey your parents and you can fill their year with joy. There's just one more thing to say as old Santa leaves, 'Merry Christmas to all.'"

Note: The story also can be presented without the aid of a costume. The presenter says, "Tonight I am going to tell you about the house were Santa Claus lives. There will be certain signs for you to use."

Pin the Pack on Santa

Adapt the game of pin the tail on the donkey using Santa and his pack. As they arrive at the party, blindfold the players and have them try this stunt. The one who pins the pack closest to the correct place is rewarded.

Santa's Pack

Seat the group in a circle with no chairs vacant and one person standing. Give each player a name of a certain thing that might be in Santa's pack, such as doll, horn, candy, and so on. One player starts walking around the circle telling a story about Santa filling up his pack. As the player mentions the names of articles, the people with those names get up and follow them around the circle, each putting their hands on the shoulders of the preceding person. When the player who is telling the story mentions "reindeer" each player tries to get a chair. The player left without a chair starts another story and the game continues.

Musical Gifts

This game works great for white elephant gifts. Seat the players in a circle and give each a gift. As the music starts they pass the gifts around the circle. When the music stops, each person opens the package they hold. If they do not want it, they may tie it up and pass it on.

Hunt and Trade

From stiff construction paper, cut several sets of Christmas items such as a star, bell, and so on. Hide them around the room before people arrive. After they arrive, explain the different objects and tell the guests that the items have different values—but don't tell them the values. Start searching all together, letting people trade for the desired pieces. After a time, stop and determine the scores.

Fishpond

All the gifts are wrapped and tied with ribbon or string and placed in the center of the floor with a row of chairs around them. Three or four fishing poles are provided with line and hook attached. The guests stand outside the chairs and secure a gift by "fishing" it out with the pole and hook.

Christmas Ring Toss

Each gift is wrapped and numbered. Nails are driven into a board and numbered corresponding to the numbers on the packages. The guests stand a few feet in front of the board and toss rings (like from canning bottles) at the nails. Each is given the gift bearing the number of the nail they ring.

Stop-Flight

If you have a real Christmas tree, decorate it after Christmas in the back yard for the birds. Plan on saving all stale bread, fat, nuts, and anything else that birds enjoy. On New Year's morning pack away the Christmas tree ornaments and redecorate the tree with the food in the back yard for the hungry winter birds. (Be careful not to put out food in quantities or locations which will attract rodents or other vermin.)

Lost Time

Hide cardboard hourglasses with different amounts of time written on them (such as, one day, thirty seconds, six hours, twenty-five minutes, and so on) about the room. The leader announces that much time has been lost during the year and that a prize will be given to the team which finds the most time in two minutes. Time is counted according to the amount written on the hourglass.

Dearly Remembered

When the Christmas cards begin to come through the mail, instead of opening them immediately, place them unopened in a bowl in the living room. Each day the number will grow, and it will be a real temptation to peek, but don't. On Christmas Eve, sit with the family in a circle on the floor and pass out all the cards. Dad reads one first, then Mom, and then the children one at a time. The small children will especially enjoy the pictures. In this way, in a relaxed mood, the cards are thoroughly enjoyed and the senders dearly remembered.

The Game of Months

One of the players is appointed to be Father Time. He appoints the other months beginning with January and proceeding through the year, giving each player a month. Then everyone lines up in front of Father Time, who throws a ball toward the line, at the same time calling out the name of a month. The player who has the name of that month must either catch the ball or get possession of it before Father Time can count to ten. If the player is unsuccessful they must take Father Time's place.

The Delicate Easter Bonnet

Each guest is given an old hat. It may be a ten-cent hat, a derby, or an old straw hat. The name of the guest is pasted inside.

Place bits of brightly colored ribbon and chiffon, flowers, feathers, and any kind of ornament on the table. Provide needles, thread, pins, and scissors as well. When the signal is given, each guest is given exactly two minutes to put some ornament on their hat. At the end of that two minutes, no matter how incomplete the work is, each guest must pass their hat to their right-hand neighbor. Trimmers are again given two minutes in which to add to the artistic developments of these hats, after which they are again passed to the right.

This continues until the hats come back to their original owners, who, it must be confessed, do not always recognize them, but may have to look inside for their name. The one whose hat is worst looking must wear it during the rest of the party.

The host or hostess may ask all the guests to wear their hats for the rest of the evening.

Easter Egg Relay

Arrange the players in two teams, lined up. Give each player a teaspoon that is held in their mouth by the handle. Place a hard-boiled egg in the spoon of the first player, who must then transfer it to the spoon of the second player without using their hands. If the egg falls during the transfer the one transferring may pick it up in their spoon and then attempt the transfer again. In picking up the egg, it may be steadied on the floor with the hands but it must be picked up with the spoon in the mouth. The team that passes the egg down the line first wins.

The Musical Egg

The host or hostess passes a hard-boiled egg to their right-hand neighbor with instructions for the player to hold it while that player sings up the scale. After the holder of the egg sings, they must quickly pass the egg on to their right-hand neighbor. This guest must also hold it until they sing up the scale before passing it on to their neighbor. The object is to sing the scale and to get rid of the egg as soon as possible in order not to be caught with it at the crucial moment. These crucial moments are determined by the host or hostess, who blows a tiny whistle at intervals of thirty seconds. Any guest caught with the egg in their hand when the whistle blows is listed. These listed guests are later on invited to pay the penalty of the game by performing impromptu for the group.

It is remarkable how many guests who "cannot sing up the scale" can sing in certain situations!

Fortune Telling Eggs

Each guest is given an Easter egg with shells painted in a light color that will easily show writing (which should be decipherable too). Give the guests pencils and have each write their initials on the large end of their egg. Collect the eggs, mix them up, and again pass one to each guest. The host or hostess then asks questions to the guests and gives them exactly one minute to answer in writing, each using the initials on the egg they now have for the first letters of the two words allowed for the answers. Answers must be written on the eggs.

Egg Tenpins

Dress up clothespins to represent children of flowers, with paper costumes of different colors. Stand up ten of them on the table in the way tenpins are placed, and roll hard-boiled eggs to knock them down. Green may count for five points, red twenty, and so on. Allow each person two eggs to roll across the table, and count the clothespins that are knocked down. Eggs do not roll as easily as balls, and they will spark a lot of fun with the results of their peculiar rolling.

Egg Pickup

Put a pile of small candy eggs on the table and give each player a pair of candy tongs, which any candy store will have. With the tongs, pick up as many eggs as possible without moving the other eggs. Baskets may be furnished, in which each person puts the eggs they pick up.

Egg Balance

Each contestant is given a spoon and a hard-boiled Easter egg. On "go" the players must balance the egg on the spoon, and run to the goal line as fast as possible without dropping the egg. The one who reaches the goal line first wins.

Romance

Distribute white paper trimmed with red hearts with the following jumbled words on them to the group. The game is to see who can unscramble the most words in ten minutes. A heart-shaped box of candy may be the prize.

1. Dipuc   (cupid)
2. Elvo   (love)
3. Tmach   (match)
4. Yitniffa   (affinity)
5. Dedwing   (wedding)
6. Ecnamor   (romance)
7. Versol   (lovers)
8. Tearhs   (hearts)
9. Shiptrouc   (courtship)
10. Riagream   (marriage)

Hearts in a Bottle

Give each person fifteen candy hearts. Set an empty bottle on the floor in the center of the room. Have the players drop candy hearts into the bottle, players holding their arms at shoulder height. The one dropping the most hearts into the bottle wins the game.

Heartstrings

Fasten pieces of red cord, several yards long and all the same length, to white cardboard darts or empty spools. Twist the cord around the dart or spool and attach red hearts to the end. Pair off players into partnerships (boy/girl) that line up at one side of the room and at a signal the girls take the hearts and walk away from their partners, unwinding the string from the darts which the boys hold. When the girl has walked as far as the cord will permit, the boy starts after her, winding the cord on the dart again. The couple who finishes first is given a heart-shaped box of candy.

Valentines

Have large sheets of heavy red or white paper with the name of each person present written on the top of each sheet. Distribute the sheets and supply magazines, glue, scissors, and pins. Each person cuts pictures, printing, and so on from the magazines and makes a valentine for the person whose name is on their paper. Specify a length of time that it must be done in. Prizes may be given for the most unique (or beautiful, and so on) valentine.

Find the Hearts

Place paper hearts around the room, some within easy reach of guests, others quite out of the way. Start a song, with each boy taking a dance partner. At a signal from the leader the music stops. Couples run in search of hearts but return to their place and start dancing as soon as the music starts again. This continues until only a few hearts remain. The couple having the most hearts at the end of the game are declared Sir and Lady Valentine and are awarded a simple, appropriate gift.

Steal the Heart

Split the group into two or four teams, with two lines facing each other, and have the players count off from opposite ends of the line. (Even up the lines as needed.) If there is an extra person, make them the score-keeper and number-caller. Place a heart-shaped box or other similar object an equal distance between the two lines and the same distance from each end of the lines. The leader or score-keeper calls out a number, and the person with that number from each line runs for the box. One person tries to pick up the box and run back to their own line before the other person touches them. If they succeed, their team gets two points. If they get caught, their team gets no points, and the other team gets one point. The two winning teams can play each other, and the two losing teams can play each other.

My Cupid

Sing to the tune of "My Bonnie Lies Over the Ocean."

My Cupid lies over the ocean,
My Cupid lies over the sea,
My Cupid lies over the ocean,
Oh bring back my Cupid to me.

Chorus:

Bring back, bring back, oh bring back my Cupid to me, to me.
Bring back, bring back, oh bring back my Cupid to me.

Actions: Perform the following motions on the words indicated.
My—point to self
Cupid—motion drawing back bow string and shoot arrow
Lies—place folded hands under cheek as if sleeping
Ocean—make ripply motion with fingers
Sea—with thumb and first finger of left hand describe letter *C*
Oh—with thumb and finger of right hand describe the letter *O*
Bring—make calling motion with both hands
Back—point to own back
To—hold up two fingers
Me—point to self

Guessing Heart Object

Before the guests arrive, have a red object cut from old magazines ready to pin on the back of each guest as they arrive. These objects do not need to be connected with Valentine's Day, but that would be more appropriate. (Allow enough paper around the object so that each is cut in the shape of a heart and the entire object is left intact.) With one of these heart-shaped objects pinned on their back, each guest finds out what their object is by asking other guests yes-and-no questions. Take care not to allow any guest to see their own object. As soon as a person discovers their object, they can sit down and continue to answer questions for others not yet finished.

Valentine Verses

Provide each guest with a pencil and paper and give them ten minutes to compose a Valentine verse of at least four lines. Have the guests sign these verses and throw them into a bowl and the host or hostess draws them forth one a time and reads them out loud, the guests trying to guess who wrote each one.

Valentine Relay Race

Divide into two or more groups. About twelve to fifteen people on a side is a good number for the relay. The members of each group stand one behind one another, facing three circles eighteen inches in diameter that have been drawn with chalk on the floor (three circles for each line). Have three Indian clubs or pop bottles for each circle that have been dressed up with crepe paper to represent valentines or cupids. Place them standing up in the circles. When the whistle is blown, the one at the front of the line runs to the circles and sets the bottles out of the circles. They must leave them all standing up. The player runs back, tags the next person in line and goes to the back of the line. The next one must place the clubs or bottles back into the circle. This continues until all have had a turn. The group that finishes first wins a prize.

Flour Heart Hunt

When the group is already divided, following a relay race or something similar, choose one person from each group for the Flour Heart Hunt. (It may be better not to tell the name of the stunt until all is ready.) When the players have been chosen, bring in saucers of flour in which are hidden cardboard hearts. They are to dig these out without the use of their hands, using only the teeth and tongue.

Attraction

When most of the guests have arrived and are seated, the leader explains the game by demonstrating it as follows. The leader walks up to a guest and says "Darling." The guest stands and says "Yes, dear?" The leader asks, "Will you be my Valentine?" and the guest says "Yes." At this the leader turns around and has the guest follow them as they go through the same procedure with another person. All three go to another guest and repeat, then repeat again, making a total of four guests who are on their feet. They are now instructed to each get as many people in their own lines as possible. The line finishing with the fewest number of people must pay a forfeit.

Heart Throb

The group separates into two lines and everyone holds hands in their own line while the leader takes hold of the hand of the person at the end of each line. The leader explains by demonstrating that he will pass to each line the "heart throb" by squeezing hands. When the last person at the end of the line feels the throb, they raise their free hand in the air. That line wins the game.

Treasure Hunt

The leader reads a mysterious letter containing directions on how to start a hunt for treasure. For example, the directions may be, "Walk twice as many steps to the east as there are steps in front of the house." Sometimes the directions may be found underneath a stone or tacked to the side of a house. The last suggestion may be, "The treasure is within thirty feet of this spot." The treasure may be a box of homemade candy or a sack of apples.

Cupid, Lover, and Arrow

Place teams in two lines. Assign one player to be a score-keeper. The first person in each line runs along their line whispering one of these three words: "Cupid," "lover," or "arrow." The person then falls in at the end of the line. The leader says, "One, two, three, go!" and each line demonstrates the word they have just been told. The "Cupids" act as if they are shooting a bow and arrow and say "twang." The "arrows" move their arms toward the other team with their fingers pointing and say "boing." The "lovers" put their hands over their hearts and say "mmmmmmm." Score is made one point for each time on the following basis: The arrow beats the lover; the lover beats Cupid; Cupid beats the arrow. In case both sides are the same, the score-keeper gets the point. The next person then goes down the line telling the group which word to demonstrate. Play until one side or the score-keeper scores five points or some other prearranged number.

The Twelve Days of Halloween

(Sing in order to the tune of "The Twelve Days of Christmas")
On the twelfth day of Halloween
My true love gave to me,
Twelve bats a-flying,
Eleven masks a-leering,
Ten ghouls a-groaning,
Nine ghosts a-booing,
Eight monsters shrieking,
Seven pumpkins glowing,
Six goblins gobbling,
Five scarey spooks,
Four skeletons,
Three black cats,
Two trick-or-treaters,
And an owl in a dead tree!

I Heard the Bells on Halloween

I heard the bells on Halloween,
Their old, familiar carols scream,
    And wild and sweet
    The words repeat
The pumpkin season's here again.
Then pealed the bells more loud and strong
Great Pumpkin comes before too long,
    The good will get,
    The bad will fret.
The pumpkin season's here again!

Pumpkin Bells

Dashing through the streets
In our costumes bright and gay
To each house we go
Laughing all the way.
Halloween is here,
Making spirits bright.
What fun it is to trick-or-treat
And sing pumpkin songs tonight!

Oh, pumpkin bells! Pumpkin bells!
Ringing loud and clear,
Oh, what fun Great Pumpkin brings
When Halloween is here!

Deck the Patch

Deck the patch with orange and black,
Fa la la la la, la la la la,
Take along your goody sack,
Fa la la la la, la la la la,
Don we now our gay apparel,
Fa la la la la, la la la la,
Troll the ancient pumpkin carol,
Fa la la la la, la la la la,
See the Great One rise before us,
Fa la la la la, la la la la,
As we sing the pumpkin chorus,
Fa la la la la, la la la la,
Follow him as he ascends,
Fa la la, la la la, la, la, la,
Join with true Great Pumpkin friends,
Fa la la la la, la la la la!

Remove the Dime

In view of all the audience, have a person lie flat on the floor and place a dime on their nose. They have to get it off without moving

269

their head, if they can. (They can't—unless they reach up and remove it with their hand.)

Nose Touch

Ask the group if they can stick out their tongues and touch their noses. After several tries on their part, show them how. Simply stick out your tongue and touch your nose with your finger.

Eighth Wonder of the World

State that you will show the folks something they have never seen before and will never see again. Then crack a nut and hold up the kernel and ask if anyone has ever seen it before. Then eat the kernel and ask them if they will ever see it again.

The Lost Sheep

The leader makes an elaborate announcement introducing a soloist who is to sing a pathetic ballad entitled "The Lost Sheep." The singer takes their position, glances at their accompanist, nods their head as a signal for the pianist to begin, stands ready as the pianist plays a prelude and then gives a plaintive "baa-aa-aa."

Thanksgiving Dinner Menu

1. I'm an article given much to reflection, but to my use there is no objection.   (Water)
2. I came from the tree top way up in the air; you'll like me first class, but I can't serve a pair.   (Toothpick)
3. I'm eaten and drunk more extensive than all, and yet in some ways I cause many a fall.   (Ice cube)
4. I've caused weeping and wailing and lots of tears, but I'll build up your health and you'll live many years. (Onion)
5. In many folks' shoes I am caught, but when I'm cooked you'll like me a lot.   (Corn)
6. Part of me is a miner's tool, if you eat too much you'll find you're a fool.   (Pickles)
7. I'm found in your mouth, so you'll know me well, when you find I've been dropped you know I'll be swell. (Gumdrop)

8. I grow in the ground and not on a tree. Animals, like men, are all fond of me. (Peanuts)
9. I am usually called poor, but that is not true, for there's really no end to the good I can do. (Prunes)
10. I'm found in some rings and on some people's heads, I've even been known to leave people dead. (Punch)
11. Sally and Lady live over the sea, and were tied up together and came to help me. (Salad)
12. I was invented in the kitchen by a cook with ease. Don't eat too many of me if you please. (Cookies)

Binoculars Race

Mark out an irregular line on the floor, or use a string about eight feet long. The victim has to walk the line looking at his feet through one end of the binoculars, and come back looking through the other end. A race is staged by having two lines or string of the same length, two players, and two sets of binoculars.

Scrambled Thanksgiving

These are things you would find at Thanksgiving. Identify.

1.	pinmkup epi	(Pumpkin pie)
2.	srrenacbei	(Cranberries)
3.	kyeutr gsresidn	(Turkey dressing)
4.	ggikistvnnha rninde	(Thanksgiving dinner)
5.	dheasm stopeoat	(Mashed potatoes)
6.	gvyar	(Gravy)
7.	tho srlol—turtbe	(Hot rolls—butter)
8.	eiutblmktr	(Buttermilk)
9.	tuanum nssoae	(Autumn season)
10.	tvrhaes item	(Harvest time)
11.	selietrva	(Relatives)
12.	euiatgrtd	(Gratitude)
13.	coaehcolt kace	(Chocolate cake)
14.	cei mrcae lorl	(Ice cream roll)
15.	srfyto rai	(Frosty air)

Pudding Feed

Several couples are called up. Blindfold the girls and tell them they are going to feed the boys their pudding, following the directions the boys give. The first couple finished with eating the pudding wins a prize.

Teaching the Play Way

Teachers and leaders like to make the subjects they teach as intriguing, challenging, and compelling as they can. As a result, teachers turn to the play way of teaching. Games may be used in two ways: solely for recreation or as teaching aids. Since any game may be used in several ways for a number of different purposes, most educational games are simply adaptations of recreational activities. While not all teaching needs to be done the play way, using recreational activities to communicate knowledge can be an effective way to increase interest in many subjects. Learning need not be a dull memorization of information. By using the play way of teaching, we may experience information.

Teaching the Play Way

The following group of games are especially designed for use in the classroom. However, they can easily be adapted for use in the family or for children's party games.

Addition Relay

Arrange the teams in parallel lines. Each row in the school room may comprise a team. Give a piece of chalk to the first player in each row. At the signal the first player runs to the blackboard and writes a number, returns, and gives the chalk to the second player who repeats the action. Continue until the last player's turn comes. This player draws a line and adds the figures and returns to his seat. Only those columns added correctly count in the winning. Of these, the team finishing first wins.

No player may write a number which already appears on the board; neither may numbers be written in succession: that is, if the first player writes "1," the second player is not permitted to write "2." Numbers ending in zero also are ruled out, or left for older children.

Arithmetic Attention

The players sit in rows, an equal number in each row. Each row comprises a team. The players number off from the front to the back. Beforehand the teacher writes on the board a number of math problems and numbers each problem. The teacher then calls out the number of a problem and a number to indicate which players should run. For example, they might say "Problem number four, number nine." The number nines on all the teams run to the board, solve the problem, and return to their seats. The player returning first having solved the problem correctly scores one point for their team. The winner is the team first scoring seven.

The teacher should call the numbers at random to keep everyone alert.

Jumbled Sentence Relay

Arrange the teams in parallel files. The rows of seats in the school room may be used for teams. This is really two contests in one. The teacher prepares in advance a sentence for each team. The teacher writes the sentence on paper, and cuts it up so that there is one word on each slip. The teacher shuffles these slips and gives one to each player on a team. At the signal, the first player on each team runs to the blackboard, writes their word, and gives the chalk to the second player who repeats. The team finishing first wins. This completes the first half of the game.

The sentences as they now appear are nothing more than a jumble of words. As soon as the last word is written, the players of each team get together and figure out the correct sentence. When they think they have it, the student chosen by their classmates runs to the board and writes it. The team wins that first writes the correct sentence.

Silent Vowel Spelling Bee

This event adds new interest to the old-fashioned spelling bee. It is a teaching contest and also serves admirably as social play for parties and social gatherings where quiet play is in order.

The players are divided into two teams facing each other, and the leader calls words to each player in turn as in the standard spelling bee, calling upon the first player of one team, then the first player of the opposing team, and so on.

Words are spelled in the regular way except that the vowels may not be spoken but are represented by the following signs:

A—Hold up right hand
E—Hold up left hand
I—Point to eyes
O- Point to mouth
U—Hold both hands up overhead in "U" shape

A player goes to the foot of the line and gives one point to their opponents whenever they (1) misspell a word, (2) speak a vowel, (3) give the wrong sign for a vowel. The team first scoring eleven points wins. When used as a social contest, do not continue for too long.

Variation: Play exactly like the above game except that in addition to using the vowel signs have the players whistle instead of speaking the letter *S*.

Picture Writing

This game is used to bring out individual talents. The teacher selects and shows three large pictures to the class. These pictures can be illustrating anything. Action pictures are very good. The pictures are put up on the board where the class can see them. Each person is to select a picture and write a short story about it. Imaginations will run wild, and many different ideas for the same picture will develop. When the stories are completed, the class will enjoy hearing them.

Finding Errors

Divide players into equal teams. The teacher writes a paragraph on the blackboard. The paragraph will have many punctuation errors and misspelled words. Each team studies the sentences and finds as many errors as possible. When the time is up, the leader of each team will go through each sentence and point out the errors. The team which found the most or all of the errors wins.

King and Queen

A circle consisting of ten players is formed. One player is selected to be "King" or "Queen." This person stands behind someone in the circle. The leader flashes a word card to these two players. If the King or Queen says the word first they remain King or Queen and move behind another player for the next turn. If the one sitting in front of the King or Queen says the word first they become the new King or Queen. The object is to see how long the King or Queen can remain in this position.

If the game is played in the schoolroom, the words on the word cards can be taken from the children's reading books or spelling lists. Children enjoy this game and it becomes very competitive.

Fish

Players sit in a circle around a reading table. Several word cards are placed word side down on the table. Each player, in turn, picks up a card. This is called "fishing for a word." The player must pronounce the word and use it correctly in a sentence.

This game also is played in the schoolroom. Children of seven through ten find it exciting.

State Charades

This is played just like Charades except that the names of states are used. The following are suggestions:

Tennessee—Ten-eye-see
Washington—Washing-ton
Arizona—Airy-zone-ah
Rhode Island-Road-eye-land
Maryland—Marry-land
Oklahoma—Oak-la-home-ah
Georgia—George-ah

Iowa—Eye-oh-ah, I-way
Ohio—Oh-high-oh
Louisiana—Louise-Anna
Carolina—Car-oh-line-ah
Colorado—Collar-ray-dough
New Hampshire—New-ham-shire

Artists of the Zoo

Divide the players into groups of four to eight people each and station them in separate corners of the room. The leader stands in the center. Give each group several sheets of paper and a pencil.

Each group sends one player to the leader. This person whispers to them the name of an animal or other nature object—for example, elephant. The players dash back and begin to draw the elephant. As soon as a player thinks they know the name of the object being drawn they venture a guess to the leader. This continues until someone succeeds. The player who names the animal first scores one point for their team. Five points win the game. No comments are allowed by the drawer as they are drawing.

The teacher should later collect the drawings and discuss them from the standpoint of the animal's characteristics.

Capitals

Arrange the players in a circle with a person chosen to be "it" standing in the center. This person tosses a handkerchief into someone's lap, names a state, and counts to ten. The person must name the capital of the state before the count is over or they become "it." If the player names it successfully, the "it" player must try someone else.

Variation: The "it" player names the capital and the player replies with the state.

Guggenheim

Divide the players into groups of four or five and seat each group at a table, giving each a paper and pencil. Ask each group to draw the chart illustrated below. Select a five-letter word, such as "cards," and ask them to write it across the top as in the illustration. Then in the column to the left ask them to write the words "trees," "birds," "animals," and "flowers."

Each group then attempts to fill in the spaces with words beginning with the letter at the top of the column and falling under the classification at the left. For example, the first line might contain the following trees: cedar, apple, redwood, dogwood, and sassafras.

	C	A	R	D	S
TREES					
BIRDS					
ANIMALS					
FLOWERS					

Allow five minutes to fill in the words. Then assemble the groups and ask the leader of each to read their words for correction or scoring. There are twenty words needed, and each team is awarded twenty points at the start—deduct one for each incorrect word or blank space.

Variation: Score ten points for each correct name listed that no other player has, nine points for each name listed that only two players have, eight for each name that only three players have, and so on. The score is written in each square over the name and the columns are added.

OTHER GAMES

Forfeits

Everyone should be prepared to entertain. When a game is played, the loser pays a forfeit by reciting a poem, singing, dancing, or one of the following might be used:

1. Pat your stomach with one hand, while you rub your head with the other. At a given signal, reverse.
2. Say "I am a donkey" four times, emphasizing a different word each time. At the end, the other players comment, "We agree!"
3. Stand on a chair and make a one-minute speech on any subject suggested by the judge or the host or hostess.
4. Say six nice things about yourself.
5. Confess your worst fault. If the judge is not satisfied, you must keep on confessing until he is satisfied.
6. Tell the truth for two minutes, answering truthfully all questions put to you by the judge or other players.
7. Smile five ways, or laugh five ways, or snore five ways.
8. Smile, frown, laugh, weep, in that order, all in half a minute.
9. Sing "Old MacDonald Had a Farm," omitting every second word.
10. Say "mixed biscuits" rapidly ten times.
11. Laugh up an octave and down again, without error, in one breath.
12. Recite, "Mary Had a Little Lamb" or any other familiar poem, counting after each word beginning with one; thus

"Mary, one, had, two, a, three, little, four. Lamb, five, Its, six, fleece, seven," and so on.

13. Have a boy act as a mirror and a girl go through all the motions she goes through while getting ready for school or an evening out.

14. Both losers talk at the same time while arguing two different subjects; the winner gets a prize.

15. Argue one of the following:

Cadillacs are better than Volkswagens.
It is better to love and lose than never to love at all.
Baby boys are better than baby girls.
It is better to love to dance than to dance to love.
Burnt toast is better than no toast at all.
It is safer to hunt four-legged "deer" than two-legged "dear."
Boys should go out with no girlfriend's roommate.
Its better to live to be one hundred than to die trying.
Who should take the garbage out.
Who should buy the groceries.
Married folks should go to dances.

16. Read as a forfeit one of the following:

If he can remember so many jokes,
With all the details that mold them,
Why can't he recall with equal skill,
How many times he's told them?

Mary had a little lamb.
But now her lamb is dead.
And so she takes her lamb to school
Between two hunks of bread.

I eat my peas with honey;
I've done it all my life.
It makes my peas taste funny
But it keeps them on my knife.

Sly Slim slipped down the slippery side street and up the steeply slanting steps to Stephen's where he saw six or seven streaked, stripped, slimy snakes, and then Slim slaughtered the serpents.

Theophilus Thistle, the thistle sifter, in sifting thousands of unsifted thistles, thrust thrice three thousand thistles through the thick of his thumb. Now if Theophilus Thistle, the thistle sifter, in sifting thousands of unsifted thistles thrust thrice three thousand thistles through the thick of his thumb, how many wouldst thou, in sifting thrice three thousand thistles, thrust through the thick of thy thumb?

Stick Twist

Grasp a broom handle or broomstick with both hands, palms down. Hold the stick horizontally in front of you. Now lower the stick and step over it. Without letting go, move the stick up your back, over your head, and back to where you started. You'll have to twist your arms a little to complete the circuit.

Heel Spring

Place your heels against a line drawn on the floor or ground, bend down and grasp your toes with the fingers of both hands, lean forward a bit to get a start, and then jump backward across the line.

Penny Catch

Bend your right arm so that your hand is in front of your chest; now raise your elbow level with your shoulder. Place several pennies in a pile on your bent elbow. Drop your elbow suddenly, move your right hand downward quickly, and try to catch the pennies before they fall.

Stretch-Out

Each contestant toes a mark. In one hand they hold a broom handle or broomstick, in the other, a piece of chalk. The contest is to see who can make a mark the farthest distance from the starting line without touching the floor or ground in front except with the stick, which is used for support.

More Tongue Twisters

One person is to take a marshmallow and place it in their mouth.

(They must not suck, chew, or swallow. It must just sit there.) Then the player repeats this tongue twister.

Betty Botter bought a bit of butter. But she said, "The butter's bitter. If I put it in my batter, it will make my batter bitter. But a bit of better butter will make my bitter batter better." So Betty Botter bought a bit of better butter and it made her bitter batter better."

or

A skunk sat on a stump. The skunk thunk the stump stunk and the stump thunk the skunk stunk.

The player continues by placing one marshmallow at a time in their mouth in succession until they can no longer say the tongue twister.

Knott Knitter

Knott was not married, and he fell in love with the knitter who knit knots with the knot knitter and the knot knotter. Knott asked her not to knit knots any longer but to become Knott forever. So Knott and the knitter tied the knot and now there will be Knott knitters forever.

Romance

A tree toad loved a she toad that lived up in a tree. She was a three-toed tree toad but a two-toed toad was he. The two-toed tree toad tried to win the she toad's friendly nod, for the two-toed tree toad loved the ground that the three-toed tree toad trod. But vainly the two-toed tree toad tried, he could not please her whim. In her tree toad bower with her tree toad power she vetoed him.

APPENDIX

Games Played with Hoops, Inner Tubes, and so on.

Games with Elastic Bands
(Purchased or cut from old inner tubes)

Relay Races

1. Run with band around ankles.
2. Run with band around knees.
3. Run and crawl through band while running.
4. Run, crawl through band, and run back.
5. Three-legged race.
6. Crawl through in couples—your partner helps.
7. Place one edge of the band under one foot, hold the other edge in your hand, straighten up, and run.

Games with Hoops
(Three feet in diameter, hula hoops, or any tough, flat material)

1. With hoop behind their heads, a couple pulls against each other while on all fours. Each person tries to pull the other over a marked line.
2. With hoop around their ankles, a couple pulls against each other while on all fours. Each person tries to pull the other over a marked line.

3. Run and crawl through the hoop.
4. Two run and crawl through the hoop at the same time.
5. Three run and crawl through the hoop at the same time.
6. Four small children run and crawl through the hoop.
7. Three run while the hoop is around their waists.
8. With the hoop around their waists, two pull in opposite directions (tug of war) while reaching for prizes.
9. With the hoop around their waists, three or four pull while reaching for prizes.

Games with Pillows

(Fill old pant legs half full of cotton, feathers, and so on; or fill pillowcases with blankets)

1. Ride the rail and pillow fight.
2. Stand on an inner tube and pillow fight.
3. Stand on an inner tube and pillow fight, touching the ground between each hit.
4. Hop on one leg and pillow fight, being out when two feet touch the ground.
5. Six stand on a mat and fight, being out when knocked off the mat.
6. The "king" stands at one end of a two-by-four inch plank. All others line up at other end. One by one they stand on the plank and pillow fight the "king." The person who knocks the king off the plank takes their place.
7. Balance the pillow on the head and run to the goal.
8. Run with a pillow between the knees.
9. Line up with the leader in front. The leader tosses a pillow to each one in the line. They toss it back and squat down, and the first line down wins.
10. Kick a pillow to the goal line.

Games with Brooms

1. Two hold a broom above their heads and grip as the broom is pulled down. The one releasing their grip loses.
2. Hold one end of the broom on the ground and crawl under

it without touching the ground with any part of the body except the feet.

Relay Races

1. Ride a broom for a stick horse.
2. Two persons ride one broom.
3. Three ride one broom.
4. Four ride one broom (if small children).
5. Sweep a can to a goal.
6. Two persons carry a broom handle that a third player sits on, with arms around the carrier's necks.
7. One sits on the bristles and another pulls the player.
8. Roll a disk with a broom.
9. Two contestants seated face to face hold a broom with the bottoms of their feet together and each tries to pull the other up.

Games with Disks

(Six-inch wooden disks one inch thick)

1. Roll for distance.
2. Roll for accuracy.
3. Balance a disk on a stick and run to the goal line.
4. Balance a disk on your head and run to the goal line.
5. Roll the disk to the goal line with a stick.
6. Push the disk to the goal line with a stick.

Games with Wheels

(Put a handle through the axis of a tricycle wheel)

1. Bend over to the ground and run while holding the handles and rolling the wheel.
2. Wheelbarrow race—one person grasps the handles while another pushes them by the legs.
3. Roll for distance.
4. Roll for accuracy.
5. Knock down pegs with wheels.
6. Roll to each other across the lawn.

Games with Rope

1. Tug of war
2. Jump rope
3. Climb rope
4. "Tarzan" with a pulley on the rope; hold on to the pulley and ride down to the ground.
5. Tie between tree for children to hang on and swing.
6. Tie to a pillow and swing the rope in a circle close to the ground for children to jump.
7. Cowboy lasso for accuracy.
8. One chases another trying to rope them.
9. Spin the rope.

Games with Inner Tubes
(or bicycle tires)

1. Roll for speed.
2. Run with an inner tube around your feet.
3. Kick the inner tube to the goal.
4. Ride and jump, feet do not touch the ground while jumping on an upright inner tube.
5. Roll for distance.
6. Throw for distance.
7. Throw for accuracy.
8. Roll for accuracy.
9. Line five or more inner tubes in one row and either hop or jump for distance, accuracy, speed, or endurance.
10. Jump on the inner tube with feet (1) separated or (2) together. Jump for balance, distance, speed, accuracy, or height.
11. Crawl through tubes or tires:
    Run and crawl through one tube or tire.
    Run and crawl through ten tubes or tires.
12. Run with one foot inside, dragging the tube.
13. Pull the tube for contests of strength.
    Two pull holding the tube with one hand each.
    Three or four pull holding with one hand each.

14. Dive through a tube or tire onto a mat.
15. Two run together with a tube around their waists.
16. Tie four tubes together. One crawls inside, another rolls them.
17. Put twenty tubes on one rope and tie the rope between trees for a swing, with one person in each inner tube.
18. Float on the water in an inner tube.

INDEX

Games with Gospel Applications

The following pages suggest possible gospel applications for games contained in this book. Subjects appear in italics without parentheses—example: **Aaronic Priesthood**. Names of games and their page numbers appear in italics in parentheses—example: (*Family Baseball, 9*). The suggested application is in ordinary type and follows the parentheses in each case—example: The first, second, and third bases . . .in this game.

Aaronic Priesthood

(*Authority*, 243) The priesthood is authority to act for God. We must meet the prerequisites (like bringing the three items) before qualifying to receive this authority.

(*Family Baseball*, 9) The first, second, and third bases can be compared to the offices of deacon, teacher, and priest in the Aaronic Priesthood. As we progress from one to another, we prepare for the blessings and responsibilities of the Melchizedek Priesthood—which could be compared to the home plate in this game.

(*Advance*, 18) Progression in the priesthood is done in steps. Each step has its own responsibilities and blessings. As we achieve each step in life, we are working towards perfection and eternal life.

(*Organization*, 29) When churches or people are not properly organized they "go all to pieces." The head bone should be connected to the neck bone, and so on (see Ezekiel 37 or Ephesians 4:11–12). The priesthood is God's organized authority here upon the earth. It must function as the Savior instructed, or it will not ensure the enduring desired results.

Apostasy

(*What's Wrong?*, 76) After the death of Christ and the Apostles, influences from within and without the Church made many small and large changes. It is important for members of the Church to heed to our prophet's counsel because the prophet can see the truth (or the way the Church was before, as organized by Christ) and address small changes that need to be corrected.

Apostles

(*Apostle Rhythm*, 13) Use this activity to help the family learn the names of apostles, both current and past.

(*Men of God,* 238) This game will help the family learn more about the leaders of the Church. (Again, this game could be used for present or past leaders.)

Appreciation

(*Home,* 53) Show family and friends how important the home is with this activity by helping them appreciate the home more fully.

(*National Anthem,* 80) This game helps families and friends to understand and appreciate the national heritage we all enjoy.

(*Peace,* 35) Peace is a wonderful blessing to have. Be sure to emphasize that we should always show appreciation to the Savior for the peace that comes through Him.

Atonement

(*Savior,* 245) Have the teams complete the exercise. Then tell them the following: "The Savior taught many principles of righteousness; but His greatest contribution was His atoning sacrifice for all mankind. We should live our lives as He would want us to." Also teach students that the Savior's sacrifice can mean many things to us, as shown by the variety of sentences written by the teams.

(*Gospel Seeds*, 15) Christ went before us and planted the seeds of life after death and of eternal life. We need to follow His teachings to reap the benefits.

(*Captain, May I?*, 19) Christ gave His life for us. We must obey His commandments in order to have the Atonement be effective in our lives.

(*Famous Partnerships*, 114) Many things work together. We could not return to our Father in heaven without Christ and His sacrifice.

Authority

(*Walk the Straight and Narrow*, 93) As we go through life, we encounter obstacles that hinder our progression on the straight and narrow path of the gospel. It is important to follow the counsel of those in authority (like the friends that could see the game's obstacles) in overcoming our obstacles and in continuing our eternal progression.

(*Patriarchal Game*, 26) Frequently, those in authority over us have been called because of their many righteous experiences. We can learn from their experiences and avoid many of life's pitfalls.

Awareness

(*Obey the Law*, 69) Teach families and friends to keep alert in obeying the laws of God. If slothful, you may miss out on opportunities.

Baptism

(*Fun with a Piñata*, 91) Seeking a worthwhile goal such as baptism involves a lot of hard work and dedication, but when we actually obtain the goal (break the pinata), the blessings come in more volume than we can contain.

(*Hold to the Rod*, 243) We grasp the rod when we are baptized. We must hang on to the rod and continue on the road to eternal progression to receive blessings. Poor choices will bring their own consequences (like the penalties).

Blessings

(*Pick-Up-Sticks*, 73) There is a great variety of blessings; some of them are easy to obtain, while others take a lot of persistent effort.

Brotherly Love

(*How Much Do You Know About Your Brother/Sister?*, 249) Very often the only difference between people you like and the ones you don't like is that you know the ones you like. Get to know the people you think you don't like and you may find that you can like them, too.

(*Humility*, 109) We must overcome our selfish attitude and concern ourselves with those around us.

(*Guess Who Loves Me*, 34) Doing nice things for family members develops love and appreciation.

(*Fox and Ducks*, 187) It is our responsibility to help others to avoid sin and destruction.

(*The Coyote and the Sheep*, 22) We must help each other do the will of the Lord and keep from sin.

(*Who Are Your Neighbors?*, 23) Getting to know our neighbors usually helps us to love them more.

(*Pick-Up*, 25) Respect for others.

(*I Have a Kindness*, 29) We should show kindness and love to other family members.

Celestial Kingdom

(*Captain, May I?*, 19) To gain our goal of reaching and qualifying for the celestial kingdom, we must be obedient to the commandments of the Lord.

Cheating

(*Spoon and Beans*, 130) Is it worth the time you save if you cheat to save it?

Cooperation

(*Keep Away*, 174) You must always act as a team if you expect to get anywhere. Individual efforts help but team work gets the job done.

(*Family Ties*, 253) Each family member is important, and each must cooperate with the other to make a happy and successful family.

(*Cooperation*, 254) We must work with our brothers and sisters to reach our gospels goals. We cannot do it alone.

Courage

(*Truth or Consequences*, 7) If we do not have the courage to meet life we have to suffer the consequences.

(*Obstacles in Man's Life*, 26) Many things in life will try to lead us astray. It takes courage to keep going on to your goal.

Covenant

(*Obstacles in Man's Life*, 26) We must stay true to our covenants regardless of outside pressure.

Creation

(*I'm Thinking*, 77) We should be aware of all of the creations of our Father in heaven.

(*Organization*, 29) When churches or people are not properly organized they "go all to pieces." The head bone should be connected to the neck bone, and so on (see Ezekiel 37 or Ephesians 4:11–12). There is order and organization in all God's creations. He created man in his own image and not from a bunch of disorganized ideas.

(*Out the Window*, 77) We should learn to develop all our senses in order to be more perceptive to the beautiful creations God has given us "to please the eye and to gladden the heart." (D&C 59:18)

(*Earth, Air, or Water*, 78) This illustrates the great wonders our Creator has put upon this earth for our enjoyment.

(*Fowl, Beast, or Fish*, 30) Learning of the animals God created.

(*Creation*, 30) Teaching children about the Creation.

(*In the Beginning*, 30) The Creation.

Dating Standards

(*Golf Ring Toss*, 20) We need to progress slowly from group activities to double dating to single dating, and so on.

(*Lost Lover*, 70) We need to search carefully for the person we will marry. We do not always see the divine capacity of others. We need the Spirit of the Lord to help us perceive whom he would have us choose.

(*Give*, 252) We need to contribute to a date for it to be successful.

(*The Storyteller*, 3) Remember who you are as you date, because sometimes actions speak louder than words.

Deceitfulness

(*How Many Times Did the Train Stop?* 4) It is easy to be deceived. We must have the Holy Ghost to prevent us from falling away from the truth.

(*Taking Vows Forever*, 117) People or things are not always as they appear.

Discernment

(*Revelation*, 27) God's word can be distorted as man passes it on through time. God's word is not distorted as we receive it through his apostles. Therefore, by following advice of apostles, we can stay on the road to eternal progression.

(*Judge*, 130) Look for the truth in things you hear.

(*False Prophets*, 245) Discernment comes by following the Spirit of Truth.

(*Where Am I Going?*, 123) It is important to recognize our goals.

(*My Eyes Are Open*, 28) Sometimes we can't see things that are right before our eyes. Some people look but never see.

(*Talking Pictures*, 28) This is the way we know of God and his attributes. Only by experiences in the Church can we visualize the things of God.

(*Horizons*, 31) Avoid narrow horizons. Life is composed of many facets.

(*Who's the Leader?*, 252) Discernment is necessary to determine the difference between true and false prophets. However, prophets can delegate authority, and we should follow our priesthood leaders.

Enduring to the End

(*Bumblebee Buzz*, 203) He who endures longest, wins.

Eternal Life

(*Message Relay*, 6) If we don't get the right message and aren't ready when Christ comes, we will miss out on eternal life.

Eternal Progression

(*Family History Relay*, 248) Instead of using a card containing name, birth date, and so on, use a card with requirements to gain the celestial kingdom—such as baptism, temple marriage, service in the Church, living the Word of Wisdom, and so on. We must know and do certain things in order to progress in our life and return to live with our Heavenly Father.

(*Finding Errors*, 275) We must Search out our errors and correct them before we can progress.

(*Question Draw*, 15, 239) If we know the scriptures and study them, we will have the opportunities to advance and progress.

(*Walk the Straight and Narrow*, 93) Be sure your steps are taking you upward, that you are not standing still but progressing.

(*Advance*, 18) By making right choices in life, we have eternal progression.

(*Golf Ring Toss*, 20) Eternal progression is gained slowly and only as one progressively meets requirements of higher laws. One must live the "lesser" law before he can live the "greater."

(*Newspaper Race*, 23) The newspapers represent steps to salvation in the gospel.

(*Gospel Steps*, 25) We must do the right things to get ahead in gospel living.

(*Overtake*, 28) We must strive every day to live the gospel or we will fall behind. When we sin we drop behind in the race for eternal life.

(*Steps to Heaven*, 32) Learning the principles of the gospel.

Eternity

(*Horizons*, 31) We sometimes lose sight of eternity because we focus all our thought on the temporal things of life.

Example

(*The Storyteller*, 3) Our actions speak louder than our words.

(*Do What I Say*, 31) Example speaks louder than words. People are converted by what they see, not by what they hear alone.

Faith

(*Famous Pioneers*, 13) History of the pioneers reveals their great faith and many efforts in preserving the Church.

(*Obstacle Race*, 221) We encounter many obstacles in our lives. We must overcome them all to return to our Father in Heaven.

(*Soul and Spirit*, 111) There is always hope of one more chance.

(*Pendulum Swing*, 105) Life's pendulum swings from failure to success—two extremes. The fulfillment of patient hope comes at the end of long and difficult trials.

(*Deer Stalking*, 68) Hope is faith, though sometimes we are temporarily in the dark.

(*Cross Country Run*, 59) The hope of a bright eternity gives us strength on running to the end.

(*Cotton Bowl Relay*, 22) We cannot rely on our senses; we must have faith to assist them or to do what they cannot achieve.

Faith and Works

(*Articles of Faith*, 6, 11, 243) It is not enough to have faith, we must have works.

(*Washer Toss*, 21) It doesn't matter how good we "think" we are it's how good we "really" are that counts.

Falsehoods

(*The Thin Line*, 21) Each time we lie we cut away from our self-respect until we fall.

Fellowship

(*I Am My Brother's Keeper*, 33) Each of us is responsible for his brothers and sisters.

(*Fellowshipping*, 253) In the Church, everyone has an opportunity to participate through Church activity. Fellowshipping comes through activity; only when you are active can you touch people's lives.

Gathering of Israel

(*Scrambled Names*, 44) (Scramble the names of the Lost Tribes.) The tribes are going to be brought together.

Family History

(*Family Ties*, 253) Just as each family member is very important to us, so should our ancestors be important to us.

(*Family History*, 32) We should learn to know our family members. We are endowed with a great heritage.

(*Family History Relay*, 248) This game is a good introduction to genealogical work.

Gift of the Holy Ghost

(*Teamwork*, 97) When you team up with the Holy Ghost you can do anything.

(*Reading Temples*, 108) The gift of the Spirit can't be seen but can be felt.

(*Which Match?*, 108) By watching for the signs from the Holy Ghost we can make the right decisions.

(*Blind Bell*, 70) Life has a blindfold. We must listen carefully to the Holy Ghost in order to know which way to go.

Goals

(*Find Your Hometown*, 92) We need to be alert and keep our eyes on the goal or we may stray.

Godhead

(*Nail Driving Contest*, 216) The Godhead works together like father and son.

Going the Second Mile

(*Do This and More*, 80) When we are called to do something we should go the second mile.

Gospel Light

(*Blowing Out the Candle*, 93) It's hard to reach goals if you attempt to do it blindly.

(*Pin the Tail on the Donkey*, 20) We fail to reach the right goals without the light of the gospel.

(*Drawing in the Dark*, 27, 112) We need the gospel's light to guide us.

Gratitude

(*Count Your Blessings*, 27) Gratitude for our blessings.

Guarding against Sin

(*Raise the Devil*, 2) The priesthood holder must rise to his calling of being the spiritual leader in the home. Satan works hard on the priesthood holder.

(*Hear No Evil, See No Evil, Speak No Evil*, 36) Be prepared against sin. Avoid even the appearance of evil.

(*King of the Walk*, 213) Don't let evil forces knock you down.

Habits

(*Habits*, 32) Bad habits are hard to break; the longer we have one the more difficult it is to overcome.

Happiness

(*Washer Toss*, 21) The person who remains closest to the Lord will receive the greatest rewards.

Harmony

(*Harmony*, 73). Harmony in the home makes things run smoother.

Heritage

(*Relative Mixer*, 199) Knowing your relatives is the first step to loving them.

(*Book of Mormon*, 231) This is a good way to get acquainted with the fathers and sons in the Book of Mormon.

(*The Family Takes a Walk*, 165) A good, strong family unit can win and accomplish anything if the members are all working and striving for the same thing.

Honor

(*Wood Sawing Contest*, 216) To honorably fulfill obligations one must do his part and not let the other person down.

(*Deception*, 109) It is difficult to hide a dishonorable character from those who are perceptive.

Honesty

(*Judge*, 130) This game can be used to develop the attitude that honesty is the best policy.

Honoring the Priesthood

(*Fireman's Drag*, 219) Fathers need to honor their priesthood, as they have the important job of helping to save or redeem their families.

Joy

(*Togetherness*, 241) When working with a group, maintain a unity through which you may reach your goal. It is through working with others that we find and receive joy.

(*Happiness*, 21) Happiness and joy are contagious. Be cheerful, and everyone among your associates will be affected by your cheerfulness.

(*Service*, 230) Progress is happiness and results from cooperation and service.

(*Happiness*, 21) After playing this game a discussion should follow. Those who strive for spiritual things, things that will really bring happiness, are always the winners, while those who go after materialistic and worldly things are losers and will not have true happiness.

(*Give*, 252) Learn the joy of giving and sharing.

Judgment

(*Tommy, Tommy, Tum*, 5) We should judge a person by what we see rather than base all facts on hearing. It is what we do that will get us to heaven, not what we say.

(*What Happened*, 98) This illustrates how differently people see things and interpret them. It shows the need for not making hasty judgments.

Justice

(*Judge and Conductor*, 239) Justice needs evidence from both sides.

Knowledge

(*Know Your House*, 51) Be aware of what is in God's eternal home. Inheriting this home pays dividends.

(*Black Magic*, 145) Having the right knowledge help you make the right choices.

(*How, When, and Where?*, 75) There are many questions we do not understand, but we can find the answers, if we will just seek.

(*Blind Alley*, 216) Often we make wrong decisions, but we learn from our mistakes.

(*Nose Touch*, 270) Sometimes we don't see the obvious things.

Marriage

(*Touch*, 77, 185) This game shows things aren't always as they seem and we need to have our eyes wide open when we are picking our mates to marry for time and all eternity.

Miracles

(*Egg in and out of Bottle*, 122, 123) Some things may appear like miracles, but in reality they are accomplished by natural laws.

(*Eighth Wonder of the World*, 270) When you first hear this, you think it can never be, but after watching it done, you know that it is simple. So it is with God. All things will be understood if we watch, study, and pray.

(*Telling Time*, 5) There are no mysteries or miracles to God. As with this game, what we think of as a mystery or a miracle is based upon laws we do not yet understand.

Missionary Work

(*Ball Throwing Contest*, 209; Archery Contest, 209; Chin-up Contest. 209; Bubble Gum Contest, 210) These games take enthusiasm to play. Good missionaries need this type of enthusiasm.

(*Seek and Find*, 252) When you are instrumental in converting a person, he helps you as a missionary.

New Testament

(*Matthew, Mark, Luke, and John*, 31) A game to memorize the books of the New Testament.

Obedience

(*Obey the Law*, 69) The laws given to us through authority are for our own benefit. Our eternal progression rests upon our ability to obey those laws. Another aspect to share is that Christ also gives us commandments. Be alert and obey the Lord's commandments.

(*Imitation*, 72) Mistakes hinder our progress.

(*Tommy, Tommy, Tum*, 25) We need to give complete obedience.

(*The Lion Hunt*, 203) In order to get to the celestial kingdom we need to follow our Prophet, the leader of the Church.

(*Statues*, 163) Obedience is necessary for entrance into the celestial kingdom.

(*Cannibals and Missionaries*, 3) We must follow certain laws of the Lord in order to obtain certain goals in life.

(*Entrance*, 4) There are requirements for entrance into the Kingdom.

(*Captain, May I?*, 19) To gain our goal of reaching and qualifying for the celestial kingdom, we must be obedient to the commandments of the Lord.

(*Following Instructions*, 28) We are not able to follow the gospel teachings until we learn to listen and follow instructions.

Opportunity

(*Wink*, 101) React quickly before opportunity slips away from you.

(*Circle Tag*, 166) Do not let opportunity slip from you.

Organization

(*Mix-up Story*, 125) When things aren't planned, we may get ridiculous combinations.

Overcoming Obstacles

(*Human Hurdle Relay*, 254) We must face each problem in life as it comes, overcoming it before going on to the next.

Peace

(*Peace*, 35) Those who seek and find peace also find a special reward. Peace is a wonderful blessing to have. Be sure to emphasize that we should always show appreciation to the Savior for the peace that comes through Him.

Perseverance

(*Newspaper Race*, 23) Some people will reach salvation faster than others, because they have the perseverance it takes to reach their goals.

(*Let's Go with the Pioneers*, 19) This game helps us to learn about courage and how to withstand hardships as the pioneers did.

Prayer

(*Listen*, 76) We have to listen or we may not know the answer to our prayers.

(*Treasure Hunt*, 134, 267) Prayer is our map to happiness and eternal life.

(*Prone to Safety*, 22) As long as you are praying you are safe.

(*Hot and Cold*, 24) We must be in tune with the Spirit in order to be guided to the best course or action.

(*Telegraph*, 251) Heavenly Father answers our prayers, but sometimes we are not in tune to receive the message he sends and thus Satan can stop the message.

Preparation

(*Back to Back*, 18) We have to be prepared or else we may be left out and not be able to receive blessings.

Priesthood

(*Knock*, 4) The priesthood cannot function without the keys of knowledge.

(*Organization*, 29) When churches or people are not properly organized they "go all to pieces." The head bone should be connected to the neck bone, and so on (see Ezekiel 37 or Ephesians 4:11–12).

Prophets

(*False Prophets*, 245) Throughout this life there are many people who would like to tell us where to go or what to do, but we must select the voice of the true prophet in order to find the truth.

Punishment for Sin

(*Pick-Up-Sticks*, 73) We must pay the penalty if we extend into the areas of others' belongings in our efforts to acquire things.

(*Monkey*, 114) We must pay the penalty if we covet what is not ours or worked for, or try to get something for nothing.

Purity

(*Translation*, 121) We purify our lives a little at a time.

Repentance

(*Forgiveness*, 24) It is important to realize that we are all capable of making mistakes. We must recognize our mistakes and repent.

(*Slam Bang*, 67) Label spools to represent coveting. Each person tries to repent by retrieving this sin. Those who are caught in the trap of covetousness must pay the penalty.

Resurrection

(*Make a Body*, 76) We can only receive a resurrected body after going through the steps of progression requisite for that quality of body.

Revelation

(*Pin the Tail on the Donkey*, 20) The Church without revelation is comparable to pinning the tail on the donkey blindfolded. We need revelation to do the things the Lord would have us do.

Scripture Reading

(*Mysterious Message*, 111) We receive messages from our Heavenly Father through the scriptures. By studying the scriptures we find out who we really are in relationship with God.

(*Gospel Relay*, 7) Helps to learn the Ten Commandments.

(*Books of the Bible*, 16) Learning the books of the Old and New Testament.

Self-Control

(*Poor Kitty*, 29) Temptations are not to be sought after. Only those with deep convictions and good control can resist them.

(*Forgiveness*, 24) We must learn to control ourselves and ask forgiveness of someone we have wronged.

(*The Queen's Headache*, 75) Self control will help overcome many obstacles in life.

Sincerity

(*Sincerity*, 252) Sincerity can sometimes be shown just by the look on a person's face.

Stewardship

(*Time*, 32) We must account for every minute of our lives spent here on the earth. We must be aware of the time and not waste it on meaningless activities.

Sustaining Authority

(*How Do You Like Your Counselors?*, 253) We have the privilege of sustaining those in authority in the Church.

Temple Work

(*Sardines*, 20) Our families should be united in truth. When one member of a family joins the Church, he should not rest until all the members are sealed together as a family unit.

Temptation

(*The Thin Line*, 21) If a person gets too close to the line between good and evil, he has to pay the penalty.

Testimony

(*Togetherness*, 241) Our belief and testimonies are strengthened as we work and associate together in the gospel.

Tithing

(*Habits*, 32) Make sure the habits you make are good ones, such as paying tithing.

Tools of Satan

(*Poison Carton*, 141) This can represent the forces of Satan that are working against us to cause apostasy from the Church.

(*Obstacles in Man's Life*, 26) Many delight in leading men away from the teachings of the apostles. We must ignore the heckling of others and seek our eternal goals.

(*Solemnity*, 200) Satan is persistent in trying to get us to do things his way. If we follow him, we eliminate blessings from our lives.

(*Handicap Relay*, 167) Satan subtly snares us with one sin at a time until we are burdened down with sins that hamper our progress to our eternal goal.

(*Getting Dressed*, 91) Satan deceives us for his own gain.

(*What's the Trick?*, 74) Beware of people who are not honest.

(*Who Hit Me?*, 91) This game illustrates how Satan works and how clever he is in his dirty work.

(*How Many Times Did the Train Stop?*, 4) This illustrates the subtleness Satan uses to lead us down the wrong path. We often look for the wrong things in life.

(*Satan Says*, 17) Withstand Satan's temptations.

(*Character*, 18) Satan leads us into darkness one step at a time.

(*Slide Right*, 21) Satan's spirits are constantly trying to get into our lives.

(*Traps*, 23) Do not get in Satan's trap.

(*Stocking Surprises*, 30) Satan can often make things appear to be what they are not.

Trust

(*Honesty*, 237) When you are honest, your conscience is clear and capable of being trusted.

Truth

(*Hunt the Ring*, 68) The truth is often hidden and we must search it out.

(*Poison Object*, 75) We must not be left with untruths; rather we should discard them at once.

(*Revelation*, 27) Truth originates in only one place and may be conveyed by only one means. Seek the proper source and heed the counsel of revelation. Do not be satisfied with what others say, because they may be misled by Satan.

Unity

(*Elbow Tug of War*, 172) After the Apostasy, there was no uniting authority in the Church. The people made no progress because of their disunity. We must be working together and pulling in the same direction to make progress.

YOUR FAVORITE
FAMILY GAMES